Hindu Mythology and Religion

HINDU MYTHOLOGY AND RELIGION

P. Singh

SUMIT ENTERPRISES
NEW DELHI - 110002

Published by :
SUMIT ENTERPRISES
4649 B/21, Ansari Road,
Daryaganj, New Delhi-110002
Phone : 011-23279353
Mob. : 9810217567
E-mail : sumit_enterprises2007@yahoo.com.in

Hindu Mythology and Religion

First Published 2011

ISBN 978-81-8420-289-2

PRINTED IN INDIA

Published by Sri Lokesh Kumar for Sumit Enterprises, New Delhi-110002, Typeset by Lucky Graphics, Printed at Nav Prabhat Printing Press, Tronicacity

Contents

Preface (*vii*)

1. Introduction 1
2. The Hindu Deities 11
3. Philosophy, Mythology and Ritual 22
4. Religion and the Epics 58
5. Classical Forms of Devotional Mysticism 94
6. Hindu Dharma 131
7. Hindu Religious Thought: Principles and Practices 174
8. Rigveda 180
9. The Golden Thread of Vedanta 211
10. Upanishads Associated with 'Esoteric Knowledge' 222
11. The Puranas 235
12. Lord Shiva 243
13. Vishnu: God of Preservation 271

Bibliography 285

Index 287

Preface

The mythology of India claims unique interest by virtue of its unparalleled length of life. Aryan mythology is comparatively recent. In mass of content and in value for mythology, however, these cannot compare with the Rigveda. Of still more importance is the fact that from the period of the Rigveda to the present day, a space of some thirty-five hundred years, we have a mythology which is in constant but organic development. Moreover, amidst the ceaseless change which is the heritage of human things, there is relative stability in the simpler thoughts of the human mind, and as in many parts of India the peasant still labours with the implements and in the mode of his ancestors in periods far remote, so his mind frames the same hypotheses to account for those phenomena of nature which in India more than elsewhere determine irrevocably his weal or his woe. The rich variety of the mythology, despite its attraction for the student of the history of myths, renders the task of concise exposition one of peculiar difficulty.

For the mythology of the present day available material is enormous: each part of the vast area of India has its own abundant store of myth and tradition, and to give detail for this period would be impossible. The same consideration applies with but slightly lessened force for the earlier epochs: the Veda, the epics, the Puranas, the literature of the Buddhists and of the Jains, each present data in lavish abundance. It has been necessary, therefore, to circumscribe narrowly the scope of the subject by restricting the treatment to that mythology which stands in close connexion with religion and which conveys to us a conception of the manner in which the Indian pictured to himself the origin of the world and of life, the destiny of the universe and of the souls of man, the Gods and the evil spirits who supported or menaced his existence. Gods and demons were very present to the mind of the Indian then as they are today, and they are inextricably involved in innumerable stories of folk-lore, of fairy tale, and of speculation as to the origin of institutions and customs.

Hindu mythology is a term used by modern scholarship for a large body of Indian literature that details the lives and times of legendary personalities, deities and divine incarnations on earth interspersed with often large sections of philosophical and ethical discourse. Despite connotations of fiction in common usage, the term *myth*, in theological and academic studies, does not necessarily imply that a narrative is untrue. The use of term mythology is a western construct applied primarily to non-Judeo-Christian religious literature. It is intellectually insincere to describe other religious literature as mythology while labelling the biblical literature as 'legends'. It must be noted that many of the topics that fall under the category of *Hindu mythology* are cherished beliefs of Hindus. All ancient religions contain stories that are accepted as literal truth by some, and as philosophical or allegorical insights by others. Thus, the biblical stories may be similarly construed as Jewish/ Christian mythology. The mythological literature is intertwined with the ethos of ancient Vedic religion and Vedic civilization, and fundamentally constructed with Hindu systems of philosophy.

The book is a comprehensive treatment of Hindu Religion and Culture. It precisely and systematically delves upon Hindu religion which is Sanatan. According is Hinduism the whole creation is Maya. Starting from pre-Indus Valley civilization, book beautifully discusses in various phases of development and growth of Hindu religion. It briefly discusses the growth of Hindu religion through Vedas, Brahmanas, Sutras, Puranas, Aranyakas, Ashram system and the various Upanishadas. It also details various systems of Indian philosophy. In addition non-Vedic system and their philosophies like Charvaka, Jainism and Buddhism.

The students, teachers, research scholars will find the book very useful and most informative.

—*Editor*

1

Introduction

Hindu mythology is a term used by modern scholarship for a large body of Indian literature that details the lives and times of legendary personalitics, deities and divine incarnations on earth interspersed with often large sections of philosophical and ethical discourse. Despite connotations of fiction in common usage, the term *myth*, in theological and academic studies, does not necessarily imply that a narrative is untrue. The use of term mythology is a western construct applied primarily to non-Judeo-Christian religious literature. It is intellectually insincere to describe other religious literature as mythology while labelling the biblical literature as 'legends'. It must be noted that many of the topics that fall under the category of *Hindu mythology* are cherished beliefs of Hindus. All ancient religions contain stories that are accepted as literal truth by some, and as philosophical or allegorical insights by others. Thus, the biblical stories may be similarly construed as Jewish/ Christian mythology.

The mythological literature is intertwined with the ethos of ancient Vedic religion and Vedic civilization, and fundamentally constructed with Hindu systems of philosophy.

Definition and Misconception: Though they are often classified as 'Hindu' or 'Indian mythology', the label does not capture the centrality of religious and spiritual affiliations of the texts that ring true today for most Hindus. They are replete with long philosophical discourses and are often seen as source books for Hindu ethics and practice. It is also to be noted that historical evidence of many acts or places of Hindu narratives have been found, establishing them as historical facts. However, evidence is extremely limited and only allows for the possibility of myths being history.

Vedic Mythology: The roots of mythology that evolved from classical Hinduism come from the times of the Vedic civilization, from the ancient Vedic religion. The characters, theology, philosophy and stories that make up ancient Vedic myths are indelibly linked with Hindu beliefs. The Vedas are said to be four in number, namely Rigveda, Yajurveda, Samaveda, and the Atharva Veda. Some of these texts mention mythological concepts and machines very much similar to modern day scientific theories and machines.

Sources: It is believed that the Hindu mythology dates back to around 7200 BC when the first hymns of the Rigveda were sung praising the elements of nature, namely, the air, the water, the thunder, the sun, the fire, etc. They found expression in early Vedic Gods, namely, Vayu, Varuna, Indra, Surya and Agni. According to modern scholars over a period of time several Vedic Gods were conceptualized. Over next several millennia, in the post-Vedic period, and during the period of the Puranas, the Gods were personified and assumed specific shapes and characteristics, with individual endowments.

This was followed by the period of the epics, when the Ramayana and the Mahabharata were composed. It is believed that they capture and depict, to a large extent, historical events and happenings, and certain modern findings also seem to corroborate this, like the finding of an ancient bridge constructed between India and Sri Lanka. However, more archaelogical evidence is required to further substantiate the actual occurrence of the events around which the two epics are based.

The Puranas deal with stories that are "mythologically" older than the epics and are set in the "Kritha" or "Sathya" yuga, the first of the four great time periods said to compose what is called the Divya yuga lasting over 4,320,000 years. The epics themselves are set in different "yugas" or periods of time in *Hindu mythology*. The Ramayana, written by the poet Valmiki, describes the life and times of Lord Rama (the seventh avatar of Lord Vishnu) and occurs in the Tretha yuga, while the Mahabharata that describes the life and times of the

Pandavas, occurs in the Dwapara yuga, a period in which Lord Krishna (the eighth avatar of Lord Vishnu) took birth.

Epics: The most important of these are an 18 voluminous group of works known as the Puranas. The two great Hindu Epics, the Ramayana and the Mahabharata, are other major works of *Hindu mythology*. The epics *Mahabharata* and *Ramayana* are very much religious scriptures. Their stories are deeply embedded in Hindu philosophy and serve as parables and sources of devotion for Hindus.

Cosmology: Hinduism presents a number of accounts pertaining to cosmology, and several explanations have been given as regards the origin of the universe. The most popular belief is that the universe emerged from Hiranyagarbha, meaning the *golden womb*. Hiranyagarbha floated around in water in the emptiness and the darkness of non-existence. Ultimately, this golden egg split and the cosmos was created. Swarga emerged from the golden upper part of the Hiranyagarbha, whereas Prithvi came out from the silver coloured lower half part.

The Wars

The Weapons: There are several weapons which were believed to be used by the Gods of the Hindu mythology, some of which are Agneyastra, Brahmastra, Chakram, Kaumodaki, Narayanastra, Pashupata, Shiva Dhanush, Sudarshan, Trishul, Vaishnavastra, Vajra, Varunastra, and Vayavastra. A particular weapon was generally associated with a particular God.

The Deluge: The story of a great flood is mentioned in ancient Hindu texts, particularly the Satapatha Brahmana. It is compared to the accounts of the Deluge found in several religions and cultures. Manu was informed of the impending flood and was protected by the Matsya Avatara of Lord Vishnu, who had manifested himself in this form to rid the world of morally depraved human beings and protect the pious, as also all animals and plants. After the flood the Lord inspires the Manusmriti, largely based upon the Vedas, which details the moral code of conduct, of living and the division of society according to the caste system.

The Peoples of the Epics: Hindu mythology is not only about Gods and men, but classifies a host of different kinds of celestial, ethereal and earthly beings.

Sapta Rishis: Lord Brahma, out of his thought, creates seven sages, or Sapta Rishis, to help him in his act of creation. *Sapta Rishis* (*sapta* means seven and *rishis* means sages in Sanskrit). They are Bhrigu, Angira, Atri, Gautama, Kashyapa, Vashishta, and Agastya. The other meaning of Saptarishis is constellation of Great Bear (Ursa Major).

Pitrs: The Pitrs, or fathers, were the first humans.

The Worlds: Hindu mythology defines fourteen worlds (not to be confused with planets)-seven higher worlds (heavens) and seven lower ones (hells). (The earth is considered the lowest of the seven higher worlds.) All the worlds except the earth are used as temporary places of stay as follows: upon one's death on earth, Yama, the god of death (officially called 'Yama Dharma Raajaa'-Yama, the lord of justice) tallies the person's good/bad deeds while on earth and decides if the soul goes to heaven and/or hell, for how long, and in what capacity.

Some versions of the mythology state that good and bad deeds neutralize each other and the soul therefore spends time in either a heaven or a hell, but not both, whereas according to another school of thought, the good and bad deeds don't cancel out each other. In either case, the soul acquires a body as appropriate to the worlds it is entering. At the end of the soul's time in those worlds, it returns to the earth (is reborn as a life form on the earth). It is considered that only from the earth, and only after a human life, can the soul reach supreme salvation Moksha, the state free from the cycle of birth and death and the place beyond the fourteen worlds where the eternal god lives.

The Higher Worlds: Swarga is the third among the seven higher worlds. In common usage, Swarga is used to refer to the 'higher worlds' or heavens in general. The higher worlds (except the earth) are populated with a variety of beings called Suras, consisting of several subdivisions: Deva, Dhanava, Gandharva, Yaksha, Kinnara, and so on. In general, beings of a higher heavenly world can freely visit a lower one. All the posts (kings, etc.) in the heavenly worlds are awarded based on the good deeds one performs while on earth.

The Lower Worlds: The term Naraka indicates the various lower worlds. The lower worlds are filled with Asuras.

Gods and Goddesses: There are many layers of gods in Hinduism. At the top are the trinity: Shiva (the destroyer), Vishnu (the protector), and Brahma (the creator), and their wives (goddesses in their own right): Shakti (also known as Paarvathi, Ambicaa) the goddess of courage and power, Lakshmi the goddess of all forms of wealth, and Saraswati the goddess of learning. The children of the gods are also gods in their own right. Interestingly, Brahma is also considered the ruler of the highest of the heavens (the world called *Sathya*), so in one sense, Brahma is not beyond the fourteen worlds as Shiva and Vishnu are.

The next lower tier of gods are those in charge of the elements: Indra (the god of thunder and lightning; he also rules the world of Swarga), Varuna (the god of the oceans), Agni (the god of fire), Kubera (the treasurer of the gods), Surya (the sun god), Vaayu (the god of wind), and Soma (the moon god). Below these are the 'garden variety' beings, who have superior powers when compared to humans but otherwise serve one of the above gods.

Swarga also has a set of famous heavenly dancers: Urvasi, Menaka, Rambhaa, and Thilottamaa (all female), whose job is to entertain the heavenly court, and upon orders from the heavenly kings, to distract people on the earth from accumulating too much good deeds so as to become a threat to the heavenly kings. Other notable inhabitants of the heavens include the celestial sages, and Naaradha the messenger of the gods. Yama (the god of death and justice) is said to live in Kailash along with his master Shiva. He rules the lower world of Naraka with a band of emissaries called the *Yama duta* (messengers of Yama), who bring the souls of dead persons to Yama for evaluation. Chitragupta is one of those lower level celestial beings who functions as the karmic accountant of all the actions of the human beings on earth.

Incarnations: As the protector of life, one of the duties of Vishu is to appear on the earth whenever a firm hand is required to set things right. The epic Bhagavatham is the chronology of Vishnu's ten major incarnations (there are totally twenty six incarnations): Matsya (fish), Kurma (turtle), Varaaha (boar), Narasimha (lion-faced human)), Vaamana (an ascetic in the form of a midget), Parasuraama (a militant Brahmin),

Rama, Balaraama (a shepherd and also the half-brother of Krishna), Krishna, Kalki (a warrior on a white horse) whose appearance also signals the beginning of the end of the epoch.

House of Ikshvaku: Ikshvaku was the son of Manu, the first mortal man, and founder of the Sun Dynasty.

Bharatavarsha: The first king to conquer all of the world was Bharata, son of Dushyanta and Shakuntala. All of this world, Vishwa, is named Bharatavarsha, or *The Land of Bharata*, or *The Cherished Land.*

King Bharata's conquests are described to have stretched over all of modern India, and Pakistan, Bangladesh and Nepal, as well as the ancient Gandhara region of Afghanistan. No account has been known to exceed these geographical boundaries

HINDU COSMOLOGY

The Rig Veda questions the *origin of the cosmos* in:

"Neither being (sat) nor non-being was as yet. What was concealed? And where? And in whose protection?... Who really knows? Who can declare it? Whence was it born, and whence came this creation? The devas were born later than this world's creation, so who knows from where it came into existence? None can know from where creation has arisen, and whether He has or has not produced it. He who surveys it in the highest heavens, He alone knows-or perhaps knows not."

(Rig Veda 10. 129)

But the Rig Veda's view of the cosmos also sees one true divine principle self-projecting as the divine word, Vaak, 'birthing' the cosmos that we know, from the monistic Hiranyagarbha or Golden Womb. The Hiranyagarbha is alternatively viewed as Brahma, the creator who was in turn created by God, or as God (Brahman) himself. The later puranic view asserts that the universe is created, destroyed, and recreated in an eternally repetitive series of cycles. In Hindu cosmology, a universe endures for about 4,320,000,000 years (one day of Brahma, the creator or kalpa) and is then destroyed by fire or water elements. At this point, Brahma rests for one night, just as long as the day. This process, named pralaya

(*Cataclysm*), repeats for 100 Brahma years (311 trillion human years) that represents Brahma's lifespan. It must be noted that Brahma is the creator but not necessarily regarded as God in Hinduism. He is mostly regarded as a creation of God/Brahman. We are currently believed to be in the 51st year of the present Brahma and so about 155 trillion years have elapsed since He was born as Brahma. After Brahma's "death", it is necessary that another 100 Brahma years pass until he is reborn and the whole creation begins anew. This process is repeated again and again, forever.

Brahma's life is divided in one thousand cycles (Maha Yuga, or the Great Year). Maha Yuga, during which life, including the human race appears and then disappears, has 71 divisions, each made of 14 Manvantara (1000) years. Each Maha Yuga lasts for 4,320,000 years. Manvantara is Manu's cycle, the one who gives birth and governs the human race. Each Maha Yuga consists of a series of four shorter yugas, or ages. The yugas get progressively worse from a moral point of view as one proceeds from one yuga to another. As a result each yuga is of shorter duration than the age that preceded it. The current Kali Yuga (Iron Age) began at midnight 17 February/ 18 February in 3102 BC in the proleptic Julian calendar.

Quoted Views on Hindu Cosmology: Professor Arthur Holmes (1895-1965) geologist, professor at the University of Durham. He writes regarding the age of the earth in his great book, *The Age of Earth* (1913) as follows:

> *"Long before it became a scientific aspiration to estimate the age of the earth, many elaborate systems of the world chronology had been devised by the sages of antiquity. The most remarkable of these occult time-scales is that of the ancient Hindus, whose astonishing concept of the Earth's duration has been traced back to Manusmriti, a sacred book."*

When the Hindu calculation of the present age of the earth and the expanding universe could make Professor Holmes so astonished, the precision with which the Hindu calculation regarding the age of the entire Universe was made would make any man spellbound.

Alan Watts, a professor, graduate school dean and research

fellow of Harvard University, drew heavily on the insights of Vedanta. Watts became well known in the 1960s as a pioneer in bringing Eastern philosophy to the West. He wrote:

> *"To the philosophers of India, however, Relativity is no new discovery, just as the concept of light years is no matter for astonishment to people used to thinking of time in millions of kalpas, (A kalpa is about 4,320,000,000 years). The fact that the wise men of India have not been concerned with technological applications of this knowledge arises from the circumstance that technology is but one of innumerable ways of applying it."*

It is, indeed, a remarkable circumstance that when Western civilization discovers Relativity it applies it to the manufacture of atom-bombs, whereas Oriental civilization applies it to the development of new states of consciousness." *Count Maurice Maeterlinck* (1862-1949) was a Belgian writer of poetry, a wide variety of essays. He won the 1911 Nobel Prize for literature. In his book *Mountain Paths*, says:

> *"he falls back upon the earliest and greatest of Revelations, those of the Sacred Books of India with a Cosmogony which no European conception has ever surpassed."*

Huston Smith (?) born in China to Methodist missionaries, a philosopher, most eloquent writer, world-famous religion scholar who practices Hatha Yoga. He has said of Hinduism:

> *"The invisible excludes nothing, the invisible that excludes nothing is the infinite – the soul of India is the infinite."*
>
> *"Philosophers tell us that the Indians were the first ones to conceive of a true infinite from which nothing is excluded. The West shied away from this notion. The West likes form, boundaries that distinguish and demarcate. The trouble is that boundaries also imprison – they restrict and confine."*
>
> *"India saw this clearly and turned her face to that which has no boundary or whatever... India anchored her soul in the infinite seeing the things of the world as masks of the infinite assumes – there can be no end*

> *to these masks, of course. If they express a true infinity... And It is here that India's mind boggling variety links up to her infinite soul."*
>
> *"India includes so much because her soul being infinite excludes nothing... It goes without saying that the universe that India saw emerging from the infinite was stupendous."*
>
> *"While the West was still thinking, perhaps, of 6,000 years old universe – India was already envisioning ages and eons and galaxies as numerous as the sands of the Ganges. The Universe so vast that modern astronomy slips into its folds without a ripple."*

Dick Teresi, author and coauthor of several books about science and technology, including "The God Particle".

"Indian cosmologists, the first to estimate the age of the earth at more than 4 billion years. They came closest to modern ideas of atomism, quantum physics, and other current theories. India developed very early, enduring atomist theories of matter. Possibly Greek atomistic thought was influenced by India, via the Persian civilization." According to Guy Sorman, visiting scholar at Hoover Institution at Stanford and the leader of new liberalism in France:

> *"Temporal notions in Europe were overturned by an India rooted in eternity. The Bible had been the yardstick for measuring time, but the infinitely vast time cycles of India suggested that the world was much older than anything the Bible spoke of. It seems as if the Indian mind was better prepared for the chronological mutations of Darwinian evolution and astrophysics."*

Carl Sagan on Hindu Cosmology: Carl Sagan was a distinguished Cornell University astronomer and Pulitzer Prize-winning author.

> *"The main reason that we oriented this episode of Cosmos towards India is because of that wonderful aspect of Hindu cosmology which first of all gives a time-scale for the Earth and the universe—a time-scale which is consonant with that of modern scientific cosmology. We know that the Earth is about 4.6 billion*

years old, and the cosmos, or at least its present incarnation, is something like 10 or 20 billion years old. The Hindu tradition has a day and night of Brahma in this range, somewhere in the region of 8.4 billion years."

"As far as I know. It is the only ancient religious tradition on the Earth which talks about the right time-scale. We want to get across the concept of the right time-scale, and to show that it is not unnatural. In the West, people have the sense that what is natural is for the universe to be a few thousand years old, and that billions is indwelling, and no one can understand it. The Hindu concept is very clear. Here is a great world culture which has always talked about billions of years."

"Finally, the many billion year time-scale of Hindu cosmology is not the entire history of the universe, but just the day and night of Brahma, and there is the idea of an infinite cycle of births and deaths and an infinite number of universes, each with its own gods."

Roger Bertschausen

"We in the West have long had trouble with time. Early Judaism, Christianity and Islam had no inkling of the long age of the universe. Cosmologies from these religions were based on the notion that the universe started at a finite point in the recent past. St. Augustine set the beginning of the universe at 5000 BCE. For centuries, this figure was embraced by most Westerners. (And some continue to believe it.) Additionally, the early Christians also believed that the end of time as we know it was close at hand."

"This view of time contrasts sharply with other religious perspectives on the age of the universe. In the Hindu tradition, for example, one day in the life of Brahma lasts 4,320,000,000 years. And Brahma lives for the equivalent of 311,040,000,000,000 human years. The historian of religions Huston Smith reports one way of conceiving of the Hindu time-frame."

2

The Hindu Deities

Ishvara: In Hinduism, when God is thought of as the supreme all-powerful person (rather than as the infinite principle called Brahman), God is called Bhagvan. *Bhagvan* is a word used to refer to the personal aspect of God in general; it is not specific to a particular deity. Bhagvan transcends gender, yet can be looked upon as both father and mother, child, or sweetheart. Most Hindus, in their daily devotional practices, worship some form of this personal aspect of God, although they believe in the more abstract concept of Brahman as well. Sometimes this means worshipping God through an image or a picture. Sometimes it just means thinking of God as a personal being.

Depending on which aspect of Bhagvan one is talking about, a different name will be used—and frequently a different image or picture. For instance, when God is talked about in the aspect as the creator, God is called Brahm. When referred to in the capacity as preserver of the world, God is called Vishnu. When referred to in the capacity as destroyer of the world, God is called Shiva. Many of these individual aspects of God also have other names and images. For example, Krishna and Rama are considered forms of Vishnu. All the various deities and images one finds in Hinduism are considered manifestations of the same God, called Bhagvan in the personal aspect and Brahman when referred to as an abstract concept.

In their personal religious practices, Hindus worship primarily one or another of these deities, known as their "ishta devat," or chosen idol. The particular form of God worshipped as one's chosen ideal is a matter of individual preference. Regional and family traditions can play a large part in influencing this choice. Hindus may also take guidance about this choice from their scriptures.

Although Hindus may worship deities other than their chosen idol from time to time as well, depending on the occasion and their personal inclinations, it is not expected that they will worship—or even know about—every form of God. Hindus generally choose one concept of God (*e.g.*, Krishna, Rama, Shiva, or Kali) and cultivate devotion to that chosen form, while at the same time respecting the chosen ideals of other people.

Devas and Devis: Krishna, an avatra of Vishnu, reveals his universal form to the devotee Arjuna in the *Bhagavad Gita*. This image indicates that all deities are forms of the One God, and that God is everything that exists. The Hindu religion speaks of many individual deities, called Devas. Goddesses are called *dev+s*. The various devas and dev+s are personifications of various aspects of one and the same God (Ishvara). For instance, when a Hindu thinks of Ishvara as the giver of knowledge and learning, that aspect of Ishvara is personified as the deity Saraswati. In the same manner, the deity Lakshmi personifies Ishvara as the giver of wealth and prosperity. This does not imply that Ishvara is the Lord of all the other deities; Ishvara is just the name used to refer to the personal God in general, when no *particular* deity is being referred to.

The *devas* (also called *devats*) constitute an integral part of the colourful Hindu culture. These various forms of God are depicted in innumerable paintings, statues, murals, and scriptural stories that can be found in temples, homes, businesses, and other places. In Hinduism the scriptures recommend that for the satisfaction of a particular material desire a person may worship a particular deity. For example, shopkeepers frequently keep a statue or picture of the Devi Lakshmi in their shops. The elephant-headed deva known as Ganesha is worshipped before commencing any undertaking, as he represents God's aspect as the remover of obstacles. Students and scholars may propitiate Saraswati, the Devi of learning, before taking an exam or giving a lecture.

The most ancient Vedic *devas* included Indra, Agni, Soma,

Varuna, Mitra, Savitri, Rudra, Prajapati, Vishnu, Aryaman and the Ashvins; important *dev+s* were *Sarasvat+*, *jc* and *Prithv+*. Later scriptures called the *Purnas* recount traditional stories about each individual deity.

Vishnu and *Shiva* are not regarded as ordinary *devas* but as *Mahdevas* ("Great Gods") because of their central positions in worship and mythology. The *Purnas* also laud other *devas,* such as *Ganesha* and *Hanumn,* and *avatras* such as *Rma* and *Krishna*. Goddesses are worshipped when God is thought of as the Universal Mother. Particular forms of the Universal Mother include *Lakshm+*, *Sarasvat+* and *Parvat+, Durg*, and *Kl+*.

There are some Hindus who consider the various deities not as forms of the one Ishwara, but as independently existing entities, and may thus be properly considered polytheistic to some extent.

Avataras (incarnations of God): Rama (centre), an avatara, shown with wife Sita, brother Lakshmana and devotee Hanuman. Rama is shown with blue skin, symbolizing divinity. Many denominations of Hinduism, such as Vaishnavism and Smartism, teach that from time to time, God comes to Earth as a human being to help humans along in their struggle toward enlightenment and salvation (Moksha). Such an incarnation of God is called an avatara. In some respects, the Hindu concept of avatara is similar to the belief found in Christianity that God came to the earth in the form of Jesus. However, whereas most Christians believe that God has assumed a human body on only one occasion, Hinduism teaches that there have been *multiple* avatars throughout history—and that there will be more in the future. Thus Krishna, an incarnation of God, says:

Whenever righteousness declines
And unrighteousness increases,
I make myself a body;
In every age I come back
To deliver the holy,
To destroy the sin of the sinner,
To establish righteousness.

The most famous of the divine incarnations are Rama, whose life is depicted in the Ramayana, and Krishna, whose life is depicted in the Mahabharata and the Srimad Bhagavatam. The Bhagavad Gita, which contains the spiritual teachings of Krishna, is one of the most widely-read scriptures in Hinduism.

Trimurti: In Hinduism, the Trimurti (also called *the Hindu* trinity) are three aspects of God in His forms as Brahma, Vishnu and Shiva.

- Brahma—the Creator
- Vishnu—the Preserver
- Shiva—the Destroyer

Some other popular Hindu aspects of God include Devi, Krishna, Ganesha, Hanuman, Murugan, Ramachandra and Lakshmi. Smarta Hindus believe that God, in whatever form they prefer, ("Ishta Devata,", *i.e.*, the preferred form of God) can grant worshippers grace to bring them closer to Moksha, end of the cycle of rebirth. The great Hindu saint Ramakrishna studied and embraced other religions, such as Christianity and Islam, and came to the same conclusion proclaimed by the Vedas, "*Truth is one; the wise call it by various names.* (*Ekam Sat Viprah Bahuda Vadanti*)

Denominations of Hinduism: Contemporary Hinduism traditionally has four major divisions, Shaivism, Shaktism, Vaishnavism, and Smarthism.

According to Adherents.com there are 580,000,000 Vaishnavas, 220,000,000 Shaivites and 22,000,000 neo-Hindus and reform Hindus.

However the Shakti sect connects God as Lord Shiva also, as the Aparabrahm while Shakti is the Parabrahm. Further the Saura sect connects itself with Lord Vishnu, one of the 12 Adityas (solar deities.) Ganesha worshippers would connect themselves with Lord Shiva as Lord Shiva is the Father of Lord Ganesha and hence, Lord Ganesha is a Shaiv deity.

Hinduism is a very rich and complex religion. Each of its four denominations shares rituals, beliefs, traditions and personal Gods with one another, but each sect have a same and different philosophy on how to achieve life's ultimate goal (Moksha, liberation).

For example a person can be a Shiva devotee and a Vishnu devotee but they can practice the Advaita Vedanta philosophy (Darshana) which believes there is no difference between the Brahman and the Soul. Conversely a Hindu may follow the Dvaita philosophy which stresses that Brahman and the Soul are not the same.

But each denomination fundamentally believes in different methods of self-realisation and in different aspects of the One Supreme God. However, each denomination respects and accepts all others, and conflict of any kind is rare.

Vaishnavism, Shaivism and Shaktism, respectively believe in a monotheistic ideal of Vishnu (often as Krishna), Shiva, or Devi; this view does not exclude other personal Gods, as they are understood to be aspects of the chosen ideal (*e.g.*, to many devotees of Krishna, Shiva is seen as having sprung from Krishna's creative force). Often, the monad Brahman is seen as the one source, with all other gods emanating therefrom. Thus, with all Hindus, there is a strong belief in all paths being true religions that lead to one God or source, whatever one chooses to call the ultimate truth.

Even Vaisnavites, like other Hindus, have tolerance for other beliefs because Lord Krishna, avatar of Vishnu, said so in the Gita. Krishna said:

> *"I am in everyone's heart as the Supersoul. As soon as one desires to worship some demigod, I make his faith steady so that he can devote himself to that particular deity. Endowed with such a faith, he endeavors to worship a particular demigod and obtains his desires. But in actuality these benefits are bestowed by Me alone." (Gita: 7.21-22).*

Another quote in the Gita states:

> *"Those who are devotees of other gods and who worship them with faith actually worship only Me, O son of Kunt+, but they do so in a wrong way." (Gita: 9.23).*

Even a Vedic verse illustrates this theme of tolerance. The Vedas are revered in Hinduism, regardless of denomination. For example, a well-known Rig Vedic hymn stemming from Hinduism states that "Truth is One, though the sages know it variously." This is in contrast with some other religious traditions, where one must believe in only one form of God and to totally reject or disdain other beliefs.

Polytheistic Gods: Although the pantheistic system allowed only a subordinate rank to the old polytheistic gods, and the actual religious belief of the people was probably but little affected by their existence, they continued to occupy an important place in the affections of the poet, and were still represented as exercising considerable influence on the destinies of man.

The most prominent of them were regarded as the appointed Loka palas, or guardians of the world; and as such they were made to preside over the four cardinal and (according to some authorities) the intermediate points of the compass.

Thus Indra, the chief of the devas, was regarded as the regent of the east; Agni, the fire, was in the same way associated with the southeast; Yama, lord of death and justice with the south; Surya, the sun, with the southwest; Varuna, originally the representative of the all-embracing heaven (atmosphere), now the god of the ocean, with the west; Vayu (or Pavana), the wind, with the northwest; Kubera, the god of wealth, with the north; and Soma with the northeast. (Note: In some traditions, an aspect of Shiva is regarded as the regent of the northeast and Nirrti the regent of the southwest.)

In the institutes of Manu the Loka palas are represented as standing in close relation to the ruling king, who is saki to be composed of particles of these his tutelary deities. The retinue of Indra consists chiefly of the Devas (angels), Gandharvas, a class of genii, considered in the epics as the celestial musicians; and Apsaras, lovely nymphs, who are frequently employed by the gods to make the pious devotee desist from carrying his austere practices to an extent that might render him dangerous to their power. Narada, an ancient sage (probably a personification of the cloud, the water-giver), is considered as the messenger between the gods and men, and as having sprung from the forehead of Brahma.

The interesting office of the god of love is held by Kamadeva, also called Ananga, the bodyless, because, as the myth relates, having once tried by the power of his mischievous arrow to make Shiva fall in love with Parvati, whilst he was engaged in devotional practices, the urchin was reduced to ashes by a glance of the angry god. Two other mythological figures of some importance are considered as sons of Shiva and Parvati, *viz.* Karttikeya or Skanda, the leader of the heavenly armies, who was supposed to have been fostered by the six Knittikas or Pleiades; and Ganesha (lord of troops), the elephant-headed god of wisdom, and at the same time the leader of the dii minorum gentium.

Smartism: Smartism, a denomination of Hinduism is a monist as well as a monotheist religion that understands different deities as representing various aspects and principles of one supreme entity, Brahman or parabrahman. Teachers such as Swami Vivekananda, who brought Hinduism to the West, held beliefs like those found in Smartism, although he usually referred to his religion as Vedanta. Other denominations of Hinduism do not strictly hold this belief. A Smartist would have no problem worshipping Shiva or Vishnu together as he views the different aspects of God as leading to the same One God. It is the Smarta view that dominates the view of Hinduism in the West. By contrast, a Vaishnavite considers Vishnu as the one true God, worthy of worship and other forms as subordinate.

Devas in the Vedas: The pantheon in the Zrauta tradition consists of various gods and goddesses. However these entities may not hold the traditional meaning of gods and goddesses in English. Instead the *devas* (which is the sanskrit word used to represent these entities) represent certain forces. For instance, the deva Agni has one aspect as the flame. But this flame symbolises the psychological power associated with Agni namely the power of will. Agni can be called God-will. Similarly Indra is the God-mind; Saraswati is the Power of Inspiration, not merely of learning.

The main devas are (vide 6th anuvaka of Chamakam):

- Agni
- Indra
- Soma
- Savitr

- Vayu
- Varuna
- Marutas
- Aditya
- Rudra
- Vishnu
- Brahma
- Uma or Shiva/Shivaa
- Pusha
- Brihaspati
- Ashwinis
- Vishvedavas
- Prithvi
- Dyaus
- Antariksha
- Dishas
- Moordha
- Prajapati

The main aspects of Devi (goddesses) are:

- Saraswati or Vaak
- Lakshmi or Shri
- Durga or Parvati

The 10 Avatars (Dashavatar) of Vishnu

1. Matsya, the fish, appeared in the Satya Yuga.
2. Kurma, the tortoise, appeared in the Satya Yuga.
3. Varaha, the boar, appeared in the Satya Yuga.
4. Narasimha, the Man-Lion (Nara = man, simha = lion), appeared in the Satya Yuga.
5. Vamana, the Dwarf, appeared in the Treta Yuga.
6. Parashurama, Rama with the axe, appeared in the Treta Yuga.
7. Rama, Sri Ramachandra, the prince and king of Ayodhya, appeared in the Treta Yuga.
8. Krishna (meaning dark or black) appeared in the Dwapara Yuga.

9. Balarama (meaning 'strong Rama'). Balarama is said to have appeared in the Dwapara Yuga (along with Krishna) or Buddha. He is also said to have been an incarnation of the Ananta Shesha.
10. Kalki ("Eternity", or "time", or "The Destroyer of foulness"), who is expected to appear at the end of Kali Yuga, the time period in which we currently exist, which will end in the year 428899 CE.

List of Hindu Gurus and Saints: These are some of the most noteworthy Gurus and Saints of Hinduism:

- A.C. Bhaktivedanta Swami Prabhupada
- Adi Shankara
- Akhandanand
- Mata Amritanandamayi
- Sri Aurobindo
- Baba Lokenath Brahmachari
- Bhakti Tirtha Swami
- Bhakti Vaibhava Puri Maharaj
- Bhagwan Nityananda
- Bhagwan Swaminarayan
- Chaitanya Mahaprabhu
- Chinmayananda
- Sri Chinmoy
- Swami Dayananda Saraswati
- Devamrita Swami
- Dharmsamrat Paramhans Swami Madhavananda
- Gurumayi Chidvilasananda
- Hrdayananda Gosvami
- Swami Janakananda
- Jayadvaita Swami
- Jayapataka Swami
- Lahiri Mahasaya
- Madhvacharya
- Mahavatar Babaji
- Maharishi Mahesh Yogi

- Shri Gurudev Mahendranath
- Malati Devi Dasi
- Mother Meera
- Muktananda
- Narayana Guru
- Neem Karoli Baba
- Nimbarka
- Swami Niranjanananda
- Nisargadatta Maharaj
- Radhanath Swami
- Raghavendra Swami
- Ramakrishna Paramahamsa
- Ramana Maharshi
- Ramanuja
- Ram Dass (Richard Alpert)
- Swami Ramatirtha
- Sri Sri Ravi Shankar
- Paramahamsa Sri Nithyananda Swamigal
- Paramahansa Yogananda
- Paramyogeshwar Sri Devpuriji
- Pramukh Swami Maharaj
- Sai Baba of Shirdi
- Sarada Devi
- Satguru Sivaya Subramuniyaswami
- Satsvarupa dasa Goswami
- Satya Sai Baba
- Swami Satyananda
- Shankaracharya
- Shree Maa
- Shriram Sharma Acharya
- Swami Shyam
- Yogiraj Gurunath Siddhanath
- Swami Sivananda
- Swarupananda

- Tamala Krishna Goswami
- Upasni Maharaj
- Swami Vivekananda
- Yogaswami
- Yukteswar Giri.

3

Philosophy, Mythology and Ritual

In every religion there are three parts, *viz.*, philosophy, mythology and ritual. Philosophy is the essence of religion. It sets forth its basic principles or fundamental doctrines or tenets, the goal and the means of attaining it. Mythology explains and illustrates philosophy by means of legendary lives of great men or of supernatural beings. Ritual gives a still more concrete form to philosophy so that everyone may understand it. Ritual consists of forms, ceremonies, etc.

Puranas contain various myths. The cosmogonic myths of the Puranas are very interesting. A certain portion of Hindu mythology is even now presented to the public in the form of dramas during days of Hindu festivals. Thus the minds of the people are saturated with sublime ideas and ideals and lifted to great spiritual heights.

Study of Mythology and its Advantages

There are great truths behind the ancient mythology of Hinduism. You cannot ignore a thing simply because it has a garb of mythology. Do not argue. Shut up your mouth. Keep your intellect at a respectable distance when you study mythology. Intellect is a hindrance. It will delude you. Give up arrogance and vanity. Cultivate love for imagery. Sit like a child and open your heart freely. You will comprehend the great truths revealed by mythology. You will penetrate into the hearts of the Rishis and sages who wrote the mythology. You will really enjoy mythology now.

You study geography through maps. There is no real country or town in a map, but it helps you to know a great deal about the different countries. Similar is the case with myths. You can grasp the subtle philosophical truths through myths.

By studying mythology, you will get several object lessons for moulding your character and leading an ideal divine life. The lives of Sri Rama, Sri Krishna, Bhishma, Nala, Harischandra, Lakshmana, Bharata, Hanuman, Yudhishthira, Arjuna, Sita, Savitri, Damayanti, Radha, etc., are sources of great spiritual inspiration for moulding your life, conduct and character. When you are in a dilemma as to what to do in puzzling situations and when there is conflict of duties, you will get the exact solutions through study of mythology.

Thus, mythology has its own benefits and advantages. It stamps on the minds the subtle and abstract teachings of the Vedas through instructive stories and illuminating discourses and paves the way for men to lead a divine life and attain perfection, freedom and immortality.

HINDU SYMBOLS

Outward symbols are necessary and beneficial. When viewed from the right angle of vision, you will find that they play a very important part in your material as well as spiritual life. Though they may look very simple and unimportant, they are very scientific and effective.

TILAKA—A MARK OF AUSPICIOUSNESS

Tilaka is a mark of auspiciousness. It is put on the forehead with sandal paste, sacred ashes or Kumkuma. The devotees of Shiva apply sacred ashes (Bhasma) on the forehead, the devotees of Vishnu apply sandal paste (Chandana), and the worshippers of Devi or Shakti apply Kumkuma, a red turmeric powder.

The scriptures say:-A forehead without a Tilaka, a woman without a husband, a Mantra the meaning of which is not known while doing Japa, the head that does not bend before holy personages, a heart without mercy, a house without a well, a village without a temple, a country without a river, a society without a leader, wealth that is not given away in charity, a preceptor without a disciple, a country without justice, a king without an able minister, a woman not obedient to her husband, a well without water, a flower without smell, a soul devoid of holiness, a field without rains, an intellect without clearness, a disciple who does not consider his preceptor as a form of God, a body devoid of health, a custom (Achara) without purity, austerity devoid of fellow-feeling, speech in which truth is not the basis, a country without good people, work without wages, Sannyasa without renunciation, legs which have not performed pilgrimages, a determination unaided by Viveka or discrimination, a knife which is blunt, a cow which does not give milk, a spear without a point-all these are worthy of condemnation. They exist for names sake only.-From this you can imagine the importance of Tilaka or the sacred mark.

Tilaka is applied at the Ajna Chakra, the space between the two eyebrows. It has a very cooling effect. Application of sandal paste has great medicinal value, apart from the spiritual influence. Application of sandal paste will nullify the heating effect when you concentrate and meditate at the Bhrumadhya. Tilaka indicates the point at which the spiritual eye opens. Lord Shiva has a third eye at the Bhrumadhya. When He opens the third eye, the three worlds are destroyed.

So also, when the third eve of the Jiva is opened, the three kinds of afflictions-Adhyatmika, Adhidaivika and Adhibhautika-are burnt to ashes. The three Karmas-Sanchita, Prarabdha and Agami-and also all the sins committed in the countless previous births, are burnt. When you apply the Tilaka, you mentally imagine:-I am the one non-dual Brahman free from all duality. May my eye of intuition open soon?-You should remember this every time you apply a Tilaka.

There are various methods of applying Tilaka. Shaivas apply three horizontal lines with the sacred ashes. The Vaishnavas apply three vertical lines (Tripundra) on the forehead. When they apply Tilaka, they say:-O Lord, protect me from the evil effects of the Trigunatmika Maya which has Sattva, Rajas and Tamas as its binding cords.-Some Vaishnavas apply only one vertical line. Only the method of application differs, but the significance is the same in both the Vaishnavas and the Shaivas.

THE TUFT—ITS UTILITY AND SIGNIFICANCE

Brahmins (Brahmanas) as well as the other castes grow

Choti or Sikha, a tuft of hair. This tuff of hair was not so small in olden days, as seen in the present day. It covered the whole brain. They allowed the hair to grow. They never cut the tuft. It protects the brain from any sudden stroke and keeps it cool. The heat of the sun does not affect the head directly. Lack of this tuff has necessitated the use of umbrellas, etc.

The tuft is most scientific as well as religious. Any religious act should be performed after tying the tuft. Only the funeral and death anniversaries are performed with tuft untied or with dishevelled hair. It is very inauspicious to remain with dishevelled hair.

It is done only in times of great sorrow or calamity. Draupadi took an oath in the assembly of the Kurus when she was molested by Dussasana that she would remain with dishevelled hair until the enemies were properly revenged. Kaikeyi remained with dishevelled hair in her apartment with the object of getting two boons from Dasaratha which were detrimental to the interests of Rama, the favourite of Dasaratha. Auspicious acts are never undertaken with tuft untied. Nowadays, very few people wear tuft, and even women are neglecting this vital point in their feverish anxiety to copy the West. The tuft of hair has a salutary effect on the essential parts of the brain and the central nervous system.

SIGNIFICANCE OF THE SACRED THREAD

Yajnopavita or the sacred thread is worn by the Brahmins, Kshatriyas and the Vaishyas. Wearing the sacred thread is a very holy and sacred ceremony amongst the Hindus. Brahmin boys between the ages of five and eight are invested with the sacred thread on a very auspicious day. By this ceremony, they become fit for the repetition of Gayatri A Brahmin becomes a true Brahmin only after this ceremony. It is said:-*Janmana Jayate Sudrah Karmana Jayate Dvijah*-By birth one is a Sudra; by Karma (*i.e.*, the investiture with the sacred thread) he becomes a Dvija or Brahmin. Upanayana or thread ceremony is the second birth; hence, the Brahmins are called Dvijas (Dvija means-born twice).

The sacred thread or Yajnopavita consists of three threads. It denotes that one should be a Brahmachari in thought, word and deed. Each thread represents a Veda, *viz.*, the Rik, Yajus and Sama. It represents also Brahma, Vishnu and Shiva. The knot in the middle represents the formless Brahman, the Supreme Principle. The three threads represent also Sattva, Rajas and Tamas of the Trigunatmika Maya, and the knot represents the Isvara who controls Maya. Those who worship God at the three Sandhyas and repeat the Gayatri holding the Brahma knot of the sacred thread, derive immense strength and power.

In days of yore, a Brahmana meditating upon the Gayatri holding the Brahma knot, had the power to bless and curse others. The educated intelligentsia of the present day are quite ignorant of the power of the sacred thread and the performance of Sandhya. That is the reason why they have ignored it. The sacred thread is a great power for the Brahmin who leads a regulated life devoted to the worship of God. Kshatriyas and Vaishyas, too, acquire power, fame and wealth by the power of the sacred thread.

A householder wears, at the time of marriage, an additional sacred thread. A Brahmachari has only one. The additional thread at the time of marriage is intended for the well-being of the partner. The sacred thread should be on the body always. The custom of washing it after removing it from the body or sending it to the washerman, is a wrong procedure. Some people are ashamed to wear the thread when they go to the office and they leave it at home. How ignorant they are!

Yajnopavita, the Choti, caste-mark, etc., are the external symbols to show that one is a Hindu. Purity, self-restraint, non-violence, patience, love for ones fellow-beings-these are the internal marks of a Hindu.

ACHAMANA AND PROKSHANA

Achamana is sipping water three times, repeating the Names of the Lord. Prokshana is sprinkling water over ones body for the sake of purity, when a bath is not possible. This is for internal as well as external purity. While sipping water, the following Mantras are repeated:-*Achyutaya Namah*-prostrations to the immutable Lord; *Anantaya Namah*-prostrations to the unlimited Lord; *Govindaya Namah*-prostrations to the Lord who is known by the Name of Govinda.-Then the various Names of the Lord-Keshava, Narayana,

Madhava, Govinda, Vishnu, Madhusudana, Trivikrama, Vamana, Sridhara, Rishikesh, Padmanabha and Damodara-are repeated, touching the various parts Of the body, *viz.*, the eyes, the ears, the face, the navel, the head, etc. One becomes pure by doing Achamana after he answers calls of nature, after walking in the streets, just before taking food and after food, and after a bath.

This reminds you of the Lord now and then. Every act, every ritual, every symbol has a deep philosophical importance. They help you in changing the mental substance from Rajas and Tamas to Sattva. They give you an opportunity to think of God frequently.

Offering Food to God, Guests and the Pancha-Pranas

Before sitting for food, the place is purified, a seat is put and in a leaf the articles of food are served. Before taking the food, a little water is sprinkled making a line all round the leaf repeating some Vedic Mantras. This repetition purifies the food. Then a little water is sipped. According to science as well as medicine, a little water, if drunk before the food is taken, is highly beneficial.

Then the food is offered to the five Pranas and Brahman seated in the heart, by repeating *Om Pranaya Svaha, Apanaya Svaha, Vyanaya Svaha, Udanaya Svaha, Samanaya Svaha,* and lastly, *Brahmane Svaha*. Just mark the importance of this offering. The person who takes the food offers it to the deities who dwell in the body in the form of Prana, Apana, etc. He does not eat for himself. The physical body is not the eater. It is the Pancha Prana that takes the food. Thus, taking food also can be converted into an act of Yoga or sacrifice.

One should daily offer to the Lord the food that he has prepared, before he partakes of it. He should say:-*Tvadiyam Vastu Govinda Tubhyameva Samarpaye*-I offer to Thee, O Govinda, this (food) which belongs to Thee only.-The custom of the Hindus is that they should feed the guest who comes to their house before they take food. The guest is a representative of the Lord. The Srutis say:-*Athhi Devo Bhava.*-

Bells, Lights, Dhupa, Camphor and Sandal Paste

Bells are rung in temples while doing Puja, to shut out the

external sounds and to make the mind inward and concentrated. Lights are waved before the Deity. This denotes that the Lord is Jyotis-Svarupa. He is all-light. The devotee says: O Lord! Thou art the self-effulgent Light of the universe. Thou art the light in the sun, moon and fire. Remove the darkness in me by bestowing your divine light. May my intellect be illumined?-This is the significance of waving lights.

Dhupa or scented incense sticks are burnt before the Deity. The smoke spreads the whole room. It acts as a disinfectant. Burning of Dhupa denotes that the Lord is all-pervading and that He fills the whole universe by His living presence. It is to remind this fact that Dhupa is burnt. The devotee prays:- O Lord! Let the Vasanas and Samskaras dormant in me vanish like the smoke of this Dhupa and become ashes. Let me become stainless.

Burning of camphor denotes that the individual ego melts like the camphor and the Jivatman becomes one with the supreme Light of lights.

The sandal paste reminds the devotee that he should, in his difficulties, be as patient as the sandal. Sandal emanates sweet odour when it is rubbed on a hard surface and made into a paste. So also the devotee should not murmur when difficulties arise, but on the other hand, remain cheerful and happy and emanate sweetness and gentleness like the sandal. He should not hate even his enemy.

This is another precept we learn from this. Though the sandalwood is crushed and made into a paste, it silently wears out emanating only very sweet odour. One should not wish evil even to his enemy.

PRASADA—ITS SACREDNESS AND GLORY

Prasada is that which gives peace. Prasada is the sacred food offering of the Lord. During Kirtana, worship, Puja, Havan and Arati, the devotee offers sweet rice, fruits, jaggery, milk, coconut, plantain and such other articles to the Lord, according to his ability. After offering them to the Lord, they are shared between the members of the house or the Bhaktas in a temple.

Water, flowers, rice, etc., are offered to the Lord in worship. This denotes that the Lord is pleased with even the smallest offering. What is wanted is the heart of the devotee. The Lord says in the Gita:-*Patram Pushpam Phalam Toyam Yo Me Bhaktya Prayacchati; Tadaham Bhaktyupahritamasnami Prayatatmanah*-Whoever offers a leaf, a flower, a fruit or even water, with devotion, that I accept, offered as it is with a loving heart. It is not necessary that one should offer gold, silver and costly dress to the Lord. The devotee offers these according to his ability and position in life, thereby denoting that the whole wealth of the world belongs to the Lord. A rich man offers costly things to the Lord. He feeds the poor and serves the sick, seeing the Lord in his fellow-beings.

Puja is done with Bael leaves, flowers, Tulasi, Vibhuti and these are given as Prasada from the Lord. Vibhuti is the Prasada of Lord Shiva. It is to be applied on the forehead. A small portion can be taken in. Kumkuma is the Prasada of Sri Devi or Shakti. It is to be applied at the space between the eyebrows (Ajna or Bhrumadhya). Tulasi is the Prasada of Lord Vishnu, Rama or Krishna. It is to be taken in. They are charged with mysterious powers by the chanting of Mantras during Puja and Havan. The mental Bhava of the devotee offering Bhog to the Lord has a very great effect. If an ardent devotee of the Lord offers anything to the Lord, that Prasada, if taken, would bring very great change even in the minds of atheists. The Grace of the Lord descends through Prasada. Go through the life of Narada. You will realise the greatness of the sacred leavings of the Lord as well as those of advanced Sadhakas and saints.

Namadeva offered rice, etc., to Panduranga Vitthala and He ate the food and shared it with Namadeva as well. If the food is offered with an yearning heart, sometimes, the Lord takes that food assuming a physical form. In other cases, the Lord enjoys the subtle essence of the food offered, and the food remains as it is in the shape of Prasada. While feeding Mahatmas and the poor people, that which is left behind is taken as Prasada.

When a sacrifice is performed, the participants share the Prasada which bestows the blessings of the gods. When Dasaratha performed Putrakameshti (a sacrifice performed wishing for son), he got a vessel full of sweetened rice which he gave to his queens, by taking which they became pregnant. Prasada is the most sacred object for a devotee. One should consider himself lucky to take the Prasada, and there is no restriction of any kind in taking Prasada. Time and place, and the condition in which one is placed-all these do not affect him in any way. Prasada is all-purifying.

The benefits of Prasada and Charanamrita are beyond description. They have the power to change entirely the outlook of a mans life. Prasada and Charanamrita have the power to cure diseases and even bring back to life dead persons. There had been ever so many instances in the past in this holy land of ours which bear witness to the potency and efficacy of Prasada. Prasada destroys all pains and sins. It is an antidote for misery, pain and anxiety. Faith is the important factor in testing the accuracy of this statement. For faithless persons, it brings very little effect.

Those who are brought up in modern education and culture have forgotten all about the glory of Prasada. Many English-educated persons do not attach any importance to Prasada when they get it from Mahatmas. This is a serious mistake. Prasada is a great purifier. As they are brought up in the western style of living, they have imbibed the spirit of westerners and forgotten the spirit of the true children of Indian Rishis of yore. Live for a week in Vrindavana or Ayodhya or Varanasi or Pandharpur. You will realise the glory and the miraculous effects of Prasada. Many incurable diseases are cured. Many sincere devotional aspirants get wonderful spiritual experiences from mere Prasada alone. Prasada is a panacea. Prasada is a spiritual elixir. Prasada is the Grace of the Lord. Prasada is a cure-all and an ideal pick-me-up. Prasada is an embodiment of Shakti. Prasada is Divinity in manifestation. Prasada energises, vivifies, invigorates and infuses devotion. It should be taken with great faith.

THE JAPA MALA

***Significance of the Number of Beads*:** Generally, the rosary or Mala used for Japa contains 108 beads. A man breathes 21, 600 times every day. If one does 200 Malas of Japa, it becomes 21, 600; thereby, he does one Japa for every breath. If he does 200 Malas of Japa every day, that amounts to remembrance of God throughout the day. Malas may contain beads which form divisions of 108 also, so that the same calculation can be maintained. The Meru (the central bead in the Mala) denotes that you have done your Japa 108 times. This also denotes that every time you come to the Meru bead, you have gone one step further on the spiritual path and crossed over one obstacle. A portion of your ignorance is removed. A rosary or Mala is a whip to goad you to do Japa. Mohammedans also have a rosary (Tasbi) in their hands when they repeat their prayers. They roll the beads and repeat the name of Allah. Christians have their paternoster.

The Raksha Stotra: Before sitting for Japa and meditation, the Raksha Stotra is generally repeated. It means:-May the Lord protect me, staying in every part of my body.-Each part is separately named and a particular Name of the Lord is repeated for the protection of that part. Anganyasa and Karanyasa also have the same effect. They drive away the evil effects of evil spirits, if any. The obstacles that stand in the way of concentration and meditation are removed. Evil thoughts will not enter the mind. This is a prayer to remove obstacles in Japa and meditation.

The Ochre Cloth and the Shaven Head

Symbols of Renunciation: The ochre colour (Gerua) of the dress of a Sannyasin indicates that he is as pure as fire itself. He shines like the burnt gold, free from all impurities of desires and Vasanas. It denotes purity. It stands for purity. For an aspirant who has taken to the path of Nivritti Marga, it is a help. He will swerve and shrink from evil actions. This cloth will remind him that he is not entitled to worldly enjoyments. Gradually his nature will be moulded. This coloured cloth serves as an external symptom to show that one is a Sannyasin.

A Sannyasin shaves his head completely. This removes from him all beauty. He will not have to take care about dressing his hair with scented oils, etc. This shows that he has renounced all external beauties and that he dwells in the Self which is Beauty of beauties. This Mundana (shaving of head) indicates that he is no more of the world. He should not desire any sensual object.

It is only an external symbol of the mental state of complete dispassion and turning away from the pleasures of the world.

He removes his Choti also at the time of Sannyasa to indicate that he is no more bound by the various Nitya and Naimittika Karmas and that they have been burnt in the fire of Vairagya. Further, this shaving of the head is suitable for a wandering life.

The existence of long hairs will prevent him from taking bath whenever he likes. Shaving will relieve him of much worry, and the time he would have otherwise spent in drying, combing and dressing his hair he may spend in prayers and meditation.

Conclusion: The Vedas and the Upanishads state that the ultimate truth in its pure and naked form, very unceremoniously. The Itihasas, Puranas and Agamas give this truth a homely, personal and symbolic touch through narration of history, legend and mythology.

Do not neglect outward symbols. Make a research study of our Vedic customs and injunctions. You will find wonderful and precious gems in every one of them. Their utility and efficacy will be revealed in following them.

May you all tread the path of Dharma and attain Kaivalya Moksha in this very birth.

Infertility, Artificial Insemination & Surrogate Mother in Hindu Mythology

Having children has always been important since time immemorial, and the continuity of the family unit has been of major significance in Hindu culture. Infertility is a social stigma even today, and Indian mythology is full of stories about what couples have done in the past to overcome their problem of infertility. Ancient tales hold the key to the unconscious desires of a people. They help us appreciate the fears and insecurities of people who visit state-of-the-art infertility clinics.

Debt to Ancestors: The following story of sage Agastya from the great Hindu epic Mahabharata (written 2000 years ago) tells us why Hindus, in particular, and Indians, in general, are so obsessed with children. Besides social factors like 'someone to take care of me in my old age', it directs our attention to a profound religious demand for a child, especially a male one.

The sage Agastya wanted moksha-, liberation from the endless cycle of rebirths. So he broke all social bonds, went to the forest, meditated and performed austerities. He believed that by refusing to succumb to any desire, by refusing to yield to the illusory pleasures of the material world, his soul would break free from the prison that was his body. He spent years mortifying himself. Liberation eluded him. Then, one night, he had a vision: he saw his ancestors hanging head down over a gaping hole.

They were crying, "We are trapped in the land of the dead. And there is no hope of escape." "What can I do to help?" asked Agastya. They replied, "Father children, so that we can be reborn. Help us return to the land of the living so that we too can work towards our moksha.

Or else, you will land up in the hell known as Put and suffer there for all eternity. Repay the debt you owe your ancestors." Thus admonished, Agastya returned to his village, got married, fathered children, and only after they had become independent did he return to the forest.

Hindus believe that all men come into this world burdened by a debt – the pitr-runa (pitr = ancestor; runa = debt). The only way to repay this debt is to father a male offspring. During funerary rites, known as shraadha, Hindu males are reminded of this debt. In the Dharmashastras, Hindu law books written between 500-1000 AD, it is said that those who fail to repay this debt end up in the Hell known as Put where they suffer for all eternity. Since the birth of a child, preferably male child, liberates a man from his debt, the Sanskrit word for son is putra (deliverer from Put). The daughter or putri is also a deliverer from Put, but to a lesser extent.

Dharma and Karma

Two words that play a crucial role in the understanding the Hindu (as well as Buddhist and Jain) attitude towards life are dharma and karma.

Dharma is essentially duty that must be performed for the sake of social as well as cosmic stability. Failure to do so leads to social anarchy and cosmic chaos. Duty is traditionally defined by one's inherited caste (teacher, protector, provider, servant) and by one's stage in life (student, householder, senior citizen, hermit). Producing a child is one's biological duty applicable all human beings. Those who wanted to renounce the world were only allowed to do so after they had fulfilled all worldly duties.

Men who could not fulfil their biological obligations because of a physical problem (impotence) or a mental quirk (homosexuality) were termed rather derogatorily kliba or napunsaka, sexually dysfunctional non-man. In the Manu Smriti, an ancient Hindu law book, such men were debarred from sacred rituals and from inheritance.

Only by producing children, were a man and woman considered biologically fulfilled. It must be remembered, that only after marriage was a man in Hindu society given the right to enjoy worldly pleasures and possess worldly wealth. A king could not be king unless he was married. And an impotent man or a man who could not father a child was not allowed to be king. Hence, in the Mahabharata, when the king Pandu learns that he will die the moment he has sex with his wife, he renounces his crown – his inability to father a child debars him from kingship.

Karma means both action and fate. Hindus (as well as Buddhists and Jains) believe that every action leads to a series of reactions. All creatures are obliged to experience the repercussions of their (conscious and unconscious) actions, either in this life or the next. Thus, every event is the result of past actions. If one is barren, it is because of events that occurred in the past, either in this life or in the one before. A folk story based on the Mahabharata illustrates this point. At the end of a great war, queen Gandhari is informed that all her hundred children are dead. She weeps and seeks a reason for this unfair situation, to which a sage replies, "In your last life, you sat on a stone under which there were a hundred turtle eggs. The eggs were crushed. So the mother-turtle cursed you that you too would experience the loss of hundred children."

A situation in governed by karma, but one's reaction to is governed by free will. Astrology helps understand what karma has in store for us. The result of karma can be either endured or it can be modified by certain occult rituals, by the power of holy men or by the grace of god. This is the reason why childless men in India visit temples, go on pilgrimages, seek the intervention of holy men or perform elaborate rituals.

White Seed and Red Seed: Why a male offspring is more important to a Hindu (besides social factors) can be traced to certain beliefs. In the Mahabharata, it is said that the soul of a man lies locked in the semen. Semen is the medium through which ancestors slip into the land of the living. The soul in semen is embodied in the womb.

According to ancient Hindu seers known as rishis, within the womb is the red seed known as rajas (the counterpart of the white male seed known as shukra). The rajas wraps the soul in flesh and blood. The shukra, besides being a medium for the soul, is also the source of bones. Thus all living creatures come into being because of the father's white seed and the mother's red seed. The former generates consciousness and transforms into the skeleton while the latter creates the flesh.

There is an interesting story in this regard from the Padma Purana. A king had two wives but no children. He asked some sages to make a potion that would make his wives pregnant. He died before the potion was ready. The two widowed queens did not want to waste the magic potion. So the elder queen drank it while the younger queen made love to her 'like a man'. In due course, the elder queen gave birth to a child, but it was only a lump of flesh. The sages said, "Since no white seed was part of the conception, the child had no bones and no consciousness." They appeased the gods and the child was 'repaired'.

Power of the White Seed: Indian men are known for their obsession with virility. Virility here refers to many things, physical strength, mental agility, sexual energy as well ability to father a male child. So when an Indian says, "I have less strength (takat kum hai)," he could refer to malaise or lethargy or impotence or inability to father a male child. Here again is an ancient belief that physical strength is reflected in semen strength.

The ancient seers believed that food consumed is transformed in the body into sap (plasma), then flesh, then blood, then bone, then marrow and finally seed (Hence the traditional Indian belief that out of a thousand drops of blood comes one drop of semen). The seed can produce a new life or if retained can transform into a magical substance called ojas that gives a man superhuman strength and occult powers. It also helps man escape from the cycle of rebirths. In women, the red seed is shed every month. Hence, women are considered to be the weaker sex–they cannot attain 'spiritual' status because they have no access to ojas.

Men on the other hand can retain their white seed and become 'holy'. This is the reason given to explain the presence of greater number of holy men than holy women in India. This is also the reason why powerful warrior gods like Hanuman and Ayyappa are associated with both virility and celibacy.

In the Mahabharata, it is said that a male child is born when the white seed is stronger than the red seed. Thus a virile man (one whose semen is strong) fathers only male children. When the red seed is strong, the child is female. When both white and red seed are equal the child is neither this nor that (this was the traditional explanation for transexuality and homosexuality).

This belief perhaps explains why, despite modern genetic data on X and Y chromosomes, it is the woman in India who is 'blamed' for the feminization of the fetus and why she is given special diets to make the fetus male. This also explains why men feel angry and ashamed when they father daughters. The sex of the child is linked to their virility, or lack of it.

The Fertile Period: According to the Dharmashastras, though sex for pleasure was permitted, greater importance was given to sex for procreation. Men who had to father male offsprings were advised not to waste semen. They were advised to have intercourse only when the woman was in 'season'. This period was known as ritu and it roughly corresponds to the fertile period, the days in the menstrual cycle when a woman is most likely to conceive. Women were advised to make themselves beautiful and present themselves to their husbands after their periods.

If a woman who was in her fertile period approached a man for sex, he was obliged to have sex with her, the reason being – a fertile period should not be wasted. Every time a fertile period was lost, an ancestor lost his opportunity to be reborn. When a woman menstruated, she was held responsible for the opportunity last. She was equated with 'death' and hence considered polluted. She was asked to isolate herself during her periods, just as men who cremate the dead are isolated from the rest of the community.

A man who turned down a woman who approached him during her fertile period was described as a eunuch and held in disdain. In the Mahabharata, there are tales of women who approached men who were not their husbands during their fertile period because their husbands were unavailable. This was legally sanctioned. The sage Aruni was horrified when his guru's wife approached him for sex. She explained, "Your guru has gone on a pilgrimage. Asking you do fulfil his biological obligations is a lesser sin than wasting this fertile period."

The time when men and women had sex affected the nature of the child conceived. In the Bhagavata Purana is the story of Diti who approached her husband, the sage Kashyapa, for sex in the evening, a time reserved for prayers to ward of malevolent spirits. As a result, she conceived children who were demons.

When a man approached a woman, before intercourse, he was expected to invoke the gods, especially Vishnu, the god who sustains natural order, and Tvastr or Vishvakarma, the god who makes things. Only through their blessings, was it believed that a child could be conceived. This was known as the garbhadhana sanskara, or the rite of conception.

The Sterile Man: When a man could not produce a child on his wife, he was given the benefit of the doubt and allowed to marry again, and again. If despite this, he failed to father a child, it was concluded (but never explicitly stated) that he was sterile. In such circumstances, the Dharmashastras suggested that another man be invited to cohabit with the wives. This practice was known as niyoga or levirate.

In the Mahabharata, when king Vichitravirya (vichitra = odd; virya = virility) dies, his mother invited the sage Vyasa to produced children on his widowed daughters-in-law. Children thus produced were called children of Vichitravirya (the legal father), not the children of Vyasa (the biological or surrogate father).

It is alleged that this practice of niyoga is followed (rather clandestinely) even today, whereby sterile men make their wives cohabit with relatives or with holy men. Though religiously sanctioned, this practice is socially frowned upon and hence no one talks about it openly.

In the Kathasaritsagar, a collection of stories written in the 11th century AD, there is the story of a king who makes an offering of rice balls to his ancestors. As he about to throw the offering in the river, three hands reach up–one of a farmer, one of a priest and one of a warrior. The oracles revealed, "The farmer is the man who married your mother, the priest is the man who made your mother pregnant and the warrior is the man who took care of you." The king is advised to give the rice ball to the farmer because scriptures describe him as the true father. Thus was the practice of surrogate fatherhood established.

Artificial Insemination: There are tales that suggest that the ancients were familiar with the 'idea' of artificial insemination. For example, we learn of 'magic potions' being created by sages for queens of childless kings that makes the women pregnant. What were these magic substances? Could they be 'fertility drugs' or could they be metaphors for 'donated semen'?

One story states that the god Shiva once spurted semen when he saw Vishnu in the form of the celestial enchantress Mohini. Sages collected this semen and gave it to the wind-god Vayu who poured it into the 'ear' (a common mythical metaphor for the womb) of Anjani, a monkey, who gave birth to Hanuman, the monkey-god. Devoid of the mythical aura, one might say that the tale refers to the practice of artificial insemination: semen is transferred to the womb without sexual intercourse).

The Surrogate Mother: In the Bhagvata Purana, there is a story that suggests the practice of surrogate motherhood. Kans, the wicked king of Mathura, had imprisoned his sister Devaki and her husband Vasudeva because oracles had informed him that her child would be his killer. Every time she delivered a child, he smashed its head on the floor. He killed six children. When the seventh child was conceived, the gods intervened. They summoned the goddess Yogamaya and had her transfer the fetus from the womb of Devaki to the womb of Rohini (Vasudeva's other wife who lived with her sister Yashoda across the river Yamuna, in the village of cowherds at Gokul). Thus the child conceived in one womb was incubated in and delivered through another womb.

Serpent Power: In India today, when a couple does not have children, they often visit shrines and pray. Some visit holy men. Others offer cradles and dolls at shrines of mother-goddesses. Still others visit serpent shrines.

Serpents in many ancient cultures have been associated with fertility (don't forget that the serpent continues to be the symbol of medicine). There are many reasons for this. Probably because the serpent could slough its skin, it was believed to possess the power of rejuvenation. Probably because the serpent lived under the earth, it was believed to be the keeper of the secret that transforms seeds into plants. Farmers in India worship serpents in the hope they have a good harvest. Women worship serpents so that they are fertile and their husbands, virile.

In modern times, these practices may seem silly and superstitious. But for centuries they have offered hope to a people who believed that producing children was their biological duty. They offer the psychological support that today counsellors provide. While these support structures can turn into crutches, their place in culture demands the be understood rather than be summarily dismissed.

'Sevikas' Serve the Cause of Religion: As we stand on the threshold of the new millennium there is a realization that the modern world is becoming increasingly complex and chaotic. Incredible progress in the field of science and technology has made man's life very comfortable but has cost him dearly in terms of his peace of mind and sense of security.

The slow dissolution of traditional codes of social customs and beliefs, the steady breakdown of inherited sanctions of religion and law, the confusion in regard to social ethics is some of the most striking features of our age. This is making man turn towards religion in his search for solutions to his conflicts and dilemmas: for religion, world over, is considered an anchor and a means of support to mankind.

Since times immemorial woman has been fostering, preserving and perpetuating human values in the framework of religion at the family level. In the present context there is an added responsibility on woman to arrive at the essence of religion and propagate it effectively for the benefit of mankind. Thanks to the increased awareness and education of woman, she is able to discharge this responsibility.

1. *The Role of Woman in Religious Education:* Hinduism recognizes the mother as the first and foremost teacher. Hindu mythology is replete with stories of prenatal learning. It is rightly believed that the attitudes and values of the mother have a direct bearing on the personality of the child. There are examples where mothers have influenced the mindsets of their children who have gone on to become nation builders, social reformers and religious leaders. Great Indian leaders like Mahatma Gandhi, Swami Vivekananda, Shivaji, have all been groomed by their mothers through simple stories, songs and lullabies subtly conveying the essence of religion to them.

Marriage and motherhood were treated as normal vocation for women all over the world until recently. In India, the role of the woman was largely confined to her own house and the upbringing of the children in a large household. There was no separate order to train woman teachers. Even now we find that women who have received modern education still adhere to household rituals religiously and identify the philosophy of life bound with these.

However, keeping with the present trends of the nuclear family and working mothers, many religious organizations are training woman in conducting religious discourses, organizing weekly workshops and religious training centres for children. These women are rightly called sevikas, for they serve the cause of religion.

2. *Dominant Values in Religious Education:* The underlying philosophy of each religion manifests itself in the value system of that religion. These values discipline the mind and a disciplined mind is the seat of happiness.

Hinduism deeply believes that material comforts do not lead to real happiness. Religious education in India is not dogmatic. It is a rational synthesis, which goes on gathering into itself new conceptions as philosophy progresses.

Hinduism believes that the fundamental truths are eternal and universal in nature. Therefore all religions have the same fundamental truths though approaches differ. Religious values form the bedrock of moral and ethical principles. Moral values are indispensable to maintain a good quality of life-set of dos and don'ts in the form of *yama* and *niyamas* are laid down in the Indian tradition. Yamas consists of concepts which discipline man like non-violence, honesty, self-control etc. Niyamas concentrate on the cultivation of virtues like purity, contentment, fortitude, devotion etc. The purpose of these is to eliminate the mental impurities such as greed, egotism, and cruelty. Ethical disciplines are prescribed depending on individual capacity and equipment. It is based on the premise that if individuals are virtuous social welfare would automatically follow.

3. *Is Religion Liberating or Restricting, Promoting or Frustrating?:* Whether religion liberates or frustrates an individual is a highly subjective question. The answer varies depending on the individual experiences and circumstances, attitude and approach. Religion should elevate an individual on to a higher plane of consciousness.

As the Hindu term for religion, *dharma*, indicates it should provide sustenance and support. The ultimate aim of religion is to lead the individual on to the path of *Moksha* or salvation. Religion can be liberating when the emphasis is on the universal principles. When religious dogmas and creeds interfere with individual lifestyles, religion can be restricting.

When the faith a person has in God generates a power, a soul force that gives him the courage to face the exigencies of life, religion is promoting. When religion imposes itself on man curtailing his freedom and thwarting his growth then it can be highly frustrating. If the supremacy of religion and of social tradition hampers the free pursuit of Philosophy, it leads to frustration.

It is sad but true that in many religions there has been a misrepresentation of facts and a misinterpretation of ideas. Most of the social evils like poverty, ignorance and hatred are offshoots of misinterpreted religion. Many of the religious rituals and customs are outdated and outmoded so they have lost their significance and have become redundant. Every fresh epoch in the progress of thought has to be accompanied by a reform in logic. When it is not so, it has invariably led to suffering or revolt. Religion has to be a perennial spring of fresh thoughts and ideas and not a stagnant pool.

4. *Various Perspectives of Continuity of Tradition, Religious Ritual and Ceremony in Family Life and Society:* The practice of religious rituals and ceremony is what gives each family its unique identity and binds the members of the family. Traditions and customs of each family are a precious heritage that is passed on from generation to generation linking them emotionally, culturally and spiritually. Every religion can be understood to have three components-philosophy, mythology and rituals. Rituals are an accepted aspect of every religion which subtly project the philosophy of that religion. These rituals intend to discipline a person and help him adhere to positive values.

The Hindu way of life is ritualistic. His daily routine like bath, prayer and eating are not mere chores for a Hindu, they are sacred rituals with religious undertones. There are sixteen important rituals in the life of every Hindu from conception to burial. These rituals help in the smooth transition from one stage to another. The Hindu concept of rebirth and the rituals followed during funerals help him in taking away the agony and sorrow at death and make it appear as the next natural stage in life.

Most of the rituals, customs and festivals bring about a strong bonding in the community leading to social harmony. An individual learns to submit his personal interest for the common good. They also ensure the participation of the community in individual growth and development. The participation of woman (wife, mother) is obligatory in almost all Indian customs. She is a *sahadharmini*, an equal partner in the man's religious quest.

To ensure a harmonious existence in a religiously plural world Tolerance and Trust should be the hallmark of all religions. When one has faith in himself and the religion he practices then one learns to trust and to be tolerant. By virtue of the qualities of Tolerance and trust women have always been the custodians of the family traditions and rituals. By the very quality of their being women are the missionaries of the civilization they belong to. In the present global scenario women are expected to take on greater responsibilities and play a more assertive role.

Mantra is a syllable or string of syllables, from the Sanskrit language, first found in Hinduism. Mantras may or may not conform to grammatical rules. Their use varies with the school and philosophy associated with the mantra. They are primarily used as spiritual conduits, words and vibrations that instill one-pointedness in the devotee. Other purposes have included religious ceremonies to accumulating wealth, avoiding danger, or eliminating enemies. Mantras originated in India with Vedic Hinduism and were later adopted by Buddhists and Jains, now popular in various modern forms of spiritual practice which are based on practices of these Indian religions.

Mantra Generally

Mantras (Sanskrit) have some features in common with spells, in that they are a translation of the human will or desire into a form of action. As symbols, sounds are seen to effect what they symbolize. Vocal sounds are frequently thought of as having magical powers, or even of representing the words, or speech of God.

For the authors of the Hindu scriptures of the Upanishads, the syllable P 'Aum', itself constituting a mantra, represents Brahman, the Godhead, as well as the whole of creation. Merely pronouncing this syllable is to experience the divine in a very direct way.

Kukai suggests that all sounds are the voice of the Dharmakaya Buddha – *i.e.* as in Hindu Upanishads and Yoga thought, these sounds are manifestations of ultimate reality. We should not think that this is peculiar to Eastern culture, however. Words do have a mysterious power to affect us. Accepted scholarly etymology links the word with 'manas' meaning 'mind' and 'trana' for protection so that a mantra is something which protects the mind – however in practice we will see that mantra is considered to do far more than simply protect the mind.

For many cultures it is the written letters that have power–the Hebrew Kabbalah for instance. Letters can have an oracular function even. But in India special conditions applied that meant that writing was very definitely inferior to the spoken word. The Brahmins were the priestly caste of the Aryan peoples. It was they that preserved the holy writings–initially the Vedas, but later also the Upanishads.

For years, they were the only ones who knew the mantras or sacred formulas that had to be chanted at important occasions. However, with the advent of egalitarian Hindu schools of Yoga, Vedanta, Tantra and Bhakti, it is now the case that intra-family and community mantras are passed on freely as part of generally practiced Hindu religion. Such was the influence of the orthodox attitude of the elite nature of mantra knowledge, that even the Buddhists, who repudiated the whole idea of caste, and of the efficacy of the old rituals, called themselves the shravakas, that is 'the hearers'. A wise person in India was one who had "heard much". Mantras then are *sound symbols*. What they symbolize, and how they function depends on the context, and the mind of the person repeating them. Studies in sound symbolism suggest that vocal sounds have meaning whether we are aware of it or not.

And indeed that there can be multiple layers of symbolism associated with each sound. So even if we do not understand them, mantras are no simply meaningless mumbo jumbo–no vocal utterance is entirely without meaning. We can look at mantra is a range of different contexts to see what they can mean in those contexts: Om may mean something quite different to a Hindu and a Tibetan Buddhist.

Tantras eventually came to see the letters as well as the sounds as representatives of the divine, it was when Buddhism travelled to China from India, that a shift in emphasis towards writing came about. China lacked a ecclesiastic language like Sanskrit, and achieved its cultural unity by having a written language that was flexible in pronunciation but more precise in terms of the concepts that each character represented. In fact the Indians had several scripts which were all equally serviceable for writing Sanskrit. Hence, the Chinese prized written language more highly than did the Indian Buddhists, and the writing of mantras became a spiritual practice in its own right. So that whereas Brahmins had been very strict on correct pronunciation, the Chinese, and other Far-Eastern Buddhists were more concerned with correctly writing something down. The practice of writing mantras as a spiritual practice, became very refined in Japan, and the writing in the Siddham script in which the Sanskrit of many Buddhist Sutras where written, is only seen in Japan nowadays. However, mantra-repetition written in Sanskrit, with any number of scripts, is well-known to many Hindu sects in India as well.

Mantra in Hinduism

Mantras was originally conceived in the great Hindu scriptures, known as the Vedas. Within practically all Hindu scriptures, the writing is formed in painstakingly crafted two line 'shlokas' and most mantras follow this pattern, although mantras are often found in single line or even single word combinations.

The basic mantra is 'Aum', which in Hinduism is known as the 'pranava mantra,' the source of all mantras. The idea behind this is the Hindu philosophy of nama-rupa (name-form), which supposes that all ideas or entities in existence, within the phenomenological cosmos, have name and form. The basic name and form is the primordial vibration of Aum, as it is the first manifested nama-rupa of Brahman. Before existence and beyond existence, there is only One reality, Brahman, and the first manifestation of Brahman in existence is Aum.

For this very reason, Aum is considered to be the most fundamental and powerful mantra, and thus is prefixed and suffixed to all Hindu prayers. While some mantras may invoke individual Gods, the fundamental mantras, like 'Aum,' the 'Shanti Mantra,' the 'Gayatri Mantra' and others, all focus on the One reality. In the Hindu Tantras the universe is sound. The supreme (para) brings forth existence through the Word (Shabda). Creation consists of vibrations at various frequencies and amplitudes giving rise to the phenomena of the world. The purest vibrations are the varna, the imperishable letters which are revealed to us, imperfectly as the audible sounds and visible forms.

Varnas are the atoms of sound. A symbolic association was built up between letters and the elements, gods, signs of zodiac, parts of the body–letters became rich in these associations. For example in the Aitrareya-aranya-Upanishad we find:

> *"Mute consonants represent the earth, the sibilants the sky, the vowels heaven. The mute consonants represent fire, the sibilants air, the vowels the sun... The mute consonants represent the eye, the sibilants the ear, the vowels the mind"*

In effect each letter became a mantra and the language of the Vedas, Sanskrit, corresponds greatly to the nature of things. Thus Vedas come to represent reality itself. The syllable 'Om', represents the underlying unity of reality, which is Brahman

Japa

Japa was a concept of the Vedic sages that incorporates mantras as one of the main forms of worship, whose ultimate end is seen as moksha/liberation. Essentially, japa means repetition, and has become an established practice of all Hindu streams, from the various Yoga to Tantra. It involves repetition of a mantra over and over again, in cycles of auspicious numbers (in multiples of three), the most popular being 108.

For this reason, Hindu malas (bead necklaces) developed, containing 108 beads and a head 'meru' bead. The devotee performing japa using his/her fingers counts each bead as he/she repeats the chosen mantra. Having reached 108 repetitions, if he/she wishes to continue another cycle of mantras, the devotee must turn the mala around without crossing the 'meru' bead and repeat.

It is said that through japa the devotee attains one-pointedness, or extreme focus, on the chosen deity or principle idea of the mantra. The vibrations of the mantra are considered extremely important, and thus reverberations of the sound are supposed to awaken the prana or spiritual life force and even stimulate chakras according to many Hindu schools of thought.

Some Hindu Mantras

The most representative mantra of all the Hindu mantras is the famed 'Gayatri Mantra':

> *Om Bhur Buvah Svah, Tat Savitur Varenyam*
> *Bhargo Devasya Dhimahi, Dhiyo Yo Nah Pracodayat*

Gayatri Mantra is the most universal Hindu mantra and invokes the Brahman as the principle of knowledge and the illumination of the primordial Sun. Many Brahmins till today, in a tradition that has continued for at least 5,000 years, perform morning ablutions at the bank of a river and while holding the sacred thread given to them at adolescence, repeat the Gayatri Mantra.

Lead me from Ignorance to Truth

asato ma Sadhgamaya, tamaso ma jyothir-Gamaya

mrityor-ma amritham Gamaya, Om santi santi santih

"Aum Asato ma sad gamaya, tamaso ma jyotir gamaya, mrityor ma aamritaam gamaya"

"Aum Lead me from ignorance to truth, from darkness to light, from death to immortality."

Hare Krishna Mantra

A very famous mantra is that created by Shri Chaitanya Mahaprabhu, a great Vaishnava bhakta (loving devotee) of the Hindu Lord Vishnu in the 15th century. It is beloved by most Hindus as very powerful, Vaishnavs and Shaivaites alike:

"Hare Krishna Hare Krishna Krishna Krishna Hare Hare / Hare Rama Hare Rama Rama Rama Hare Hare"

When A.C. Bhaktivedanta brought his ISKCON (International Society for Krishna Consciousness) brand of Hindu Vaishnavism to the West, he framed the "Hare Krishna" mantra as the sole mantra for moksha/liberation and his sect is now commonly known in the West by the name 'Hare Krishnas.'

Shanti Mantra : The Mantra of Peace:

Aum Saha Navavatu / Saha Nau Bhunaktu / Saha Viryam Karvavahe / Tejaswi Navadhi Tamastu / Ma Vidvishavahe / Aum Shanti Shanti Shantihi / Hari Hi Aum

(Om, May the Lord protect us, May the Lord allow us to enjoy, May we work together. May our studies be thorough and faithful, May we never misunderstand each other, Om, Peace, Peace, Peace!)

Universal Prayer

Sarvesaam Svastir Bhavatu/Sarvesam Santir Bhavatu/ Sarvesam Purnam Bhavatu/Sarvesam mangalam Bhavatu (May good befall all, May there be peace for all, May all be fit for perfection, and May all experience that which is auspicious.)

Sarve Bhavantu Sukhinaha/Sarve Santu niramayaha/Sarve Badrani Pasyantu/ma Kascidh-dhuhkha Bhaga-Bhavet (Om, May all be happy. May all be healthy, May we all experience what is good and let no one suffer, Om, Peace, Peace, Peace!)

Thou Are That

Tat Twam Asi

To list most of the main Hindu mantras would take reams of paper. Indeed, simple two-lined shlokas from holy Hindu texts like the Vedas, Upanishads, Bhagwad Gita, Yoga Sutra, even the Mahabharata and Ramayana, are considered powerful and finely honed enough to be repeated to great effect.

A very common mantra is formed by taking a deity's name and saluting it with in such a manner: 'Aum namah' or 'Aum Jai (Hail!)' or several such permutations. Common examples are 'Aum namah Shivaya' (Aum to Lord Shiva), 'Om Jai Jagadish Hare' (Salutations to the Universal God Vishnu), 'Aum Shri Ganeshaya Namah' (Aum to Shree Ganesha) and 'Jai Ma Kali.' Needless to say, there are more mantras of this sort than names of the Hindu deities. Another example of Hindu mantras is seen in the Surya Namaskara, whose practice is found recorded as far back as in the Hindu scripture of the Ramayana. As each of the twelve postures is performed, a salutatory mantra is recited to the Lord Surya, the Sun.

The Hindu Bija Mantra

In Hinduism the concept of mantra as mystical sounds was carried to its logical conclusion in 'seed' (Sanskrit *bija*) mantras that have no precise meaning but instead are thought to carry within their sounds connections to various spiritual principles and currents. For example, worship of the Mother Goddess Kali, in mantra form, is famously reduced to the powerful Bija mantras of the Shakti tradition of Hinduism:

"Aum Kreeng Kreeng Kreeng Hoong Hoong Hreeng Hreeng Dakshina Kalike |

Kreeng Kreeng Kreeng Hoong Hoong Hreeng Hreeng Swaha | |"

Of course, the most revered of all Bija mantras is Om/Aum.

The Bija mantra is part of the Hindu monist theory that while reality manifests itself as many/multiple, it is ultimately one.

Hindu Scriptures

Hindu scripture, which is known as "Shastra" is predominantly written in Sanskrit.

Classification of Hindu Scripture

Hindu scripture is divided into two categories: Sruti – that which is heard (*i.e.*, revelation) and Smriti – that which is remembered (*i.e.*, tradition, not revelation).

The Sruti scriptures are of divine origin, whose truths were directly revealed to ancient rishis (sages) in their deep meditations. The Smriti scriptures are of human origin and were written to explain the Sruti writings and make them understandable and meaningful to the general population. Sruti scriptures include the four Vedas (Rig, Yajur, Sama and Atharva) and the Bhagwad Gita, and constitute the highest religious authority. Smriti literature includes Itihasas (epics like Ramayana, Mahabharata), Puranas (mythological texts), Agamas (theological treatises) and Darshanas (philosophical texts). Hindu texts are typically seen to revolve around many levels of reading, namely the gross or physical, the subtle, and the supramental. This allows for many levels of understanding as well, implying that the truth of the texts can only be realized with the spiritual advancement of the reader.

Vedas

The Vedas are referred to as the Shruti. The Vedas are the oldest extant Hindu texts. The ideas expressed in the Vedas were traditionally handed down orally from father to son and from teacher to disciple. Therefore, these ideas had been in circulation for a long time before their codification and compilation, which are attributed to a Rishi named Veda Vyasa (literally, "the splitter of the Vedas,"). He was named that way as it was he who was accredited with forming the large mass of knowledge and hymns of the Vedas and 'splitting' them into comprehensible sections for the rest of humanity.

The Vedas have been divided in various ways. One simple way is to divide the Vedas into two sections according to their subject matter:

1. The Karma Kanda ("the action part"), deals with karma, rituals, and sacrifices the purpose of which is to attain material prosperity on earth and the benefits of heaven after death, and
2. The Jnana Kanda ("the knowledge part"), is concerned with the spiritual Knowledge that brings liberation from ignorance and realization of the Ultimate Truth. The Upanishads constitute a major portion of the Jnana Kanda.

The Vedas are four in number. The Rig-, Yajur-, Sama-and Atharva Vedas represent various shakhas, or branches, of knowledge.

Upanishads

The Upanishads ("Sittings Near) (a Teacher]") are part of the Hindu Shruti; these religious scriptures primarily discuss philosophy and "cosmic reality"; they also contain transcripts of various debates or discussions. They are commentaries on the Vedas and their branch of Hinduism is called Vedanta.

Bhagwad Gita

Many a Hindu has said that the most succinct and powerful abbreviation of the overwhelmingly diverse realm of Hindu thought is to be found in the Bhagwad Gita. Essentially, it is a microcosm of Vedic, Yogic, Vedantic and even Tantric thought of the Hindu fold. Bhagwad Gita (literally: Song of the God) is a part of the epic poem Mahabharata and is revered in Hinduism. It speaks not only to Vaishnavas but to all people, and it is accepted by the members of all Hindu streams as a seminal text. Indeed, the "tag line" of each chapter of the Bhagwad Gita refers to the book as the "Gita Upanishad" and as a "scripture of yoga," thereby establishing that in this text, Lord Krishna speaks the truths of yoga and the Upanishads for all. What holds the devotee's mind foremost is Krishna's repeated injunction to abandon the mortal self to the infinite love of the Lord. He not only speaks to the mind and to the Hindu's innate sense of Dharma, but calls for overwhelming love. By loving God one also loves the immortal Self, finds harmony in oneself, and finds oneself at peace with the entire cosmos. The Gita speaks of cultivating the intellect, properly using the body, and always remaining equipoised in relation to the greater Self. The Bhagwad Gita truly presents itself as a liberation scripture universal in its message.

Itihasas

The Itihasas (itihasa is Sanskrit for "history" or "thus verily happened") are narrative traditions composed as supplementary Vedic literature to helps explain the rituals of the Vedas and the highly compressed philosophy of the Vedanta-sutras by using historical events of the universe and factual stories of many great sages, and so forth.

Mahabharata

Included in the Itihasas is the Mahabharata, written by Srila Vyasadeva. It is an historical epic about the great kingdom of Bharatavarsa, or the region of India. It contains 110,000 couplets making it the longest poem and greatest epic in world literature. It is divided into 18 sections called parvas, such as the Adi Parva, etc.

It is a treasure house of Indian lore and holds within it a code of life for ethical, social and spiritual relations. Throughout this great epic every sort of human situation is described and every kind of emotion is aroused. There is a saying that if it is not in the Mahabharata then it is not to be found.

Ramayana

The Ramayana consists of 24,000 verses, and first written during the time of Lord Ramachandra by the great poet Valmiki, which describes the life of Lord Ramachandra, an incarnation of God, and His wife Sita. This is also a most touching and exciting adventure which explains how Lord Ramachandra lived in the forest and fought against and killed the great demon Ravana and his armies in order to rescue His wife, Sita, who had been kidnapped.

Many other stories are included in this storehouse of wisdom that has been an inspiration for thousands of years to all people who have read it. In the incarnation of Lord Ramachandra, God appears as the perfect king and ruler, and inspires all His subjects with the greatest love for Him.

Written in high Sanskrit in the form of rhyming couplets, the Ramayana contains seven sections (kandas):

1. Bal Kanda-Rama's boyhood
2. Ayodhya Kanda-Rama's life in Ayodhya until his banishment
3. Aranya-Rama's life in the forest and his abduction by Ravana
4. Kishkinda-Rama's stay at Kishkinda, the capital of his monkey ally Sugriva
5. Sundara-Rama's journey to Sri Lanka
6. Yuddha (or Lanka)-Rama's battle with Ravana, the recovery of Sita and their return to Ayodhya
7. Uttara-Rama's life as king in Ayodhya, the birth of his two sons, Sita's test of innocence and return to her mother, and Rama's demise

Puranas

The Puranas are a vast literature of stories and allegory. There are 18 primary Puranas, 18 upa-puranas, and numerous minor Puranas. 18 are considered to be Mahapuranas, or Great Puranas, and thus authoritative references on the Gods and Goddesses, religious rites and holy places (most of which are in the Indian subcontinent, known as Bharat). Six devoted to worship of Shiva, six to Vishnu, and six to Brahma. The primary Puranas describe these five subjects: sarga (creation), pratisarga (recreation), vamsa (history of the sages), manvantara (periods of Manu), and vamsanucarita (geneology of kings).

The most important Puranas are:

- Vishnu Purana
- Bhagavata Purana (Krishna)
- Shiva Purana
- Markendeya Purana (to the Goddess)

Lord Vishnu is the predominating Deity of the following six Puranas:

- Bhagavata Purana has 18,000 verses, and is a jewel of the Vedas, providing all instruction on the science of self-realization.
- Vishnu Purana has 23,000 verses, including stories of various devotees, a description of varnasrama, the six angas of the Veda, a description of the age of Kali, a description of Sveta Varaha Kalpa, and Vishnu dharmotara.
- Naradiya Purana has 25,000 verses, and contains a synopsis of the complete philosophy. It describes Jagannath Puri, Dwarka, Badrinath, and other holy sites.
- Padma Purana has 55,000 verses, and contains the glory of Srimad-Bhagavatam, and stories of Rama, Jagannath, Matsya, Ekadasi, Bhrgu, and others.
- Garuda Purana has 19,000 verses, and discuss the subject of Bhagwad-gita, reincarnation, Vishnu-sahaasra-nama, and a description of Tarsya Kalpa.
- Varaha Purana has 24,000 verses, and describes the different vratas and Lord Vishnu's glories.

Lord Brahma is the predominating Deity of the following six Puranas:

- Brahmanda Purana has 12,000 verses, and describes the vedangas and the Adi Kalpa.
- Brahmavaivarta Purana has 18,000 verses, and describes the glories and pastimes of Sri Sri Radha-Krishna.
- Markandeya Purana has 9,000 verses, and tells the stories of Rama and Krishna.
- Bhavisya Purana has 14,500 verses, and describes the glories of devotional service to Sri Krishna, along with the prediction of Lord Chaitanya.
- Vamana Purana contains 10,000 verses, and tells the story of Lord Trivikrama.
- Brahma Purana has 10,000 verses, and describes the teachings of Lord Brahma to Daksa.

Lord Shiva is the predominating Deity of the following six Puranas:

- Matsya Purana has 14,000 verses, and describes the Vamana and Varaha Kalpas, and temple construction.
- Kurma Purana has 17,000 verses, and describes the conversation between Krishna and the Sun-god, Dhanvantari, and the Laksmi Kalpa.
- Linga Purana has 10,000 verses, and describes the glories of Lord Nrsmhadeva, the stories of Janardhana and Ambarisa, and the glories of Gayatri.
- Shiva Purana has 24,000 verses, divided into six samhitas. It was recited by Vedavyasa's disciple Romaharshana.
- Skanda Purana has 81,000 verses, and describes the slaughter of the demon Tarakdsura by Skanda (Subrahmanya). Skanda Purana is very similar to the Kumarasambhava of Kalidasa.
- Agni Purana has 15,400 verses, and describes Salagrama and the Isana Kalpa.

Agamas & Tantras

Scriptures of the three major theological traditions: Shaivism, Vaishnavism, and Shaktism.

Darshanas

Manuals of Philosophy

The Sutras

- Brahma Sutra: Vedanta philosophy of Sage Vyasa
- Mimamsa Sutra: Philosophy of rites and rituals of Sage Jaimini
- Nyaya Sutra: Logical analysis of Sage Gautama (not Buddha)
- Vaisheshika Sutra: Atomic school of philosophy of Sage Kanada
- Sankhya Sutras: Sankhya philosophy of Sage Kapila
- Yoga Sutras: Yoga philosophy of Sage Patanjali

Essence of Hindu Scriptures for Mankind

During their spiritual quest, the ancient rishis experienced sparks of divinity in all things and beings of the world. The vision of the Hindu scriptures is thus a vision of the unity of all existence, summarized as follows:

- There are many ways of conceiving the Supreme Reality (Brahman) and numerous ways of approaching It. To insist that one's own way is the only way is thus wrong and harmful.
- God is the source of goodness and truth. Man's goal in life is to seek union with Him. This union can be sought in many ways, all requiring sincerity of purpose, self-sacrifice and discipline.
- The highest religious experience is the one in which an individual transcends the intellect and realizes God immediately.
- The concept of "survival-of-the-fittest" is God's law for the animals. Harmlessness to all creatures is His law for humans.
- There is natural order (rita) inherent in the natural world. There must be moral order (dharma) inherent in human life. Everyone must be responsible for his (or her) actions and their consequences (karma). We cannot blame God for our ills.
- Individual responsibility and one's ethics are a foundation for individual happiness and social stability.
- The universe is a wheel of sacrifice (yajna). At the beginning the Supreme Lord performed self-sacrifice to create the universe and set the wheel in motion. The water sacrifices to form clouds, the clouds sacrifice to make rains, the rains sacrifice to grow food, and the food sacrifices to feed humans. In turn, humans must sacrifice for the welfare of the Mother Earth and all its creatures.
- There is no intrinsic evil in Nature nor any evil force in the world to oppose God. Man commits evil only due to ignorance (maya).
- Love, freedom and peace are fruits of the tree of divine consciousness, which can be planted by worshipping God regularly and systematically through yoga, meditation, study of scriptures, by performing religious rites and ceremonies-as enjoined by scriptures-and selfless work.

Hindu Scriptures and Authoritative Texts

Hindu authoritative writings constitute an immense literature. Keep in mind that the vast family (of religions, beliefs, sects, traditions) that constitutes Hinduism, not all that is listed here is considered sacred (or is even known) by every Hindu.

The categories of literature mentioned here are those that have had the most effect on the last 3000 years of Hindu thought.

The writings of Hinduism fall into two sections: *Shruti* and *Smriti*.

Shruti is considered a closed canon, and cannot be added to. Smriti, which is based in Shruti, is considered an open canon, and can be added to—even to this day. The two most well-known texts of Hinduism are the *Rig Veda* and the *Bhagwad Gita*. The Rig Veda (Shruti) is not only the oldest text in Hinduism, it is one of the oldest texts of any Indo-European language. The Bhagwad-Gita (Smriti) is but one book of the epic *Mahabharata*.

Shruti means *that which is heard*, and refers to the works of ancient, unknown poets and writers considered to be fully authoritative as Holy Scripture. Modern scholarship classifies Shruti in four main collections called *Vedas*. These are the *Rig Veda, Sama Veda, Yajur Veda,* and *Atharva Veda*.

Each Veda contains several kinds of writings or general components:

- *Samhitas*—collections of hymns, verses and sayings.
- *Brahmanas* (9 existing)—texts that explicate the homologies, the mystical, philosophical, anthropological and cosmological meanings of the Vedic sacrifice.
- *Aranyakas*—or Forest Books—texts featuring esoteric meditations about the meaning of the sacrifice and the structure of the cosmos.
- *Upanishads* (108 in total, of which 12-18 are considered of principal importance). A codified collection of texts said to reveal hidden eternal truths regarding the metaphysical connections between the ultimate and the human worlds.

SMRITI means *that which is remembered*, and refers to less ancient writings and oral traditions that are not considered as authoritative as Shruti. Among the various literary forms of Smriti are:

- *Puranas*—Ancient Narratives. Compendiums of Hindu mythology, history, philosophy, ritual and much else. Many discuss technical subjects such as architecture, ethics and medicine (human and veterinary). It is traditionally agreed that there are 18 major Puranas, however, it is not always agreed upon as to which these 18 are. The 29 listed here were composed between ca 200 CE-1700 CE
- *Epics*, of which there are two—the Mahabharata and the Ramayana.
  - o *Mahabharata—The Great War of the Bharata Tribe*, consists of 18 books, including the *Bhagwad-Gita or The Song of the Lord*, which is the 6th book. This epic, composed over a time span of 600-800 years (ca. 300 BC.-300 CE), is ten times the size of the *Illiad* and the *Odyssey* combined.
  - o *Ramayana—The Deeds of Rama.* This epic was composed over a 400 year time span (roughly ca. 200 BC.-200 CE).
- *Dharmashastras, Dharmasutras* (lawbooks). Texts of classical teachings pertaining to the proper conduct of virtually every aspect of human life including life-cycle rituals, correct livelihood, the order of society, statecraft and law.
- *Tantras.* Dating from about the 7th century CE, these writings deal with esoteric practices (sometimes quite unorthodox to the Hindu societal laws).
- *Darshana Literature.* Treatises of the various schools of Indian philosophy.

Mahabharata Epic: The Bhagwad-Gita (another translation) (another translation) The Bhagwad-Gita (Prabhupada) The Bhagwad-Gita (Arnold) The Bhagwad-Gita (Beck) .

4

Religion and the Epics

Ramayana

The Ramayana of Valmiki consists of about 24,000 verses and describes the life of Prince Rama, an incarnation of Vishnu. The author, Valmiki, according to later tradition, belonged to the shudra varna and made his living by robbing travellers. After an encounter with the sage Narada, Valmiki turned his life around and became a poet and scholar.

Classical Hinduism recognizes him as a brahman and as India's first poet. Rama and his wife Sita embody virtue and righteousness, and their lives demonstrate dharma in various spheres of activity. Their life stories contain lessons for Hindus on ideal behaviour in various roles, such as son, brother, wife, king, and married couple. Rama's reign ushers in a golden age, and the expression *Rama-rajya* (rule of Rama) describes the best of times in which the divine presence rules on Earth.

Mahabharata

The Mahabharata, an epic story of 100,000 verses, is attributed to a sage named Vyasa and considered to be the longest poem in the world. It traces the descendants of two sets of cousins, the Kauravas and the Pandavas, whose disputes eventually lead to the Mahabharata war. Krishna, an avatar of Vishnu, is central to the story. Like the Ramayana, the Mahabharata addresses many questions related to dharma and the actions of individuals and society. These discourses have provided inspiration for Hindus in many areas of life.

Bhagwad-Gita

One part of the Mahabharata, the Bhagwad-Gita, functions virtually as a text on its own in Hinduism. On the eve of the Mahabharata war, the hero Arjuna suddenly develops a disinclination to fight. Arjuna's decision leads to a prolonged dialogue with Krishna during which Krishna tries to resolve Arjuna's moral and metaphysical dilemmas in 700 verses. The way in which Krishna seeks to guide Arjuna has endeared the text to the Hindus as a guide to their faith.

In the Bhagwad-Gita Hinduism comes closest to possessing a universal scripture. Since the Gupta period (AD 320 to 550; *see* Gupta Dynasty) it has inspired a stream of commentaries, summaries, and translations, all of which attest to its wide popularity. The process shows no signs of letting up. The Bhagwad-Gita's doctrine of *svadharma* (understanding one's own role and responsibility) implies a cosmic mirroring of the essential nature of reality (Brahman) in the reality of the individual's essential nature (atman). This implication has proved spiritually intriguing for practitioner, believer, and scholar alike.

The Mahabharata and the Bhagwad-Gita carry meaning on multiple levels. In one interpretation, the Pandavas and Kauravas represent the forces of good and evil that exist within each person, and the contest between them represents the perpetual battle between these tendencies. The Bhagwad-Gita describes the techniques and paths by which the individual can attain realization of the Ultimate Reality with Krishna as the guide. As part of the Mahabharata, the Bhagwad-Gita technically falls in the category of smriti rather than shruti. However, it virtual enjoys the status of shruti by representing the words of the divinity, incarnated as Krishna and addressed to human beings through Arjuna.

Tantric Literature

Tantra represents another vast body of Hindu literature. After centuries of neglect, it has gradually begun to receive fuller recognition. The word *tantra* has two meanings. In one sense it refers to sacred literature which appeared from the 5th century onward and focused not only on Vishnu and Shiva, but also on the cults of earlier deities: Ganapati (another name for the elephant-headed god, Ganesha), Kumara (a son of Brahma), Surya (sun) and Shakti (the goddess). The second sense restricts *tantra* to texts that deal with the worship of Shakti.

After the Gupta age ended in the 6th century the Tantric tradition heavily influenced Hinduism, Buddhism, and Jainism. If elite or intellectual Hinduism is Vedic in nature, then mainstream Hinduism is Tantric in orientation. Some accounts consider both traditions equally revelatory. Tantric literature largely eliminates caste distinctions in terms of religious practices. It also holds women in high regard. It thus provides a useful corrective to the negative stereotypes of Hinduism as *patriarchal* (male-controlled). Although smriti literature can be described as male oriented, Tantric literature is female oriented.

Consider these statements from Tantric literature. The *Gautamiya Tantra* clearly states that tantra is open to women and members of all castes. The *Mahanirvana Tantra* requires a man to fast for a day for talking rudely to a woman. The *Kubjikamata Tantra* states that all houses of women should be worshipped as holy shrines. In the *Shakta* model of Hinduism, which focuses worship on the Great Goddess, all women are regarded as gurus and may initiate others by reading out the mantra from an authoritative text. Men have no authority to do so. In addition, the Devi (goddess) is worshipped in her own right, rather than in relation to a male god.

Hindu gods are regularly displayed with their female counterparts. When they are invoked together, the female partner is named first, as in Sita-Rama and Radha-Krishna. In the case of Shiva and Shakti the relationship gets so close that they are represented as inhabiting a single body in the *Ardhanrishvara* (Lord-who-is-half-female) form. Tantra at times involves the balancing of these two aspects—Shiva (representing consciousness) and Shakti (representing energy)—in a manner reminiscent of *yin and yang* in Daoism.

Literature in Regional Languages

Most Hindus first encounter Hinduism through their regional languages, despite the special significance of Sanskrit. Almost every regional language in India has produced its own version of the Ramayana and the Mahabharata, sharing in the religious admiration given to the original versions. Deservedly famous translations of the Ramayana include one in the Tamil language by the 9th-century Hindu scholar Kamban and one in Hindi and by the 16th-century poet and saint Tulsidas. A wave of literature in Tamil appeared in the 7th to 9th centuries as the result of a surge of devotion of Vishnu and Shiva. Most of the influential works of modern Hinduism were originally composed in English. Masters who have realized Brahman continually renew the Hindu tradition and express themselves in a language appropriate to their time and place.

The utilization of these various bodies of literature provides insight into how Hinduism tries to sanctify what it touches. Thus the title of Veda came to be conferred on any worthwhile body of knowledge, including writings on architecture, on music, and even on military science. Highly esteemed sacred texts that came after the Vedas have come to be described as the fifth Veda.

History of Hinduism

Hinduism does not attach the same religious significance to historical events that Judaism, Christianity, and Islam do. Some have compared Hinduism's indifference to the history of a religious idea or practice to a scientist's indifference to the history of science. What is of value to both is the idea or practice as such.

The history of Hinduism thus becomes a history of its quest to incorporate the various developments it has encountered or generated, rather than a history of conquest of or triumph over these historical developments. The contrast is apparent in the Biblical injunction to believe in one God who is the only God and the Vedic perception that "Truth is one, sages call it variously." Considerable controversy remains over Hinduism's historical origins. At one time scholars believed that the arrival of the Aryan people in India about 1500 BC represented a critical moment in the history of Hinduism. The Aryans replaced the earlier Harappan culture in the Indus valley, and they are the people described in the Vedas, the earliest sacred literature of Hinduism.

Although linguistic evidence tends to support the notion of an Aryan migration, most scholars now believe this view awaits confirmation by archaeology, especially because it has been challenged by the discovery of extensive sites in northwestern and western India. So far there is no clear-cut answer to the key question: Did Hinduism as described in the Vedas originate in India or did it arise as a result of migrations from outside? What is clear is that the Hinduism of the Vedas goes back at least to 1200 BC in India and perhaps much earlier.

Vedic Hinduism

The beginnings of Vedic Hinduism, no later than 1200 BC, trace back to the Rig-Veda, which contains hymns of praise to various deities called devas. *Agni* (deva of fire) and *Indra* (king of devas and deva of the atmosphere, storms, rain, and battle) were prominent, judging by the number of hymns addressed to them. Fire was the deity of the domestic hearth as well as of public ritual. The Rig-Veda calls the deity "smoke-bannered" as it carries the offering made into it toward the gods. Indra was a martial leader in the Rig-Veda who carried his followers to victory in battle and also battled drought as a rain-god. An entire book of the Rig-Veda is devoted to soma, a plant whose juice produced ecstatic experiences. It is already clear in the Rig-Veda that all these devas were aspects of one underlying reality.

By the 4th century BC Vedic Hinduism had appeared in virtually all of India and had assimilated and absorbed various local religious beliefs and practices. The resulting mixture is what we refer to comprehensively as Vedic Hinduism.

Classical Hinduism

The period from the 3rd century BC to the late 7th century AD is known as classical Hinduism. Even as Vedic Hinduism flourished throughout India, various aspects of its world-view had come under challenge by the 6th century BC. This challenge came from Upanishadic thinkers and from the rise of new sects including the Jains and the Buddhists.

The Upanishadic thinkers considered themselves in the line of descent from Vedic seers, while the followers of Buddhism and Jainism tended to question Vedic authority, although they retained many concepts from the Vedas. All were concerned about release from eternal rebirth and generally agreed that release was obtained not by sacrifice but by meditation and contemplation.

Buddhism and Jainism gradually gained strength in India during the centuries just before and just after the beginning of the first millennium. Buddhism benefited in the 3rd century BC from the patronage extended to it by King Ashoka, who ruled almost all of India. Jainism similarly benefited from royal patrons. By the start of the Gupta period, which lasted from about AD 320 to 550, Hinduism resurged, having integrated a variety of Buddhist and Jain beliefs and practices. These included the doctrine of *ahimsa* (nonviolence) and an emphasis on vegetarianism. The Gupta period is celebrated as a glorious epoch of classical Hindu culture.

During this classical Gupta period, Hindu thought and its systematization flourished. By then many *shastras* (classical works) of Hindu philosophy had been compiled. These shastras include the *Arthashastra* (principles of statecraft), *Nayashastra* (aesthetics of performing arts), poetry and dramatic works by writers such as Kalidasa and Bhavabhuti, grammars by Panini and Patanjali, works on human sexuality such as the *Kamasutra,* and the medical compendia of Charak and Susruta. In addition, the major epics—the Ramayana and Mahabharata—received their present form. Also during this period, rules were developed for representations of the deities and for building structures to house these statues and images.

Medieval Hinduism

As a vigorous and multifaceted Hinduism unfolded in India during the 7th century, a new religion made its appearance in Arabia: Islam. Within a century, Islam's dominions extended from Spain to Sindh (now part of Pakistan). By the 10th and 11th centuries the followers of Islam consolidated their hold on northwestern India. By 1200 Islamic rule was established in the city of Delhi in northern India, and it then spread in two waves over nearly the whole of India. The first wave of expansion occurred under the Delhi Sultanate, which ruled from 1206 to 1526. During the second wave, under the Mughal Empire (1526-1858), Islamic rule achieved its maximum extension.

This encounter between Hinduism and Islam lasted more than 800 years. During most of this time, Islam had the upper hand politically, a fact that had enormous consequences for Hinduism and that presented challenges for both Hinduism and Islam which continue to this day. Islam's military victories outside India were followed by the conversion of the masses to Islam, with the possible exceptions of Spain and the Balkans. In India, however, Islam succeeded in converting barely a quarter of the population to Islam by 1900. Although Hinduism had successfully incorporated all previous invaders and political conquerors within the Hindu religious system—from the Persians in 6th century BC to the Huns in the 6th century AD—its powers of assimilation failed in the face of Islam.

One response of Hinduism to the presence of Islam was political. It included the emergence of the Hindu Vijayanagar kingdom, which held power in southern India from about 1336 to 1565, and the Hindu Maratha state in western India during the 17th and 18th centuries. The rise of Sikhism and the Sikh Empire (1767-1846) in the Punjab can also be considered part of this response. Willing to use violence in self-defense, Sikhs took a militant stance toward the conquerors.

The Islamic presence evoked a paradoxical Hindu religious response that blended hostile rejection and active emulation. Mainstream Hinduism retreated into a defensive position under the protective cover of *orthodoxy* (conformity to rule), judging by the number of Hindu religious codes produced during this period. At the theological level, however, Hinduism witnessed the rise and flowering of the *bhakti* (devotion) movement.

This movement of ecstatic devotion to Vishnu or Shiva had gained a firm foothold in the south by the 9th century, and it swept over the rest of the country by the 17th century. Devotion to the divine (*bhakti*), rather than knowledge of the divine (*jnana*), became the dominant form of Hinduism, perhaps reflecting the historical circumstances. Bhakti poetry expressed love for the divine, often in the forms of Krishna and Rama. Among the mystical bhakti poets were Chaitanya, Tulsidas, Mirabai, and Kabir.

The bhakti movement also provided a point of contact with a mystical movement in Islam known as Sufism. Sufis were religious figures known for their piety and love of God. As they carried out their work in India, the two traditions of Hinduism and Islam came together in their love of God. This coming together, however, never crossed over from communion to union, but the rise of Sikhism points to a possible crossover. Sikhism rejects image worship and ritualism in keeping with Islam, while retaining many aspects of the Hindu world-view.

Modern Hinduism

Following the decline of the Mughal Empire during the late 17th century, the British gradually succeeded in establishing themselves as the paramount power in India during the next century. The process began with a British victory in the Battle of Plassey in 1757, followed by the defeat of the Marathas in 1818. British victory over the Sikhs in 1846 completed the process. By this time the British had made two decisions of far-reaching importance for the future of Hinduism: to allow Christian missionaries to operate within the British dominions, in 1813; and to introduce English as the language of public instruction, in 1835.

These decisions forced Hinduism to confront Christianity and Western modernity. At the same time, the Western world was exposed to Hindu scriptures translated into European languages.

Movements for Reform

One response to the encounter with Europe was reform. The Bengali scholar Ram Mohan Roy set the tone for reform in the early 19th century. Roy campaigned against medieval or regional Hindu practices that were objectionable in the modern world. He advocated allowing widows to remarry and abolition of the relatively rare practice of *sati* (self-immolation of a wife after her husband's death, *see* suttee). In 1828 Mohan Roy founded the Brahmo Samaj (Society of Brahma) to spread his ideas.

Another movement kept India from moving too far toward imitation of the modern Christian West. The movement was named after Ramakrishna, a Hindu spiritual leader who served as a priest at the Dakshineshwar Temple in the city of Kolkata (Calcutta). His reputation as a mystic drew many to him, including Swami Vivekananda, who founded the Ramakrishna movement after Ramakrishna's death in 1886.

Vivekananda, a representative Hindu product of India's new English-language education system, became a devotee of Ramakrishna and renounced the world after the priest's death. His message was a return to the timeless wisdom of the Vedas. As an unknown swami, he turned up uninvited at the Parliament of World Religions in Chicago in 1893 to present Ramakrishna's teachings. He won instant celebrity and was hailed as a hero in India for his vigorous advocacy of Hinduism. In 1895 he founded the Vedanta Society in New York City to promote Hindu ideas.

Vivekananda primarily used English in his work of reforming Hinduism and stressing the inclusive aspects of Hindu spirituality over ritual and rules. Another reform-minded leader of the 19th century, Dayananda Saraswati, used Hindi in responding to the challenges of Christianity and modernity. Saraswati founded the Arya Samaj, a movement also dedicated to modernizing Hindu practices and asserting the universality of the Hindu tradition. These movements helped revitalize Hinduism.

Another issue that engaged Hindu reformers was the plight of the lowest social class, the panchama jatis who are also known as untouchables. Local movements, such as one led by Sri Narayana Guru in Kerala, were most successful at reform. Narayana, who was born in 1856, believed that education and greater self-esteem, rather han confrontation and blame, would elevate the untouchables. He established temples where all castes could pray together.

RAMAYANA

The *Rmyaga* is an ancient Sanskrit epic attributed to the poet Valmiki and is an important part of the Hindu canon (*smrti*). The name *Rmyaga* is a tatpurusha compound of *Rma* and *ayana* "going, advancing", translating to "the travels of *Rma*". The *Rmyaga* consists of 24,000 verses in seven cantos (*kgas*) and tells the story of a prince, Rama of Ayodhya, whose wife Sita is abducted by the demon (*Rkshasa*) king of Lanka, Rvana. In its current form, the Valmiki Ramayana is dated variously from 500 BC to 100 BC, or about co-eval to early versions of the *Mahabhrata*. As with most traditional epics, since it has gone through a long process of interpolations and redactions, it is impossible to date it accurately. The Ramayana had an important influence on later Sanskrit poetry, primarily through its establishment of the Sloka meter. But, like its epic cousin Mahabharata, the Ramayana is not just an ordinary story. It contains the teachings of ancient Hindu sages and presents them through allegory in narrative and the interspersion of the philosophical and the devotional. The characters of Rama, Sita, Lakshmana, Bharata, Hanumn and Ravana (the villain of the piece) are all fundamental to the cultural consciousness of India.

One of the most important literary works on ancient India, the Ramayana has had a profound impact on art and culture in the Indian Subcontinent and Southeast Asia. The story of Rama also inspired a large amount of later-day literature in various languages, notable among which are the works of the sixteenth century Hindi poet Tulsidas and the Tamil poet Kambar of the 13th century.

The Ramayana is not just a Hindu religious tale. Starting from the 8th century, the colonisation of Southeast Asia by Indians began. Several large empires like the Khmers, the Majapahits, the Sailendras, the Champas and Sri Vijaya were established. Because of this, the Ramayana became popular in Southeast Asia and manifested itself in text, temple architecture and performance, particularly in Indonesia (Java, Sumatra, Bali and Borneo), Thailand, Cambodia, Laos, Malaysia, Myanmar, Philippines and Vietnam.

Structure of Valmiki Ramayana: Valmiki's *Ramayana*, the oldest version of Ramayana is the basis of all the various version of Ramayana that are prevalent in the various cultures. The text survives in numerous complete and partial manuscripts, the oldest surviving of which is dated from the eleventh century AD. The current text of Valmiki Ramayana has come down to us in two regional versions from the north and the south of India. Valmiki Ramayana has been traditionally divided into seven books, dealing with the life of Rama from his birth to his death.

1. *Bala Kanda* – Book of the young Rama which details the miraculous birth of Rama, his early life in Ayodhya, his slaying of the demons of the forest at the request of Vishvamitra and his wedding with Sita.

2. *Ayodhya Kanda* – Book of Ayodhya in which Dasharatha comes to grief over his promise to Kaikeyi and the start of Rama's exile.
3. *Aranya Kanda* – Book of the Forest which describes Rama's life in the forest and the abduction of Sita by Ravana.
4. *Kishkindya Kanda* – Book of Kishkinda, the Vanara kingdom in which Rama befriends Sugriva and the Vanara army and begins the search for Sita.
5. *Sundara Kanda* – Book of Sundara (Hanuman) in which Hanuman travels to Lanka and finds Sita imprisoned there and brings back the good news to Rama.
6. *Yuddha Kanda* – Book of the War, which narrates the Rama-Ravana war and the return of the successful Rama to Ayodhya and his coronation.
7. *Uttara Kanda* – Epilogue, which details the life of Rama and Sita after their return to Ayodhya, Sita's banishment and how Sita and Rama pass on to the next world.

There have been speculations on whether the first and the last chapters of Valmiki's *Ramayana* were indeed written by the original author. Many experts are of the opinion that they are integral part of the book in spite of the many differences in style and some contradictions in content between these two chapters and the rest of the book. These two chapters contain most of the mythological interpolations found in the Ramayana, such as the miraculous birth of Rama and his divine nature as well as the numerous legends surrounding Ravana.

'Main Characters'

- Rama is the hero of this epic tale. He is portrayed as an incarnation of the god Vishnu. He is the eldest and the favourite son of the King of Ayodhya, Dasharatha. He is a popular prince loved by one and all. He is the epitome of virtue. Dasharatha, forced by one of his wives Kaikeyi commands Rama to relinquish his right to the throne for fourteen years and go into exileand by his father. While in exile, Rama kills the demon king Ravana.
- Sita is the wife of Rama and the daughter of king Janaka. Sita is the epitome of womanly purity and

virtue. She follows her husband into exile and there gets abducted by Ravana. She is imprisoned in the island of Lanka by Ravana. Rama rescues her by defeating the demon king Ravana.

- Hanuman is a vanara belonging to the kingdom of Kishkinda. He worships Rama and helps find Sita by going to the kingdom of Lanka crossing the great ocean.
- Lakshmana, the younger brother of Rama, chose to go into exile with him. He spends his time protecting Sita and Rama. He is deceived by Ravana and Maricha into believing that Rama was in trouble while Sita gets abducted.
- Ravana, a rakshasa, is the king of Lanka. He received a boon from Brahma that he will not be killed by either gods, demons or by spirits, after performing a severe penance for ten thousand years. He was also the most intelligent and erudite living being of his time. He has ten heads and twenty arms. After getting his reward from Brahma, Ravana begins to lay waste the earth and disturbs the deeds of good Brahmins. Rama is born a human to defeat him, thus overcoming the boon given by Brahma.
- Dasharatha is the king of Ayodhya and the father of Rama. He has three queens, Kousalya, Sumitra and Kaikeyi, and three other sons, Bharata, Lakshmana and Shatrughna. Kaikeyi, Dasharatha's favourite queen forces him to make his son Bharata heir apparent and send Rama into exile. Dashatara dies heartbroken after Rama goes into exile.
- Bharata is the second son of Dasharata. When he learns that his mother Kaikeyi had forced Rama into exile and caused Dasharata to die broken hearted, he storms out of the palace and goes in search of Rama. When Rama refuses to break his exile to return to the capital to assume the throne, he requests and gets Rama's sandals and places them on the throne. Bharata then rules Ayodhya as a representative of Rama.
- Vishvamitra is the sage who takes Rama into the forest at the behest of defeating the demons destroying his

Vedic sacrifices. On the way back he takes Rama into Mithila where Rama sees and falls in love with Sita.

Synopsis: Rama, the hero of *Ramayana*, is a popular deity worshipped by Hindus, the route of his wanderings being, each year, trodden by devout pilgrims. The poem is not a mere literary monument, it is a part of Hinduism, and is held in such reverence that the mere reading or hearing of it, or certain passages of it, is believed by the Hindus to free them from sin and grant every desire to the reader or hearer. According to Hindu tradition, Rama is an incarnation (Avatar), of the god Vishnu, who is part of the Hindu Trinity. The main purpose of this incarnation is to demonstrate the righteous path (dharma) for the life on earth.

Rama's Youth: Brahma, creator of the universe, could not revoke a boon he gave the demon king Ravana, as a reward for his severe penances, that he should not be slain by gods, demons, or spirits. Having been then rewarded, Ravana began with the help of his evil supporters, the *Rakshasas*, to lay waste the earth and to do violence to the good, especially the Brahmin priests, disturbing their sacrifices. All the gods, watching this devastation, went to Brahma to find a way to deliver themselves and the earth of this evil. Brahma went to Vishnu and conveyed the anguish of the gods and requested that Vishnu incarnate on earth as a human to destroy Ravana, as Ravana had not asked for protection against humans or beasts in his wishes to Brahma.

Meanwhile, the good king Dasharatha of Ayodhya, who had ruled over his kingdom of Kosala for a long time, was beginning to become anxious about his successor, for he had no sons to take over the kingdom after him. Taking advice from his ministers and priests Dasharatha organised a *Putrakameshti Yagna*, a sacrifice for progeny. Vishnu decided to be born as the eldest to Dasharatha and caused a divine being to emerge from the sacrificial fire. The divine being gave Dasharatha a golden vessel filled with nectar and asked him to give it to his queens. Dasharatha divided it amongst his three queens, Kausalya, Sumitra and Kaikeyi. In due course they became pregnant and gave birth to four sons: Queen Kausalya gives birth to the eldest son, Rama. Bharata is born to Queen Kaikeyi, and twins, Lakshmana and Shatrughna, are born to Queen

Sumitra. The boys grew up learning the scriptures and the art of bowmanship from the sage Vasishta. One day, the sage Vishvamitra visited the kingdom and asked King Dasharatha to send Rama to protect him from demons who had been disturbing his sacrifices. Although very reluctant, Dasharatha agreed to send Rama and Lakshmana with Vishvamitra. As the brothers fulfilled their duties, Vishvamitra was pleased with them and bestowed upon them various celestial weapons.

Towards the end of their stay with Vishvamitra, Rama chanced to pass near the kingdom of Mithila and heard that its king, Janaka, had offered his peerless daughter, Sita, in marriage to the man who could bend the mighty bow of god Shiva, which had been kept at Janaka's court. Rama at once determined to accomplish the feat, which had been tried in vain by so many suitors. When he presented himself at court Janaka was at once won by his youth and beauty. Five thousand men drew in the mighty bow, resting upon an eight-wheeled chariot. Rama, without any apparent effort, bent it until it broke and Janaka gladly gave him his beautiful daughter. After the splendid wedding ceremonies were over, the happy pair travelled back to Ayodhya.

Rama's Exile: King Dasharatha, began to feel weary of reigning, and decided to make Rama, his eldest son and heir-apparent, the co-regent (*Yuvaraja*). His happy people received the announcement of his intention with delight and the whole city was in the midst of the most splendid preparations for the ceremony. Dasharatha went to discuss the celebrations with his favourite wife Kaikeyi. However, Kaikeyi's jealousy was aroused by her evil maid Manthara, because the son of Kausalya and not her own son Bharata, at that time absent from the city, was to be made king. She fled to an ante-chamber where Dasharatha found her in tears..

To Dasharatha's concerned queries, Kaikeyi recalled that, ages ago, the old king had granted her two boons. She now demanded the fulfilment of these before she would consent to smile upon him. Dasharatha agreed and Kaikeyi revealed her demands. She required him, first, to appoint her son Bharata as co-regent and, second, to exile Rama for fourteen years to the terrible forest of Dandaka. Dasharatha was heart-broken, but had to abide by his promise. Rama, the obedient son, immediately agreed to relinquish his claim to the throne and started to leave for his exile. His faithful wife Sita and his loving brother Lakshmana also decided to go along with Rama. With Dasharatha lying grief-stricken, Rama left for the forest, followed by the lamenting people of Ayodhya. Soon after, king Dasharatha died, overcome by grief.

Sita's Abduction: Rama, Sita and Lakshmana left behind Ayodhya and its people, crossed the river Ganges and went into the forest. They found an idyllic place called Chitrakuta to establish their hermitage. No more beautiful place could be imagined. Flowers of every kind, delicious fruits, and on every side the most pleasing prospects, together with perfect love, is stated to have made their hermitage a paradise on earth. In the forest, Rama befriended the old vulture-king, Jatayu.

Meanwhile, Bharata returned to Ayodhya and, being also devoted to Rama, became furious with Kaikeyi for her role in exiling Rama and for the death of his father. Determined to bring back Rama, he headed for the forest. When he found Rama and pleaded with him to return and assume the throne, Rama politely refused, saying that he was duty-bound to see that his father's promise was fulfilled. Reluctantly Bharata agreed to return to the kingdom, requesting that Rama give to him his sandals. Back in Ayodhya, Baratha placed Rama's sandals on the throne of Ayodhya, and ruled as Rama's proxy from a village called Nandigrama near Ayodhya, awaiting his return. He also vowed to end his own life if Rama failed to return after fourteen years.

One day, the rakshasi Surpanakha, a sister of the demon king Ravana, chanced upon Rama's hermitage and saw the handsome Rama and became enamoured. Taking the form of a beautiful young girl, she tried to seduce Rama. Rama, ever faithful to his wife Sita, did not respond and asked her to approach Lakshmana. Lakshmana too refused, stating his duty towards his brother and his sister-in-law while in exile. An infuriated Surpanakha blamed Sita for the men scorning her charged at her in her original demonic form. However, Lakshmana saved Sita by severing Surpanakha's nose and ears. Surpanakha flew back to Ravana complaining about the young exiles. Ravana, after hearing of the beautiful Sita from Surpanakha, resolved to kill Rama in revenge and take Sita for himself. He enlisted the aid of the demon Maricha. Maricha turned himself into a golden deer that Sita wanted for herself. She asked Rama to get it for her, but after Rama left to find it, Maricha began screaming to trick Lakshmana. Lakshmana, convinced Rama was in danger, resolved to go out and find his brother. Before leaving Sita alone in the hut, Lakshmana drew a circle in the dirt saying that Sita would be safe as long as she stayed in the circle. Ravana approached the hermitage in the guise of an old man and asked Sita to give him some food. Initially hesitant to step out of Lakshmana's circle, Sita finally stepped out to give the old man some food. At this moment Ravana grabbed Sita and fled in his airborne vehicle, (Pushpaka Vimana). Jatayu, seeing them fly, attempted to save Sita, but Ravana engaged Jatayu in combat and chopped off the vulture's wings. On returning to the hermitage, Rama and Lakshmana found it empty and anxiously began a search. Through Jatayu, whom they found lying mortally wounded, Rama and Lakshmana learnt of Sita's fate.

Vanara Kingdom: Continuing their search, they encountered the vanara king of Kishkindha, Sugriva, and Hanuman, one of his generals, among whom Sita had dropped from the chariot her scarf and some ornaments. Sugriva had been deposed from his kingdom by his brother, Vali, who had also taken his wife Roma from him. Rama agreed to defeat Vali if Sugriva would assist in the search for Sita. The agreement made, Sugriva challenged Vali to a duel. While the duel was progressing, Rama shot from his bow and killed Vali. Sugriva regained his kingdom and his wife.

Sugriva and Rama sent the vanara soldiers in various directions in search of Sita. However, their efforts didn't bear fruit until they met another ancient vulture, Sampati, who was the brother of the slain Jatayu. Sampati was earthbound and deformed-his wings were burnt when he flew too close to the Sun (a story that can be considered to be similar to that of Icarus's). His brother, being hardier, had saved him from falling to his death. While Jatayu was the physically stronger of the two, Sampati possessed a compensating gift of vision. Sampati's vision was incredibly powerful, spanning several hundred yojanas and enabling him to see farther than anyone else. On hearing of Ravana's killing his brother, he readily agreed to help the vanaras. He was soon able to spot Sita in the southern direction. He could see her imprisoned in a garden of Ashoka trees on the island of Lanka, beyond the southern ocean.

Hanuman in Lanka: Sugriva dispatched his army to the south with his nephew Angada at the head. Hanuman went with Angada as his general. When they reached deep south, they found a great ocean stretching between them and land of Lanka. They could find no means by which to cross the ocean. Commanding his soldiers to remain where they were, Hanuman expanded his body to enormous proportions, leaped the vast expanse of water, and alighted upon a mountain *Trikuta* from which he could look down upon Lanka. Perceiving the city to be closely guarded, he assumed the form of a cat, and thus, unsuspected, crept through the barriers and examined the city.

He found Ravana in his apartments, surrounded by beautiful women, but Sita was not among them. Continuing his search, he at last discovered her, her beauty dimmed by grief, seated under a tree in a beautiful asoka grove, guarded by hideous rakshasas with the faces of buffaloes, dogs, and swine. Assuming the form of a tiny monkey, Hanuman crept down the tree, and giving her the ring of Rama, took one from her. He offered to carry her away with him, but Sita declared that Rama must himself come to her rescue, and as proof of finding her Sita gave Hanuman a priceless jewel to take back to Rama. While they were talking together, Ravana appeared, and, after fruitless wooing, announced that if Sita did not yield herself to him in two months he would have her guards "mince her limbs with steel" for his morning repast.

In his rage, Hanuman destroyed a mango grove and was captured by the rakshasa guards, and brought before Ravana. Hanuman proclaimed that he was a messenger of Rama, and demanded that Ravana restore Sita to Rama or fall victim to Rama's wrath. Furious at hearing Hanuman's words, Ravana ordered Hanuman's death.

Vibhishana, Ravana's righteous brother, intervened and counselled Ravana to follow the scriptures, reminding that it was improper to execute a messenger, and instead told him to exact the appropriate punishment for Hanuman's crime. Ravana accepted and ordered his rakshasas to set fire to Hanuman's tail. As soon as this was done, Hanuman made himself very small, slipped from his bonds, and, jumping upon the roofs, spread a conflagration through the city of Lanka. He leaped back to the mainland, conveyed the news of Sita's captivity to Rama and Sugriva, and was soon engaged in active preparations for the campaign.

Battle of Lanka: Rama decided that as long as the ocean was not bridged, it was impossible for any one but Hanuman to cross it. Rama meditated for three days without food or water, but in vain. In his anger at being so ignored, Rama turned his weapons against the ocean, until from the terrified waves arose Varuna, the god of the ocean, who promised him that if Nila and Nala from his army built a bridge, the waves should support the materials as firmly as though it were built on land.

Terror reigned in Lanka at the news of the approach of Rama. Vibishana, Ravana's brother, deserted to Rama, because of the demon's rage when he advised him to make peace with Rama. Fiercely fought battles ensued, in which even the gods took part—Vishnu and Indra taking sides with Rama, and the evil spirits fighting with Ravana.

After the war had been fought for some time, with varying results, and a great number of troops on both sides were killed, it was decided to determine the victor by single combat between Ravana and Rama. Even the gods were terrified at the fierceness of the conflict. At each shot Rama's mighty bow cut off a head of Ravana, which at once grew back, and the hero was in despair until Vibhishana told him to aim at Ravana's belly-button. Rama took careful aim.

As Ravana fell by this weapon, flowers rained from heaven upon tho happy victor, and his ears were ravished with celestial music. Touched by the grief of Ravana's widow, Mandodari, Rama ordered a splendid funeral for his foe, and then sought the conquered city.

Sita was led forth, beaming with happiness at finding herself re-united to her husband, but her happiness was destined to be of short duration. Rama received her with coldness and with downcast eyes, saying that she could no longer be his wife, after having dwelt in the house of Ravana. Sita assured him of her innocence; but on his continuing to revile her, she ordered her funeral pyre to be built, since she would rather die by fire than live despised by Rama. The sympathy of all the bystanders was with Sita, but Rama saw her enter the flames without a tremor. Soon Agni, the god of fire, appeared, bearing the uninjured Sita in his arms. Her innocence thus publicly proved by the trial by fire, she was welcomed by Rama, whose treatment she tenderly forgave.

The conquest won, Ravana defeated, and Sita restored, Rama returned in triumph to Ayodhya, and assumed the governance to the great delight of Bharata and the people of Ayodhya.

Sita Banished: Ayodhya was prosperous, the people were happy, and for a time all went well. It was not long, however, before whispers concerning Sita's long stay in Lanka spread through the city, and Rama came to hear the whisperings that a famine in the country was due to the guilt of Sita, who had suffered the caresses of Ravana while in captivity. Under the pressure from the citizens of Ayodhya, Rama banished her to the forest in which they had spent together the happy years of their exile.

Without a murmur the unhappy Sita dragged herself to the forest, and, torn with grief of body and spirit, found the hermitage of Valmiki, where she gave birth to twin sons, Lava and Kush. Here she reared them, with the assistance of the hermit, who was their teacher, and under whose care they grew to manhood, handsome and strong.

It chanced that about the time the youths were twenty years old, Rama began to think the gods were angered with him because he had killed Ravana, who was the son of a Brahman. Rama became determined to propitiate them by means of Ashvamedha, the great sacrifice, in which he caused a horse to be turned loose in the forest. When his men went to retake it, at the end of the year, they found it caught by two strong and beautiful youths who resisted all efforts to capture them. When his men couldn't retake the horse, Rama went to the forest in person, only to learn that the youths were his twin sons, Lava and Kush. Struck with remorse, Rama recalled the sufferings of his wife Sita, and on learning that she was at the hermitage of Valmiki, requested her to come with him.

Sita had time to recover from the love of her youth, and the prospect of life with Rama, she felt, was not altogether pleasant. She appealed to the earth, if she had never loved any man but Rama, if her truth and purity were known to the earth, let it open its bosom and take her to it. While the people stood trembling with horror, the earth opened, a gorgeous throne appeared, and the goddess of earth, seated upon it, took Sita beside her and conveyed her to the realms of eternal happiness, leaving the too late repentant people to wear out the remaining years in penitence.

Morals in Ramayana: In his *Ramayana,* Valmiki expresses his view of human code of conduct through Rama: life is evanescent and the hedonistic approach to it is meaningless. However, that should not allow one to be indifferent to one's own rights and duties laid down in the ancient texts. He thus adopts the view that Dharma is what is proclaimed in the Veda and it should be followed for its own sake, not for what it brings you in pain or pleasure. Doing this will ensure one's welfare in this and the next world. In addition, Ramayana also reinforces the need for thinking about the consequences before making promises, for if you make them you must keep them, no matter how hard it may be.

Sankshepa Ramayana, the brief narration of the entire Ramayana story by the sage Narada to Valmiki, forms the first *sarga* of Valmiki Ramayana. Narada lists the sixteen qualities of the ideal man and says that Rama was the complete man possessing all sixteen of these qualities. Although Rama himself declares "he is but a man, and never once claims to be divine, Rama is regarded by Hindus as one of the most important Avatar of the god Vishnu and as an ideal man.

Valmiki portrays Rama not as a supernatural being, but as a human with all the attendant shortcomings, who encounters moral dilemmas but who overcomes these by simply adhering to the *dharma*—the righteous way. There are several instances narrated in Valmiki Ramayana which cast shadows on the pristine character of the hero and reinforce the theme of Ram struggling with mortal flaws and prejudices whilst struggling to follow the path of dharma. When Rama killed Vali to aid Sugriva regain his throne, it was not in fair combat, but while hiding behind a tree. When Sita was freed from Ravana's prison, Rama forced Sita to undergo an ordeal by fire to prove her purity and later as the king, Rama killed the Shudra Shambuka for performing a yogic penance not in keeping with his perceived low station in the society, though this latter incident is contested and may have crept in because of reinterpretation later on.

Concept of Dharma-Artha-Kama as per Ramayana: The concepts of Dharma, Artha, Kama (and Moksha) are very old Hindu concepts. They are also known as Purusharthas. There are two prominent instances of it being defined in *Ramayana*. The first was when Bharat came to forest (Chitrakoot) to meet Rama. Rama asked him whether he followed the rules of Dharma, Artha and Kaama properly. As per Rama it is defined as: Artha should not interfere with Dharma and vice versa. Similarly Kaama should not interfere with either Dharma or with Artha. Since Bharat was already knowledgeable he was to be reminded in very short words.

But Dharma here means the duties and welfare one does for the society. Making wells, for example, is part of the dharma of a king. Arth means earnings. As it is further asked by Rama: The king has to see that there is enough income from taxes, the salaries of the employees are given at proper time and the tax should not be more than 1/6th (16.6%) of a person's income. Kaama means pleasure here. One is allowed to have pleasure but without affecting the duties and earnings.

The other instance of this concept comes in Yudha Kanda. Here Kumbhakarna, Ravana's brother, advises Ravana that one should use dharma in the morning, artha in the daytime and Kaama at night. He further says to Ravana that he (Ravana) is busy with Kaama all the time and this will take him to destruction. Interestingly one of Ravana's ministers Mahodara scolds Kubhakarna and to please his master says that a King can enjoy Kaama at any time.

Textual History: Traditionally the epic belongs to the Treta Yuga, one of the four eons of Hindu chronology and is attributed to Valmiki, is an active participant in the story.

It is composed in Epic Sanskrit, an early variant of Classical Sanskrit, so that in principle the core of the work may date to as early as the 5th century BCE. Since in its current form, after hundreds of years of transmission through recitations and in manuscript form, the epic has gone thorough numerous variations, it cannot be dated by linguistic analysis as a whole, and should be considered to have emerged over a long process, spanning from the 5th to 1st centuries BC.

The core events told in the epic may well be of even greater age, the names of the characters, Rama, Sita, Dasharata, Janaka, Vasishta and Vishvamitra are all known in the Vedic literature such as the Brahmanas which are older than the Valmiki Ramayana. However, nowhere in the surviving Vedic poetry is a story similar to the Ramayana of Valmiki. Brahma, one of the main characters of *Ramayana*, and Vishnu, who according to *Bala Kanda* was incarnated as Rama are not Vedic deities, and come first into prominence with the epics themselves (and further during the 'Puranic' period of the later 1st millennium AD).

There is general consensus that books two to six form the oldest portion of the epic while the first book *Bala Kanda* and the last the *Uttara Kanda* are later additions. The author or authors of *Bala Kanda* and *Ayodhya Kanda* appear to be familiar with the eastern Gangetic basin region of northern India and the Kosala and Magadha region during the period of the sixteen janapadas as the geographical and geopolitical data is in keeping with what is known about the region. However, when the story moves to the *Aranya Kanda* and beyond, it seems to turn abruptly into fantasy with its demon-slaying hero and fantastic creatures. The geography of central and south India is increasingly vaguely described. The knowledge of the location of the island of Sri Lanka also lacks detail. Basing his assumption on these features, the historian H.D. Sankalia has proposed a date of the 4th century BC for the composition of the text. A. L. Basham, however, is of the opinion that Rama may have been a minor chief who lived in the 8th or the 7th century BC.

The events of the epic have also been dated to as early as 6000 BC by adherents of archaeoastronomy.

Variant Versions: The epic story of Ramayana was adopted by several cultures across Asia. Shown here is a Thai historic artwork depicting the battle which took place between Rama and Ravana. As in many oral epics, multiple versions of the Ramayana survive. In particular, the Ramayana related in north India differs in important respects from that preserved in South India and the rest of South-East Asia. There is an extensive tradition of oral storytelling based on the Ramayana in Thailand, Cambodia, Malaysia, Laos, Vietnam, and Indonesia.

In many Malay versions, Lakshmana is given greater importance than Rama, whose character is considered somewhat weak.

Within India: There are diverse regional versions of the Ramayana written by various authors in India. Some of them differ significantly from each other. During the twelfth century AD, Kamban wrote *Ramavatharam*, known popularly as Kambaramayanam in Tamil. Although based on Valmiki Ramayana, Kambaramayanam is a true classic and unique in that Kamban has modified and reinterpreted many anecdotes in Valmiki Ramayana to suit the Tamil culture and his own ideas. Valmiki's Ramayana inspired the Sri Ramacharit Manas by Tulasidas in 1576, an epic Awadhi (a dialect of Hindi) version with a slant more grounded in a different realm of Hindu literature, that of Bhakti.

It is an acknowledged masterpiece of India. It is popularly known as *Tulsi-krita Ramayana*. Gujarati poet Premanand wrote a version of *Ramayana* in the 17th century. Other versions include, a Bengali version by Krittivas in the 14th century, in Oriya by Balarama Das in the 16th century, in Marathi by Sridhara in the 18th century, a Telugu version by Ranganatha in the 15th century, a Kannada Ramayana by the 16th century poet Narahari, Kotha Ramayana in Assamese by the 14th century poet Madhava Kandali and Adhyathma Ramayanam Kilippattu, a Malayalam version by Thunchaththu Ezhuthachan in the 16th century.

There is a sub-plot to Ramayana, prevalent in some parts of India relates to the adventures of Ahi Ravana and Mahi Ravana, the evil brother of Ravana, which enhances the role of Hanuman in the story. Hanuman rescues Rama and Lakshmana after they are kidnapped by the Ahi-mahi Ravana at the behest of Ravana and held prisoner in a subterranean cave, ready to be sacrificed to the goddess Kali.

There have been reports of a version of the Ramayana story prevalent amongst the Mappilas of Kerala. This version, known as *Mappila Ramayana*, forms a part of the Mappillapattu. *Mappillapattu* is a genre of folk singing popular amonst the musims of Kerala and Lakshadweep. Being of Muslim origin, the hero of this story is a sultan. There are no major changes in the names of characters except for that of Rama's which is changed to 'Laman'. The language and the imagery projected in the Mappilapattu are in accordance with the social fabric of the earlier Muslim community.

Southeast Asian Versions: Many other Asian cultures have adapted the Ramayana, resulting in other national epics. Aspects of the Chinese epic Journey to the West were inspired by the Ramayana, particularly the character Sun Wukong, who is believed to have been based on Hanuman. Kakawin Rmayaga is an old Javanese rendering of the Sanskrit Ramayana from the ninth century Indonesia. It is a faithful rendering of the Hindu epic with very little variation. Phra Lak Phra Lam is a Lao language version, whose title comes from Lakshmana and Rama. The story of Lakshmana and Rama is told as the previous life of the Buddha. In Hikayat Seri Rama of Malaysia, Dasharatha is the great-grandson of the Prophet Adam. Ravana receives boons from Allah instead of Brahma.

Thailand's popular national epic Ramakien is derived from the Hindu epic. In *Ramakien*, Sita is the daughter of Ravana and Mandodari (*T'os'akanth* (=Dasakand) and *Mont'o*). Vibhisana (*P'ip'ek*), the astrologer brother of Ravana, predicts calamity from the horoscope of Sita. So Ravana has her thrown into the waters, who, later, is picked by Janaka (*Janok*). While the main story is identical to that of the *Ramayana*, many other aspects were transposed into a Thai context, such as the clothes, weapons, topography, and elements of nature, which are described as being Thai in style. It has an expanded role for Hanuman and he is portrayed as a lascivious character. Ramakien can be seen in an elaborate illustration at the Wat Phra Kaew temple in Bangkok. Other Southeast Asian adaptations include Ramakavaca of Bali, Maradia Lawana of the Philippines, the Reamker of Cambodia and the Yama Zatdaw of Myanmar.

Contemporary Versions: Contemporary versions of the

Ramayana include Sri Ramayana Darshanam by Dr. K. V. Puttappa (Kuvempu) in Kannada and Ramayana Kalpavrikshamu by Viswanatha Satyanarayana in Telugu, both of which have been awarded the Jnanpith Award. The modern Indian author Ashok Banker has so far written a series of six English language novels based on the Ramayana. In September 2006, the first issue of Ramayana 3392 A.D. was published by Virgin Comics, featuring the Ramayana as reinvisioned by author Deepak Chopra and filmmaker Shekhar Kapur.

Ramayana Landmarks: Amongst the ruins of the Vijayanagara empire near Hampi, is a cave known as Sugriva's Cave. The cave is marked by coloured markings. The place holds its similarity to the descriptions of 'kishkinda' in Sundarakanda. Rama is said to have met Hanuman here. The place is also home to the famous Hazararama temple (Temple of a thousand Ramas).

MAHABHARATA

The *Mahabharata* (Devanagari), is one of the two major Sanskrit epics of ancient India, the other being the *Rmyaga*. With more than 74,000 verses, plus long prose passages, or some 1.8 million words in total, it is one of the longest epic poems in the world. Taken together with the Harivamsa, the *Mahabharata* has a total length of more than 90,000 verses.

It is also of immense religious and philosophical importance in India, in particular for including the Bhagavad Gita, an important text of Hinduism.

The title may be translated as "Great India", or "the great tale of the Bharata Dynasty", according to the *Mahabharata*'s own testimony extended from a shorter version simply called *Bhrata* of 24,000 verses The epic is part of the Hindu *itihsas*, literally "that which happened", along with the *Ramayana* and the *Purgas*.

Traditionally, the *Mahabharata* is ascribed to Vyasa. Due to its immense length, its philological study has a long history of attempting to unravel its historical growth and composition layers. In its final form, it was completed by the first century, with its central core *Bharata* (consisting of 24,000 verses) dating back to the 6th century BCE, and some parts possibly dating back as far as the 8th century BCE. The events depicted in the *Mahabharata* are thought to have taken place around the 12th century BCE.

Influence: With its philosophical depth and sheer magnitude, a consummate embodiment of the ethos of not only India but of Hinduism and Vedic tradition, the *Mahabharata*'s scope and grandeur is best summarized by one quotation from the beginning of its first *parva* (section): "What is found here, may be found elsewhere. What is not found here, will not be found elsewhere." This quotation rightly sums up Mahabharata, within which one finds myriads of relationships, stories and events.

In its scope, the *Mahabharata* is more than simply a story of kings and princes, sages and wisemen, demons and gods; its author, Vyasa, says that one of its aims is elucidating the four goals of life: kama (pleasure), artha (wealth), dharma (duty) and Moksha (liberation). The story culminates in Moksha, believed by Hindus to be the ultimate goal of human beings. Karma and dharma play an integral role in the *Mahabharata*.

The *Mahabharata* includes large amounts of Hindu mythology, cosmological stories of the gods and goddesses, and philosophical parables aimed at students of Hindu philosophy. Among the principal works and stories that are a part of the *Mahabharata* are the following (often considered isolated as works in their own right):

- Bhagavad Gita (Krishna instructs and teaches Arjuna. Anusasanaparva.)
- Damayanti (or Nala and Damayanti, a love story. Aranyakaparva.)
- Krishnavatara (the story of Krishna, the *Krishna Lila*, which is woven through many chapters of the story)
- Rama (an abbreviated version of the Ramayana. Aranyakaparva.)
- Rishyasringa (also written as Rshyashrnga, the horned boy and rishi. Aranyakaparva.)
- Vishnu sahasranama (the most famous hymn to Vishnu, which describes His 1000 names; Anushasanaparva.)

Textual History and Organization: It is undisputed that the full length of the *Mahabharata* has accreted over a long period. The *Mahabharata* itself (1.1.61) distinguishes a core portion of 24,000 verses, the *Bharata* proper, as opposed to additional "secondary" material, while the Ashvalayana Grhyasutra (3.4.4) makes a similar distinction. According to the *Adi-parva* of the *Mahabharata* (shlokas 81, 101-102), the text was originally 8,800 verses when it was composed by Krishna Dwaipayana Vyasa and was known as the *Jaya* ("*Victory*"), which later became 24,000 verses in the *Bharata* recited by Vaisampayana, and finally over 90,000 verses in the *Mahabl arata* recited by Ugrasravas.

Not unlike the field of Homeric studies, research on the *Mahabharata* has put an enormous effort into recognizing and dating various layers within the text. Oldenberg (1922) stipulated that the supposed original poem once carried an immense "tragic force", but dismissed the full text as a "horrible chaos".

The earliest known references to the *Mahabharata* and its core *Bharata* date back to the 6th-5th century BCE, in the Ashtadhyayi (sutra 6.2.38) of Pgini (c. 520-460 BCE), and in the *Ashvalayana Grhyasutra* (3.4.4), while various characters from the epic are also mentioned in earlier Vedic literature. This indicates that the core 24,000 verses, known as the *Bharata*, as well as an early version of the extended *Mahabharata*, were composed by the 6th-5th century BCE, with parts of *Jaya*'s original 8,800 verses possibly dating back as far as the 9th-8th century BC.

However, the earliest testimony of the existence of the full text of the *Mahabharata* is by the Greek Sophist Dion Chrysostom (c. 40-105), who mentions that "the Indians possess an Iliad of 100,000 verses". The later copper-plate inscription of the Maharaja Sharvanatha (533-534) from Khoh (Satna District, Madhya Pradesh) also describes the *Mahabharata* as a "collection of 100,000 verses" (*shatasahasri samhita*). The redaction of this large body of text was carried out after formal principles, emphasizing the numbers 18 and 12.

The addition of the latest parts may be dated by the absence of the *Anushasana-parva* from *MS Spitzer*, the oldest surviving Sanskrit philosophical manuscript dated to the first century, that contains among other things a list of the books in the

Mahabharata. From this evidence, it is likely that the redaction into 18 books took place in the first century. An alternative division into 20 parvas appears to have co-existed for some time. The division into 100 sub-parvas (mentioned in Mbh. 1.2.70) is older, and most parvas are named after one of their constituent sub-parvas. The Harivamsa consists of the final two of the 100 sub-parvas, and was considered an appendix (*khila*) to the *Mahabharata* proper by the redactors of the 18 parvas.

According to Mbh. 1.1.50, there were three versions of the epic, beginning with *Manu* (1.1.27), *Astika* (1.3, sub-parva 5) or *Vasu* (1.57), respectively. These versions probably correspond to the addition of one and then another 'frame' settings of dialogues. The *Vasu* version corresponds to the oldest, without frame settings, beginning with the account of the birth of Vyasa. The Astika version adds the Sarpasattra and Ashvamedha material from Brahmanical literature, and introduces the name *Mahabharata* and identifies Vyasa as the work's author. The redactors of these additions were probably Pancharatrin scholars who according to Oberlies (1998) likely retained control over the text until its final redaction. Mention of the Hunas in the *Bhishma-parva* however appears to imply that this parva may have been edited around the 4th century.

Historicity: The historicity of the Mahabharata war is unclear. The epic's setting certainly has a historical precedent in Vedic India, where the Kuru kingdom was the centre of political power in the late 2nd and early 1st millennia BCE.

Ancient Indian scholars have calculated chronologies for the *Mahabharata* war, the 5th century mathematician Aryabhatta arriving at an approximate date for the Kurukshetra battle of 3137 BCE. The Aihole inscription of Pulakesin II (7th century CE) dates the Kurukshetra War to 3102 BCE. Vriddha-Garga, Varahamihira and Kalhana dated the War to 653 years after 3102 BCE.

Contentious and disputable attempts to date the events of the *Mahabharata* with the help of archaeoastronomy have claimed dates in the 6th millennium BCE..

According to Varahamihira, Yudhisthira lived 2526 years before the beginning of the Saka era (Brhatsamhita 13.3).

According to the Puranas, there is a time gap of 1015 or 1500 years between Parikshit's birth during the *Mahabharata* war and the coronation of king Mahapadma Nanda (ca. 364-382 BCE). Between Mahapadma Nanda and the last Andhra king Pulomavi, the Puranas count 836 or 829 years. Vayu Purana has the Saptarsi in Magha when Yudhisthira lived, in Purvasadha when Nanda lived and in Satabhisaj at the end of Andhra rule. This could correspond to a difference of 1000 (or more) years between Pariksit (seven generations after Pratipa) and Nanda, and 400 (or more) years between Nanda and the end of Andhra rule.

The Brhadaranyaka Upanisad has eight generations between Pariksit and Yaska. Pargiter remarked that the Great Bear (the rksas or the Saptarsi) "was situated equally with regard to the lunar constellation Pusya while Pratipa was king." The Puranas list a number of kings between the Mahabharata War and Mahapadma Nanda which indicates that 1451 or 1503 years could have passed between them. Pargiter has argued that there were 26 kings between Adhisimakrishna and Mahapadma Nanda.

Synopsis: The epic employs the story within a story structure popular in many Indian religious and secular works. It is recited to the King Janamejaya by Vaisampayana, a disciple of Vyasa.

The core story of the work is that of a dynastic struggle for the throne of Hastinapura, the kingdom ruled by the Kuru clan. The two collateral branches of the family that participate in the struggle are the Kauravas, the elder branch of the family, and the Pandavas, the younger branch.

The struggle culminates leading to the Great battle of Kurukshetra, and the Pandavas are ultimately victorious. The *Mahabharata* itself ends with the death of Krishna, and the subsequent end of his dynasty, and ascent of the Pandava brothers to Heaven. It also marks the beginning of the Hindu age of Kali (Kali Yuga), the fourth and final age of mankind, where the great values and noble ideas have crumbled, and man is speedily heading toward the complete dissolution of right action, morality and virtue. Some of the most noble and revered figures in the *Mahabharata* end up fighting on the side of the Kauravas, due to conflicts of their dharma, or duty. For example, Bhishma had vowed to always protect the king of Hastinapura, whoever he may be. Thus, he was required to fight on the side of evil knowing that his Pandavas would end up victorious only with his death.

Authorship: The epic is traditionally ascribed to Maha Rishi Veda Vyasa, who is one of the major dynastic characters within the epic. The first section of the *Mahabharata* states that it was Ganesha who, at the behest cf Vyasa, fixed the text in manuscript form. Lord Ganesha is said to have agreed, but only on condition that Vyasa never pause in his recitation. Vyasa then put a counter-condition that Ganesha understand whatever he recited, before writing it down. In this way Vyasa could get some respite from continuously speaking by saying a verse which was difficult to understand. This situation also serves as a popular variation on the stories of how Ganesha's right tusk was broken (a traditional part of Ganesha imagery). This version attributes it to the fact that, in the rush of writing, the great elephant-headed divinity's pen failed, and he snapped off his tusk as a replacement in order that the transcription not be interrupted.

Bhishma: Janamejaya's ancestor Shantanu, the king of Hastinapura has a short-lived marriage with the goddess Ganga and has a heroic son, Devavrata (later to be called Bhishma). Devavrata, a young man already with a reputation as a fearsome warrior, is the heir apparent to the throne.

Many years later, when the king goes hunting, he spots Satyavati, the daughter of a fisherman, and wants to marry her. Eager to secure his daughter's and her children's future happiness, the fisherman refuses to consent to the marriage unless Shantanu promises to make the future son of Satyavati the king upon his death, instead of Devavrata. To solve the king's dilemma, Devavrata agrees to that. Finding that the fisherman, though convinced of Devavrata's commitment, is not sure about the prince's children honouring the promise, Devavrata makes a severe vow of lifelong celibacy to guarantee his father's promise. Hearing such a vow, unheard of amongst warriors, the heavens bestow Devavrata with the name Bhishma, 'the person of the terrible oath'.

When King Shantanu is on his deathbed, his concern for his children and the stability of the kingdom delays his death. To ease the king's pains Bhishma promises to stay alive until the kingdom is safe and secure. Again, an awesome promise as all kingdoms are under constant threat. This promise was to cost him dearly, giving him a long life with constant tribulations and battles. Later, though seriously wounded, Bhishma could not give up his soul until the final battle resulted in the rule of the righteous Pandavas.

The Pandavas: Unfortunately Satyavati's sons die young and her grandson Pandu ascends the throne as his elder brother Dhrtarashtra is blind. Pandu whilst out hunting deer, is however cursed by a sage (whom he accidentally kills while he is having sex with his wife, mistaking their moans of pleasure to be the sounds of a deer) that he can never engage in sexual act with any woman. He retires to the forest along with his two wives. Kunti, using a boon granted by another sage whom Kunti, tended and cared for with great dilligence to summon the gods Dharma, Vayu, and Indra, his elder queen Kunti gives birth to three sons Yudhishthira, Bhima, and Arjuna through their respective "fathers".

The sons of course inherit the primary character of their respective father. Kunti shares her boon with her "sister" queen Madri, who bears the twins Nakula and Sahadeva through the Ashwini twins. However Pandu and Madri cannot resist temptation, indulge in sex and die in the forest and Kunti returns to Hastinapura with her sons. The rivalry between the Pandavas and the Kauravas starts from childhood itself. Dhrtarashtra's sons, the Kauravas, led by the eldest Duryodhana, detest their cousins the Pandavas. However, they were the favourite of their teacher Drona and (the Pandavas) grow up to be exceptional. Each one of the Pandavas is said to have one exceptional strength or virtue-Yudhisthira is the most virtuous, Arjuna the bravest warrior, Bhima the strongest, Nakula the most handsome and Sahadeva wise and able to predict the future.

When the princes of Hastinapura come of age, a tournament is held to display their strength and skill. When Arjuna was hailed as a master of archery, a young man challenges him for a duel. He declares his name is Karna, and he is the son of a charioteer. When asked to prove that he is of royal birth, which is the criterion for joining the tournament, Duryodhana, spotting a potential ally, jumps over to his side and gives his kingdom of Anga. Karna is forever grateful for this act. Because of this, he becomes Duryodhana's closest friend and plays a crucial role in the war.

The House of Wax: Meanwhile Duryodhana plots to get rid of the Pandavas and tries to kill the Pandavas secretly by burning their palace which is made of lac. However, the Pandavas are warned by their uncle, Vidura who sends them a miner to dig a tunnel. Therefore, when Duryodhana's servants set the house on flames, they will be able to escape in safety. After escaping from the tragedy, the Pandavas arrive in a forest and rest. Bhima and Arjuna want to confront the Kauravas, but Kunti and Yudhisthira decide against it. Bheeshma goes to the river Ganga to perform the last rites of the Pandavas. Vidura then informs him that the Pandavas are alive and to keep the secret to himself.

City of Ekchakra: The Pandavas stay in the city of Ekchara in the guise of Brahmans. Kunti and Bhima then learn of a cruel and terrible rakshasa named Bakasura who has made a deal with the villagers that if he receives 1 villager a month to eat, he will not harm the villagers. Bhima sets out to eliminate this rakshasa. A great fight arises and Bhima with his might kills him. In order to avoid being caught by the villagers, the Pandavas leave the City of Ekchakra and move on.

Draupadi: In course of this exile the Pandavas are informed of a "competition" called a swayamvar taking place with the prize being the hand of the Panchal princess and the daughter of King Drupad, Draupadi. The Pandavas enter the competition in disguise as Brahmans, the task being to string a mighty steel bow and shoot with a steel arrow the eye of a rotating fish on the ceiling while concentrating on the reflection underneath. No king manages to come close to do so. They fail to even pick up the bow! Karna, the only one who picks up the bow, is about to try is halted by Draupadi by the excuse that he is the son of a charioteer and may not participate.

Arjuna becomes successful and manages to complete the task. When he returns with his bride, Arjuna goes to his mother to show her his prize, exclaiming, "Mother, I have brought you a present!". Kunti, not noticing the princess, tells Arjuna that whatever he has won must be shared with his brothers. To ensure that their mother never utters a falsehood even by mistake, the brothers take her as a common wife. All of the Pandavas love Draupadi dearly. In some interpretations, Draupadi alternates months or years with each brother. At this juncture they also meet Krishna who would become their lifelong ally and guide.

Indraprasth: Duryodhana and Shakuni are furious when they learn that the Pandava brothers are alive and that King Dhritrashtra has sent Vidur to call them back to Hastinapura. Karna, as usual, is ready to fight them, but Shakuni realizes that with King Drupad and Krishna on the side of the Pandavas it would be difficult to defeat them. Dhritrashtra consoles Duryodhana and assures him that his rights as the Heir Apparent to the throne of Hastinapura will be fully protected.

In Kampilya, King Drupad and Shri Krishna advise Yudhisthira to fight for his right to the throne of Hastinapura. Just then Vidur arrives and tells the Pandava brothers that they have been invited back to Hastinapura along with their bride. The Pandavas and Draupadi return to Hastinapura. Dhritrashtra conceals his disappointment and orders everyone to welcome them. Determined to establish peace between the Kauravas and the Pandavas, Bhishma suggests giving half the Kingdom to Yudhisthira.

Dhritrashtra agrees to this suggestion. Krishna and Balram, also give their consent and it is decided that Yudhisthira's coronation as King of Indraprasth be held in Hastinapura. This land given to them again becomes another unjustice to the Pandavas as it neither has any agricultural soil neither any buildings nor people. Krishna consolidates the Pandavas saying that Indraprasth is not a waste but instead a Land of Action. Taking the advice of Krishna, the Pandavas make Indraprasth a beautiful town where justice is always met and the inhabitants are happy.

The Rajsuya Yagna: Shortly after this, Arjuna and Subhadra (Krishna's sister) get married and return to Indraprastha to be welcomed by Draupadi. Here, Yudhisthira seeks Sri Krishna's advice on performing the Rajsuya Yagna which will make him the emperor of India. Krishna advises him that Jarasandha who has imprisoned 86 kings must be killed as he may interfere in the ceremony. Hence Yuddhisthira decides to send Krishna, Bhima and Arjuna to challenge Jarasandh for combat. Jarasandh chooses to fight with Bhima. Bhima and Jarasandh were so equally matched in strength that they fought for nearly fourteen days without rest. When Jarasandha finally showed signs of exhaustion, Krishna prompted Bhima to make an end of him. After Jarasandha had been destroyed, Jarasandha's son was crowned King of Magadha. The Rajsuya Yagna is celebrated and Yudhisthira is recognized as an Emperor.

The House of Illusion: Duryodhana is unhappy about the prosperity of the Pandavas, Shakuni consoles him and later loses in a game of dice to Yudhisthira. Duryodhana walks around Yudhisthira's 'Maya Mahal" ("The House of Illusion") and falls into one of the pools. Draupadi calls him the "blind son of a blind father." Duryodhana, Karna and Shakuni plan to avenge Draupadi for her taunting remarks.

Duryodhana's Game: Duryodhana, who now has a friend in the peerless warrior Karna becomes aware of Yudhisthira becoming the emperor. This proves too much for Duryodhana who feels death would be better than watching one's foes prosper. His maternal uncle Shakuni, convinced that however brave his nephew may be, he was no match for his cousins, decides to use a ruse to destroy the Pandavas. He forces Dhrtarashtra to invite the Pandavas for a game of dice in which he wins everything from Yudhisthira, including himself, his brothers and Draupadi through the use of a trick. The jubilant Kauravas insult them in their helpless state and even try to disrobe Draupadi in front of the entire court. Her honour is saved by the grace of Krishna. When the elders intervene and Dhrtarashtra has to restore everything to the Pandavas, Shakuni forces another game of dice which he again wins. The Pandavas are required to go into exile for 13 years, and on the 13th year they must remain hidden. If discovered by the Kauravas, they will be forced into exile for another 12 years.

The Years in Exile: The Pandavas having lost the game of dice go on exile for 12 years and a year of hiding. During the period of exile, they visit many religious places and are often visited by Krishna. Draupadi who has been insulted by Dushasana (Duryodhana's brother), takes a vow never to tie up her hair until she had blood from Dushasana's thigh to wash her hair with. This constantly reminds her husbands of how war was inevitable. Krishna advises Arjuna that since war was inevitable, he should enter heaven to seek the divine weapons held by Gods and that he who is favoured by Lord Indra would be able to do so.

Through the prayer of Lord Indra, Arjuna gains access to heaven from where he obtains the divine weapons and also learns how to use them. Finally, Lord Indra advises Arjuna to learn the art of dance as it would come to his aid in the 13th year of hiding. It is during this time that the Pandavas get to face a demon called Hidumba. Bhima kills him and marries his sister, Hidumbi. With her, he begets a son called Ghatothkacha.

The Battle at Kurukshetra: When the Pandavas return from their exile after many hardships, they request for a peace treaty with the Kauravas to gain Indraprastha back. However, Duryodhana disagrees and argues that since the Pandavas where "caught" in their year of hiding, they must go into another 13 years of exile before they can have Indraprastha. The Pandavas on Krishna's advice again ask for a peace treaty asking for at least five villages for the five brothers, from the Kauravas' vast kingdom. Duryodhana refuses to give in. Krishna intervenes to mediate peace but is unsuccessful. War becomes inevitable.

The two sides summon vast armies to their help and line up at Kurukshetra for a war. The Kingdoms of Dwaraka, Kasi, Kekaya, Magadha, Matsya, Chedi, Pandya and the Yadus of Mathura and some other clans like the Parama Kambojas from Transoxiana were allied with the Pandavas; the allies of the Kauravas comprised the kings of Pragjyotisha, Anga, Kekaya (Kekaya brothers who were enemies of the Kekeya brothers on the Pandava side), Sindhudesa (including Sindhus, Sauviras and Sivis), Mahishmati, Avanti in Madhyadesa, Madras, Gandharas, Bahlikas, Kambojas (with Yavanas, Sakas, Tusharas etc.) and many others. Prior to war being declared, Krishna's brother, Balarama, had left to go on pilgrimage, thus he does not take part in the battle itself.

Arjuna, seeing himself facing grandsire Bhishma and his teacher Drona on Duryodhana's side due to their vow to serve the state of Hastinapura is heartbroken and at the idea of killing them he fails to lift his Gandiva bow. Krishna who has chosen to drive Arjuna's chariot wakes him up to his call of duty in the famous Bhagavad Gita section of the epic. Though initially sticking to chivalrous notions of warfare, the Kauravas and Pandavas soon descended into dishonourable warfare. At the end of the 14 days slaughter only the Pandavas and Krishna survive with a few old warriors from the Kaurava side.

The end of the Pandavas: Beholding the carnage, the noble mother of the Kauravas, Gandhari who had lost all her sons, curses Krishna to be a witness to a similar annihilation of his family, for though divine and capable of stopping the war, he had not done so. Krishna who had incarnated precisely to destroy the wicked kings accepts the curse, which bears fruit 36 years later. He then departs from the world and the Pandavas who had ruled righteously all along, now tired, decide to renounce everything. Clad in skins and rags they retire to the Himalayas and ascend the peaks towards heaven in their bodily form. Legend reveals that a mangy, stray dog travels along with them. One by one the Pandavas and Draupadi fall on their way.

As each one stumbles, Yudhishtra gives the rest the reason for their fall (Draupadi was partial to Arjuna, Nakula and Sahadeva were vain and proud of their looks, Bhima and Arjuna were proud of their strength and archery skills, respectively). Only the virtuous Yudhisthra who had tried everything to prevent the carnage and the dog remain. The dog reveals himself to be the god Dharma, who reveals the nature of the test and assures Yudhishtra that his fallen siblings and wife are in heaven. Yudhistra alone transcends to heaven in his bodily form for being just and humble.

Arjuna's grandson Parikshita rules after them and dies bitten by a snake. His furious son, Janamejaya, decides to perform a snake sacrifice (sarpasattra) in order to destroy the snakes. It is at this sacrifice that the tale of his ancestors is narrated to him.

5

Classical Forms of Devotional Mysticism

WE have described the ideal of supreme self-control and of the extinction of all desires as an indispensable requirement for the attainment of high perfection. This end is believed to be reached by replacing egoism with unlimited universalism, the individual learning to desire his own good by desiring the good of others. But such an unlimited universalism could hardly be practiced within the limited sphere of the duties and activities of a householder. The ideal yogin who renounced the world and spent a life of supreme self-control and suppression of all desires, and who practiced his yoga courses in which all movements of his body are inhibited, could not live in society and follow the ordinary vocations of life. Cut off from society, he pursued a goai of individualistic perfection.

But the general Hindu system of life was not monistic, individualistic, or separatistic. Hindu society was divided into four castes. We find (1) Brahmins, who followed the scholarly and the priestly line of work, studied the Vedas, gave spiritual instruction and performed the sacrifices; (2) Kshatriyas, the warrior caste who protected the weak from the attacks of the strong, governed kingdoms as kings, and gave to the Brahmins all protection and encouragement in their scholarly and priestly works; (3) Vaishyas, or the trading and pastoral caste, who increased the wealth of the country by trading and farming; and (4) Shudras, or the servant caste, recruited from the non-Aryans who found a home in the Aryan societies and served as menials to the Brahmins, Kshatriyas and Vaishyas.

The Brahmin went to live with his teacher from the age of eight and remained with him until he had completed the study of the Vedas. He then returned from the house of his teacher and was bound according to the injunction of the scriptures to get married, to perform regularly the sacrifices, to be united with his wife and procreate sons, to teach students, and to make gifts or charities to proper persons at auspicious times and at holy places. Upon reaching the age of fifty he had to retire to forest life with his wife, and give himself up to holy thoughts and the leading of a holy life. In the last stage of his life, it was necessary for him to renounce even his forest life of retirement. He had to sever himself from all his attachments, lead the life of a hermit and get his food by begging. Of these four stages of life, called Brahmacharya, Grihastha, Vanaprastha, and Yati, the householder's life was regarded as the best. For this stage (*ashrama*) provided an opportunity for the doing of good to the people of all the other stages of life, by gifts, by the performance of sacrifices, by instruction to teachers,

and by the procreation of good sons who might become the future supporters of society. Performance of sacrifices, teaching, and the procreation of sons were regarded as debts with which every Brahmin was born, and no Brahmin had any right to seek the individualistic goal of a hermit's life unless and until he had discharged these duties for the major portion of his life.

Similarly, it was regarded as the duty of a Kshatriya to protect the weak and to fight in a good cause, and of a Vaishya to carry on trading and farming. The performance of the class of duties belonging to each caste at its specific stage of life is the imperative duty (*dharma*); transgression of it was held to be transgression of duty and hence vicious (*adharma*). What was expected of every man was that he follow the specific duties allotted to his caste, satisfy his desires of life, and enjoy the pleasures of life.

It was a balance in which equal attention was paid to the performance of the allotted duties and to the satisfaction of personal needs and desires that was regarded as the true ideal of life for all normal persons. Only in exceptional cases did the Hindu scheme of life admit the renouncement of this life (*trivarga*) of threefold duties in a search for the attainment of the goal of liberation (*apavarga*). The yearning after a higher life was an actual and soul-stirring experience among spiritually-minded persons. They were allowed the privilege of renouncing the life of ordinary pleasures, and of seeking to kill all other desires and to attain true knowledge, by intuition, moral elevation, yoga or even by asceticism.

In their case alone, however, was this exception made. But even then the exception was not very readily admitted in orthodox Hindu circles. We remember the great effort that Shankara, the great Vedanta teacher, had to make, especially in his commentary on the Gita, to establish this point. He taught that those who attained higher knowledge (*jnana*) were exempt from the allotted duties of ordinary persons. These duties were obligatory only for those who did not attain the higher knowledge. But Shankara's interpretation of the Gita was objected to by other authorities.

The Gita is a work of great sanctity and popularity among the Hindus. It consists of seven hundred simple verses, of which the first chapter of forty-six verses forms the introduction. It is written in the form of a dialogue between Lord Krishna and Arjuna, the great warrior who, on the battlefield of the terrible Indian civil war described in the classic heroic poem Mahabharata, is appalled at the prospect of the fearful impending destruction and refuses to fight. Lord Krishna tries to persuade him, in the Gita, that as a Kshatriya, (a man of the military caste) it is his duty to fight. To add strength to his persuasion he makes use of many moral and religious arguments. Traditionally this theme forms a part of the fifth canto of the Mahabharata. Though its date is uncertain, it may well be believed to have been written about the second or the third century B. C. It discards self-mortification and believes in three kinds of *tapas*: first, bodily discipline—respect to gods, Brahmins and the wise, purity, sincerity, chastity and non-injury; second, speech discipline—sweet and truthful speech, and study; and third, mental discipline—contentment, self-control, amiability, purity of mind, and meditation.

But the great solution of the Gita is the compromise it advances between the worldly life of allotted duties and the hermit life of absolute renouncement, and between a life of lawful and proper enjoyment and the absolute extinction of desires. The programme that it proposes is, on the one hand, that we purify our minds, purging them of all attachments and passions by dedicating all the fruits of our actions to God; and yet, on the other hand, that we continue to perform all the duties belonging to our particular caste or stage of life. It is not the actions but our own inclinations and passions that really bind us. But if we can augment our faith in and our affection for God to such an extent that in our love for Him we free ourselves from all other attachments while yet we continue to perform the allotted and normal duties, the actions can in no wise bind us to a lower goal. A life dedicated to God, and lived for and in love of Him, is a life which is inevitably ennobled to the highest degree.

A seer who has been able to liberate himself from the tendency to self-seeking and from attachment is never over-pleased at any good fortune nor over-sorry at any misfortune. His is a calm and unruffled life. He takes the pleasures and sorrows of life without the least perturbation; he has no fear and no anger; he is firm in himself, unshakeable and unmoved. Yet he follows the daily routine of social and other duties.

The Gita seems to reject the doctrine that the body and mind may be made entirely motionless or inactive. Simple physical conditions could make the body move; and it urges that it is only a false show of morality when the body is controlled and yet one continues to think of doing bad things or to harbour thoughts of attachment. The mysticism of the Gita consists in the belief that the performance of actions without personal attachment or self-seeking motive, and with a dedication of their fruits to God, leads a man to his highest realization or liberation.

Knowledge is praised, but only because true knowledge is conducive to the acceptance of such a life of desireless self-surrender to God. A man who has no personal motive in an action really does not perform the action though to all appearances he may seem to be so doing. It is only such a person who my truly be called a yogin. His is a mind that is constantly fixed on God, and he performs all his duties for the sake of duty, out of reverence to the law, and with complete self-surrender to God. Self-surrender to God, or self-abnegation, however, does not in the Gita involve a personal relationship of communion and love so much as it does the moral qualities of compassion, universal friendship, humility, contentment, want of attachment, self-control and purity. The expectation is emphasized that a person possessed of these moral qualities will be equally unruffled in sorrow and in happiness and that he will be the friend of all. Mind and intellect are to be concentrated on God, and all actions are to be surrendered to Him. This does not necessarily mean a superabundance of love. It may be an offshoot of the old yoga ideal of Patanjali. Here it is enjoined that the mind and intellect be concentrated on God, for, if this is done, God, being satisfied by this attachment, will help the yogin, and by His divine grace the yogin may achieve his goal much more easily than would otherwise be possible.

The idea of the surrender of all actions to God is also to be found in the yoga of Patanjali. Though the writer of the Gita admits breath-control as a discipline, yet his whole emphasis is laid on self-abnegation and self-surrender to God. Breath-control seems to be given only a subordinate value, that of a means of purifying the mind. We have, therefore, in the Gita a new solution of how a man may attain his highest liberation. He may remain a member of society and perform his allotted duties provided he has the right sort of moral elevation, has fixed his mind on God, has dissociated himself from all attachment, and, by self-surrender and self-abnegation, has devoted himself to God. It is faith in the special grace of God to those who have surrendered themselves to Him that forms the essence of the Gita

Though the idea of love for God does not show itself in any prominent way in early Sanskrit literature, except in the Pancharatra literature, it is very improbable that the idea was not known from very early times. For some of the monotheistic Vedic hymns reveal an intimate personal relation with the deity, implying affection; and in the Buddhist literature we find frequent references to love for the Buddha.

In the Vishnu Purana we are given the story of Prahlada. Because of his devotion to Hari, his father tormented him in various ways and sought to put him to death by throwing him into fire or into the sea, by administering poison, and by various other methods. But he was saved from all these perils by the grace of Hari, and as a true devotee of the great Lord he was not in the least angry with his father. In all the adoration to Hari, whether on the part of Prahlada or as otherwise reported in the Vishnu Purana and in many of the other early Puranas, the great Lord is adored and praised metaphysically or philosophically as the great Being from whom everything has come forth and to whom everything will return, as the great controller of the universe and the great lord who is residing within us and is controlling us, and as the prime mover of the material cosmic world which is only a manifestation of his power.

The subtle and primal cosmic matter is a concrete expression of the energy of the Lord. By His will it is set in active operation and transforms itself into the visible universe. The universe, therefore, though in a sense different from Him, is ultimately sustained and supported by Him; created by Him, it will ultimately return to Him. Many are the hymns in the Puranas which praise God in this philosophical manner and extol His great powers. There are also numberless instances in which God is said to be pleased by philosophic meditation, and in consequence appears to the devotee, to speak with him, and to grant him the boon he seeks.

The earlier literature does not always emphasize the feeling element in devotion. In the Vishnu Purana, however, we find that when God came face to face with Prahalad and asked him if he had a boon to crave, he besought the same attachment for the Lord that ordinary people have for sense enjoyments. The devotion that Prahalad had previously shown was a concentration on God and a serene contemplation in which he became one, as it were, with the Lord. Ramanuja, the great Vedanta commentator of the 11th century, also defines devotion (bhakti) as a contemplation of God unbroken as the smooth and ceaseless flow of oil.

But that such a contemplation necessarily implies love of God as its inner motive cannot be denied, and Ramanuja also describes this ceaseless contemplation as having its main source in love for God, who was so dear to the devotee. But all that I wish to point out in this connection is that, in this aspect of devotion, contemplation and communion are more prominent than any exuberance of feeling. Prahalad was attached to God by his love of Him; God was the dearest of all dear things to him. It was this inmost and most deep-seated love for God that stirred him to withdraw his mind from all other things and to enter into such a contemplation of God that he became absorbed in Him, his whole personality lost in an ecstatic trance unity with God. But this did not satisfy Prahalad. He desired such a devotion to God that the very thought of Him would bring the same sort of satisfaction that persons ordinarily have in thinking of sense-objects. He desired not only contemplative union but longed also to taste God's love as one tastes the pleasures of the senses.

It is the contemplative union with God that we find in the Gita, and the transition to it from the state of yoga concentration is not difficult to understand. Self-surrender to God, the higher moral elevation, and concentration on God are all present in Patanjali's yoga. But here the objective was the destruction of the mind through psychical exercises accompanied by the complete inhibition of bodily and mental activity. Later the devotee seeks to attain liberation through the special grace of the Lord, which he can hope to acquire by such contemplative union.

In later Indian thought the method of yoga on the one hand receded in favour of that of bhakti or devotion; on the other hand, its pure form became greatly complicated by the development of many mysterious doctrines and rites which became associated with it, sought its support, and claimed to be forms of it. But my time is limited and I cannot enter into these latter forms of mysticism. Nor can I describe those mystical religious movements which, arising as a reaction against the dominant religious ideal of extreme sense-control and the practice of desirelessness, tried to formulate certain principles and methods by which one could attain his highest goal not by sense-control but by sense-enjoyments.

In these schemes, sense-indulgence under certain specified conditions was considered not only harmless but an indispensable desideratum. They probably started among some of the Buddhist schools and they soon became very common among certain sects of the Hindus. But the elucidation of these ideas would require a special course of lectures. I shall, therefore, leave them and pass directly to the development of the mysticism of love to God, as it is presented in the Bhagavata Purana and other relevant later literature.

It is in the Bhagavata Purana, whose date is probably the eleventh century AD, that we first meet with the idea of devotion as the supreme source of a bliss or spiritual enjoyment that is itself the highest goal and so completely usurps the place of wisdom or philosophical knowledge. Even in the Gita true wisdom was regarded as a fire which reduces to ashes, as it were, all the past deeds whose fruits were not yet on the point of being enjoyed. But in the Bhagavata we read (11.14) that it is bhakti which destroys all the past sins. The old principle of self-surrender to God and a life spent in God-intoxication is the happiest of all lives. A man of such self-surrender has nothing else but God as his possession: he is supremely self-controlled, and the enjoyment that he has from his constant association with God keeps him absolutely happy and content with all things.

Such a man does not aspire to any heavenly happiness or even to liberation. Devotion is regarded as having also a protective virtue. Even an ordinary devotee who is often led away by his sense attachments is so purified by this devotion that he is no longer overcome by external attachments or passions. The Lord can be realized by bhakti and by nothing else. Neither the performance of the allotted duties nor knowledge combined with the austere discipline of tapas can purify a man who is devoid of all bhakti. This bhakti, however, is no longer the old contemplative meditation of God, stirred by a deep-seated love.

It is the evolution of feelings and emotions of attachment to God. It manifests itself in the soft melting of the heart and expresses itself in tears, inarticulate utterances of speech, laughter, songs and dances, such as can only be possible through a mad intoxication of love. This kind of bhakti is entirely different from the calm contemplative life of complete self-abnegation and self-surrender to God and a mind wholly immersed in God and the thought of God.

The Bhagavata Purana is aware of the three methods of approach by knowledge, work and devotion, and also of the approach through yoga. Moreover, while emphasizing the superiority of devotion, it does not deny the efficacy of the other methods of approach. The latter are also described in the Gita; indeed, the Gita also emphasizes the bhakti method. Both the Gita and Bhagavata criticize the older course of the Vedic sacrifices, but neither of them has the boldness to pass an unconditional condemnation. The Gita says that one should perform these sacrifices, which are obligatory, with a pure and desireless mind.

The fault of those who devote themselves to sacrifices is that they are filled with ordinary desires for pleasures and are not acquainted with any higher goal of life. To one who is infused with the higher ideal of life and can emancipate himself from desires by self-surrender to God, the performance of sacrifices, as of any other kinds of action, can do no harm. Indeed, it is good that under these circumstances one should not forsake his allotted duties.

The Bhagavata holds that the only efficacy of the Vedic restrictions and prohibitions is to be found in the fact that they offer a check on the natural inclinations of man and ultimately help him to desist from sense-activities and sense-propensities. The promise of heavenly rewards as the result of the performance of sacrifices is only a trick to incline people to accommodate themselves to modes of life offering only a restricted scope of sense-gratification. Its appeal is therefore only to those of the lowest plane. Those who are of the next higher order and have been able to accommodate themselves to a life of desirelessness would perform the obligatory duties without in the least looking forward to their fruits. In the next higher stage, a man may follow the path of yoga, or the path of wisdom respecting the supreme unity of Brahman, or any other line of devotion.

The path of devotion, however, is most fitted for those who are neither too much attached to sense-desires nor too much detached from them. Such men may adopt the line of bhakti and thereby purify their minds and, by self-surrender to God and the taste of supreme human happiness in their love, become averse to all other desires and enjoyments. Thus they learn to live a life of supreme devotion. They come to experience such intense happiness that all their limbs and senses become saturated therewith and their minds swim, as it were, in a lake of such supreme bliss that even the bliss of ultimate liberation loses its charm. Such an individual desires to live on, enjoying the love of God with heart, soul and body. When he acquires such a bhakti, it purifies his mind from all passions and impurities, and destroys all the bonds of his deeds and their fruits. For such a person is so attached to God that there is nothing else for which he cares; without any effort on his part, other attachments and inclinations lose their hold over him. So great is his passion for God that it consumes all his earthly passions. It is so great that it is its own satisfaction; it seeks nothing beyond itself. It stands by itself. As a great spring of happiness, it is ultimate and self-complete.

The bhakta who is filled with such a passion does not experience it merely as an undercurrent of joy which waters the depths of his heart in his own privacy, but as a torrent that overflows the caverns of his heart into all his senses. Through all his senses he realizes it as if it were a sensuous delight; with his heart and soul he feels it as a spiritual intoxication of joy. Such a person is beside himself with this love of God. He sings, laughs, dances and weeps. He is no longer a person of this world. The germ of this love is already found in the Vishnu Purana, where Prahalad seeks as a boon that bhakti which is an attachment for God no less strong than the attraction to sense-objects felt by ordinary sensual persons.

Vallabh, a later writer, defines bhakti as a great, firm feeling of love, associated with a sense of God's superiority and greatness. It places the bhakta or the devotee in a subordinate position. The latter is described as approaching God as one approaches his master, desiring mercy and protection and soliciting His special grace. But this idea of seeking protection and special grace, with a sense of God's supreme superiority, and finding oneself happy in thinking of the greatness of the superior Being, is by no means restricted to Hindu circles. There are numerous evidences of Buddhists praising the Buddha and seeking his protection, and finding great joy in extolling his great qualities and powers. Bhaktishataka of Ramachandra Bharati of the 13th century may be referred to as a typical instance.

This kind of bhakti is also associated with the doctrine of prapatti, or taking refuge in God, and is to be found among many classes of Vaishnavas, including the followers of

Ramanuja. Prapatti consists in taking refuge in God with great faith and with the strong conviction that it is God and God alone who can help one to attain one's end. Like the fabled bird Chataka that would rather die of thirst than drink any water other than that falling from the clouds, the devotee looks to God for succour, and would seek no other help. Believing that God alone is the saviour, the devotee depends entirely on Him, and refuses to take any other course than that of remaining in entire dependence upon Him. God, for him, is the great master of whom he is the humble servant; God is the controller alike of his mind and his body.

This is only a detailed method of the self-surrender already referred to in the Gita. Naturally the latter also is based on a belief in the great mercy of God, who is sure to free the devotee who with complete reliance has taken refuge in Him as his master and Lord. But in this case the prapatti or taking refuge in God is always with a purpose. It is for the realization of an end that the devotee relies on the mercy, goodness or grace of God. He believes that he can by this means alone attain what he wants. But the bhakti praised in the Bhagavata is of a sort superior to this. It is a devotion without motive of any kind. It is the love of God proceeding directly from the heart and not prompted by any reason. The true bhakta does not love God because he seeks something from Him, but he loves Him freely and spontaneously. He sacrifices everything for this love. It is his only passion in life and he is filled with God. God is attracted by such love and always abides with such a bhakta and encourages his great love for him. All distinctions of caste, creed or social status vanish for those who are filled with this true and sincere devotion to God. It is a great leveller. To the eye of a true bhakta all beings are but manifestations of God's power, and they are all equal. Impelled by this idea of universal equality and by the idea of God being in all things and all things in God, he is filled with such a sweetness of temper that howsoever he may be tyrannized over by any one he cannot think of inflicting any injury in return. Nor can he remain unaffected when he sees the sufferings of his fellow-beings, however lowly or depraved they may be.

The question is sometimes asked whether such devotional systems of mysticism are pantheistic. To this no satisfactory reply can be given without a proper definition of pantheism. Without entering into any discussion regarding the meaning of this term or the distinctive metaphysical features of the different systems of Vaishnavism, I can here say only that all these systems in a manner agree as to the duality of God and man. They consider man as a manifestation of the power of God. Though ultimately sustained and always controlled by God, man is for all empirical purposes different from Him.

This psychological, logical and ontological difference between God and man is the basis of devotion and worship. In the development of devotion there may, however, come a stage in the mind of the devotee when he becomes one with the Lord in the exuberance of his feelings. But at the next instant the experience may again be differentiated into a feeling of duality and of distinction between him and God. The devotee may then come to regard himself as a servant of God or His son, or friend, or spouse. It cannot be said, in this inner dialectic of feeling, which of the phases is the truer and has a greater claim to our acceptance.

For we have here an alternation of feeling which sometimes expresses itself as an experience of communion or contemplative unity with God and then by its own inner movement passes for its own realization into the various other modes of relationships through which ordinary human love expresses itself. It is a circular movement. At one stage within it, man becomes God, but, at the other, God slowly becomes man and participates with him in diverse human relationships of love and its joys.

Love of God is not a thing which we produce in ourselves by excessive brooding or by self-hypnotism or by any other method. It is a permanent flame, slowly burning in the caverns of all our hearts. Only, however, when it gains strength through study, and through association with other devotees at an opportune moment, do we come to know of it. The basis of all religions is this love of God. For if this love of God were not vital to us, all that the great prophets have been trying to preach would have been unreal and futile. If it were not a real experience which in some sense is shared by us all, an experience which ennobles us and raises us far above the selfish pettinesses of life, no prophet and no religious deed would be able to appeal to our higher natures and establish the claims of religion. Religion is by nature an other-worldly attitude of life—one which we have along with our worldly attitude. "Man does not live by bread alone," is a very elastic proposition.

If we by nature wanted only that which satisfies our appetites, there would have been no art, no philosophy, and no religion. Our being is such that side by side with the tendencies that take us to the satisfaction of our appetites or to sense-gratifications, there are others which in an unaccountable manner lift us higher. The senses when properly exercised give us sense pleasures; the mind, through its activities of logical thinking, affords the corresponding joys and the satisfaction of truth-seeking; and the spirit longs to associate itself with some higher ideal, with a greater and superior being, or with a transcendent unspeakable something of which it has at first only an indistinct vision.

Reason moves within a circle and cannot get beyond it. When the ultimate reason of reasoning is to be sought, we have to rest in a tendency, temperament or feeling. Ask a philosopher why he engages in philosophical speculation. He may say that he seeks to know the truth of some particular or some universal problem. But ask him again why he so seeks and he will probably say that he does it because he finds therein a special satisfaction. The satisfaction, though not measureable in physical terms, is yet enough for him. He possesses intellectual curiosity and it must be gratified. Ask a scientist and you will probably receive the same answer. One can never explain our endeavours in any of the higher planes of life, philosophy, art or religion, by reference to any of the ordinary needs and objects of life. These higher activities are apparently without any reason, but still they justify themselves and they are our very existence. That bread alone should not satisfy man is part of his very nature and there is no getting away therefrom. It is an absolute fact with man.

The case of religion is very similar. There is a spiritual longing in the heart of man, indistinct and undefined, but steady like a flame tapering upwards to some divine goal. The mystics of the Bhagavata Purana of whom I am now speaking called it the love of God. They felt that there is nothing higher than the culture of this love. The seed of it they regarded as latent within the individual. Hearing and singing the praises of God stimulates its growth—sprinkles it with water, as it were—until it ascends higher and higher and eventually reaches God. Like an expert gardener the individual has always to see that no beast of a sin, tramples this tender creeper, and that no offshoots, no branches of worldly desires, obstruct its upward growth. Whenever he is tempted by worldly desires or to pray to God for worldly good, he is allowing offshoots to grow on the body of the tender creeper of God's love and to interfere with its upward growth. He must cut them off and make the creeper of love grow freely in one direction, until it connects him with God and he thus comes to enjoy its sweet fruits.

The type of bhakti which is preached in the Bhagavata Purana is well illustrated in the life of Chaitanya, who was born in Navadvip, in Bengal, in 1486 and died in 1534. In his life we find an exemplification of how love of God may be cultivated for its own sake, without any kind of ulterior motive whether of liberation or of happiness. In the accounts which his biographers have given of his mysticism, a distinction is drawn between the experience of God's love as self-surrender to Him, or taking refuge in Him through attachment to Him, and a driving passion of love for God, *i.e.*, between what they call *rati* and *preman*. A distinction is also drawn between a course of attachment and love of God adopted out of a sense of duty or of reverence for the scriptures and a passion of love which springs spontaneously and overflows unrestrainedly.

A distinction is further made between love of God with an overwhelming sense of His greatness and superiority, awe and reverence, and love of God as an easy flow of affection to one who is nearest and dearest to us. Real intimacy with God is only possible in the case of the latter alternative, when a free flow of passionate love springing spontaneously from within associates us with God as the most intimate friend and beloved without whom we cannot live. Chaitanya acknowledges, of course, the peaceful calm and tender love for God called *shanta*, and the submission of the heart to God in obligation and service to Him, called the service attitude, *dasya*; but to look upon God as one's own most intimate friend, *sakhya*, is regarded by him as higher than either of the first two attitudes. To look upon God as one's dearest beloved or lover, or to love Him with a feminine love as that with which a woman loves her beloved, he considers the deepest, sweetest and most perfect love, *madhura*.

According to the legend, Lord Krishna was born of Devaki and Vasudeva in a prison-house where the King Kansa, who was afraid of the birth of the infant who was foretold to be his future destroyer, had confined his mother Devaki. Later Krishna was carried to the house of a cowherd chief, Nanda. There he grew up, having as his associates cowherd boys with whom he was very friendly. He came to be regarded as God incarnate, as the result of a number of miracles which he performed.

The wives of most of the cowherd people, who were, in reality but the female incarnations of God's energy, became attached to him and loved him dearly. They were sorely pained over the separation when he later on left for Mathura, a city at some distance from Brindaban, the scene of his early activities. Krishna's early life illustrates the love for him of his fostermother Yashoda, wife of the cowherd chief Nanda, the love for him of his cowherd friends, and the love of the cowherd girls for him as their lover. Inasmuch as Krishna was considered to be God, these three kinds of love for Krishna as described in the tenth chapter of the Bhagavata Purana, together with the other two time-honoured modes of loving God, viz., the peaceful quiet love of God and the love of God as God's servant, came to be considered as the five fundamental modes of loving God.

The attention of the later Vaishnavas was so much drawn to the excellence of the three kinds of love described in the Bhagavata, and particularly of the love of God as one's lover, that no less than fourteen commentaries have been published dealing with this portion of the Bhagavata Purana. Love of Krishna was the most absorbing passion of Chaitanya's life and, though he came to taste all the different ways of loving God, it was the sweet love of Krishna as the lover, husband and Lord that was the most important feature of his life.

Chaitanya's elder brother had turned a recluse. So his mother Sachi Devi would not at first send Chaitanya to school, since she believed that it is through knowledge that one learns the transitoriness of all things, and she thought it better that her son should grow untutored than that he become learned and renounce the world. So Chaitanya, or Nimai as he was called in his early life, grew wild.

But he gradually grew so wild that he could no longer be tolerated, and so he was sent to school. He mastered Sanskrit grammar and logic very thoroughly and at twenty started a school himself. Numerous anecdotes are told by his biographers of his great scholarship and of occasions when he defeated reputed scholars in open debates. At this period he scoffed at all religions and was considered by many to be absolutely godless. In the meanwhile he had settled down in life. His first wife having died, he married again.

But at this time Chaitanya's deeper nature began to reveal itself and he wanted to visit the temple of the God Krishna at Gaya, several hundred miles distant from his village. On his way thither he met a great Vaishnava saint and at his sight his higher spiritual life was stirred into life. When he reached the temple of Gaya he experienced a rapturous fervour of love for Krishna, and he became an entirely different man. "Where is my God Krishna," became his chief cry. In thinking of Krishna, in seeking Him, in relating his vision of Him, he would be so overpowered as often to become unconscious. It was in this condition that he was brought home from Gaya by his friends. He spent his days and nights in reciting and singing the name of God. He, his intimate friend Nityananda, and his other friends used thus to sing the name of God and to dance about with a particular type of music produced by special musical instruments. This music touched the inner, spiritual chords of life and brought on a great religious intoxication in all the hearers, and particularly in Chaitanya and his followers. Chaitanya lived continually in this state of religious intoxication. He had no respect for caste or creeds but was a friend of all. He could not continue this sort of life midst the worldly conditions of his native village. Hence he renounced the world to preach the love of God all over India.

In this work he spent the rest of his years, going about from place to place, thousands of miles, on foot. The vision of God was always before him in the form of Lord Krishna. His whole life was a passionate flow of love for this deiity, and this emotion was generally so intense that as he sang and danced like a mad man he often became unconscious. He had so thoroughly identified himself as a partner in the episodes of the life of Krishna as described in the Bhagavata that the slightest incidents deriving either from personal conversations and relations or from the scenes of nature sufficed to suggest to him similar adventures or events in the life of Krishna.

Chaitanya described God's love in its most exalted form as being like the love of a woman in deep attachment to a man, where the attachment is so deep that all sex considerations have ceased a love so intense that only an insatiable desire of union in love remains and all the earthly relations of man and woman have ceased. God, he taught, is himself a great controller of us all, and in His eternal love is always attracting us, drawing us up toward greater and greater perfection. Love is His very nature. So it is only through a passionate love of Him that we can enjoy His deep love for us. The older ideals of liberation, of heavenly happiness, of the destruction of the mind and the like were considered by Chaitanya to be absolutely insignificant for a person whose mind has been fired by a great passion that flows in torrents to God, the great ocean of love, who washes away all his sins and defects. In the end, Chaitanya, in an outbreak of divine passion which he was unable to restrain, jumped into the deep blue ocean on the South and was lost forever to human eyes. So passed away one drop of God's love in human shape into that eternal and limitless Ocean of divine love from which it had descended upon the earth.

POPULAR DEVOTIONAL MYSTICISM

The chief features of the passionate devotion for God described in the last lecture are its spontaneity and its transference of human relations and emotions to God through the medium of the Krishna legend described in the Bhagavata Purana. It presupposes the theory of the incarnation of God as man, which makes it possible to think of God in human relations and in human ways. The idea of God as father is indeed as old as the Vedas. It is expressed also in several passages of the Gita (9.17, 11.43, 11.44, 14.4) and in the Puranas, in the Nyaya-bhashya of Vatsyayana, as well as elsewhere.

Nevertheless it did not, during this period, seem to gain much strength in the way of fostering an intimate relation with

God or of affecting worship. Wherever it appears it seems to be but one of the many passing phases in which God's relation to man is viewed when God is praised and extolled in His greatness as Lord and Master. But in the new school of bhakti the conception of God as creator, supporter, father, lord and master, or as the ultimate philosophical principle, is subordinated to the conception of god as the nearest and dearest. The most important feature is His nearness to and His intimacy with us—not His great powers, which create a distance between Him and us.

That He is the greatest of the great and the Highest of the high, that there is nothing greater and higher than Him is admitted by all. His greatness, however, does not reveal the secret of why He should be so dear to us. He may be the greatest, highest, loftiest and the most transcendent, but yet He has made His home in our hearts and has come down to our level to give us His affection and love. Indeed He is conceived as so near to us that we can look upon Him and love Him with the love of a very dear friend, or with the devotion and the intensity of love of a spouse. Love is a great leveller; the best way of realizing God is by making Him an equal partner in life by the force of intense love.

The legend of Krishna supplies a human touch to God's dealings with men. With the help of this legend the bhaktas of the new school, by a peculiar mystical turn of mind, could conceive of God as at once a great being with transcendent powers and also as an intimate friend or a dear lover maintaining human relations with his bhaktas. The episodes of Krishna's life in Brindaban are spiritualized. They are often conceived to happen on a non-physical plane where both Krishna and his partners are thought to play their parts of love and friendship in non-physical bodies.

Thus they are not regarded as particular events that took place at specific points of time in the life of a particular man, Krishna. They are interpreted as the eternal, timeless and spaceless play of God with His own associates and His energies, with whom He eternally realizes Himself in love and friendship. The part that his bhaktas had to play was to identify themselves, by a great stretch of sympathy, as partners in or spectators of God's love-play, and find their fullest satisfaction in the satisfaction of God. For a true bhakta, it is not necessary, therefore, that his sense-inclinations should be destroyed. What is necessary is merely that these should be turned towards God and not towards himself, *i.e.*, that he use his senses not for his own worldly satisfaction but to find enjoyment and satisfaction in the great love-drama of God by identifying himself with one of the spiritual partners of God in his love-play. Hence it is not essential that all desires and sense-functions, as the Gita says, be destroyed, or that the individual behave as if he had desires while yet being absolutely desireless.

It was required that the bhakta have the fullest satisfaction of his sense and inclinations by participating in the joys of Krishna in his divine love-play. For such participation and vicarious enjoyment was regarded as true love (*preman*), while the satisfaction of one's own senses or of one's own worldly purposes was viewed as a vicious passion. Thus here we have a new scheme of life. The ideal of desirelessness and absolute self-control is replaced by that of participation in a drama of divine joy, and the desires are given full play in the direction of God. Desires are not to be distinguished; only their directions are to be changed.

Though this form of bhakti has in various circles at times been debased and encroached upon by diverse kinds of eroticism or erotic mysticism, it cannot be denied that many of the immediate and later followers of Chaitanya achieved great spiritual success in this form of bhakti-worship. In the Narayaniya chapter of the fifth canto of the Mahabharata God is spoken of as a father, mother and teacher; and in the Yoga Sutra of Patanjali and elsewhere the idea is often expressed that God originally taught the Vedas to the sages and that He is therefore the original teacher. In all these writings, however, the love of God supercedes deep reverence.

The true bhakta looked upon God as the divine dispenser; he considered all that he had—kingdoms, riches, wife and all that he could call his own—to be God's. Love of God as the mother of the world plays an important part in the religious attitude of many bhakti worshippers. This is particularly true in the case of Ramprasad and others, notably the sage Ramakrishna of recent times. And in this attribution of motherliness to God both Ramprasad and Ramakrishna view

Him as a tender mother who is always helping her child, condoning his sins and transgressions, partial to his weaknesses and concerned to better him. Nevertheless He cannot be attained by mere formal worship but only through a whole-hearted worship, with a proper control of the sense-inclinations.

The theory of bhakti seems to have its original source in the Pancharatra school of Vaishnavism. However, the doctrine of supreme self-surrender to Narayana, Hari or Krishna as the one and only God in disregard of all other mythical gods, represents a teaching of the Gita, the chief work of the Ekanti school of Vaishnavas; and this doctrine forms the universal basis of all kinds of bhakti worship, though among the Shaktas or Shaivas the supreme deity went by the name of Shakti or Shiva. The Gita plainly teaches, as we have already pointed out in our previous lecture, that there is no other God but Narayana or Krishna, that He alone is great and that we should lay aside all other modes of religious worship and take refuge in Him.

In Chaitanya this devotion to God developed into a life-absorbing passion; yet in all advanced forms of bhakti the chief emphasis is on supreme attachment to God. The sort of bhakti which Prahalad asked as a boon from Hari was such an attachment for Him as worldly persons have for the objects of their senses. Such a bhakti, as described in the Bhagavata or the Shandilya sutra, is not worship out of a sense of duty or mere meditation on God or mere singing of His name, but it is deep affection (*anurakti*). It is therefore neither knowledge nor any kind of activity, but is a feeling. And the taking of refuge (*prapatti*) in God is also not motivated by knowledge but by a deep affection which impels the individual to take his first and last stay in Him. But though a feeling, this bhakti does not bind anyone to the world. For the world is but a manifestation of God's maya, and God so arranges for those who love Him that His maya cannot bind His bhakta to the world.

But how is such a bhakti possible? For this also we have ultimately to depend on God. There is a passage in the Upanishads (Katha II. 23) which states that He can be attained by him whom He (God) chooses. This text has often been cited to indicate that it is only the chosen man of God who has the privilege of possessing a special affection for God. Vallabh declares this special favour (*pushti*) of God indispensable for the rise of such an affection for God.

He further holds that according to the different degrees of the favour of God one may have different degrees of affection for Him, though by avoiding the commission of sinful actions, by cleansing the mind of the impurities of worldly passions, and by inclining the mind towards God, one may go a great way in deserving His special favour. It is only by the highest special favour of God that one's affection or attachment for Him can become an all-consuming and all-engulfing passion (*vyasana*—see the Prameyaratnarnava). True devotion to God, affection or love for Him, must always be an end in itself and never a means to any other end, not even salvation or liberation, so much praised in the classical systems of philosophy. This all-absorbing passion for God is the bhakta's eternal stay in God, and dearer to him than liberation or any other goal of religious realization.

It is not out of place here to mention that among various Hindu sects it was held that an engrossing passion of any kind may so possess the whole mind that all other mental functions may temporarily be suspended, and that gradually, through the repeated occurrence of such a passion, the other mental functions may be altogether annihilated. Thus, absorption in a single supreme passion may make the mind so one-pointed that all other attachments are transcended and the individual attains Brahmahood (see the Spandapradipika).

In the Upanishads (Brihadaranyaka IV. 3.21) we find that the bliss of Brahman is compared with the loving embrace of a beloved woman. To love one's husband and to serve him as a god was regarded from very early times as the only spiritualizing duty for a woman. Hence the idea that ordinary man-and-woman love may be so perfected as to become a spiritual force easily won acceptance in certain circles. This man-and-woman love developed an absorbing and dominant passion, completely independent and unaided by other considerations of marital and parental duties.

In its non-marital forms, it was considered to be capable of becoming so deep as to become by itself a spiritualizing force. Moreover, it was thought that the transition from human love to divine love was so easy that a man who had specialized in the experience of deep man-and-woman love of a non-marital type could easily change the direction of his love from woman to God, and thus indulge in a passionate love for God. The story is told that in his early career the saint Bilvamangala became so deeply attached to a courtesan named Cintamani that one night he swam across a river supported by a floating corpse, then scaled a high wall by holding on to the tail of a serpent, and finally well-nigh broke his limbs in jumping down from the wall into the yard of Chintamani. The woman, however, rebuked him, saying that if he entertained toward God a little of the love that he had for her he would be a saint. This produced such a wonderful change in Bilvamangala that he forthwith became a God-intoxicated man. Later, in his saintly life, when he once again felt attracted by a woman, he plucked out his eyes so that external forms and colours might not further tempt him. This blind saint became one of the best-reputed among all the saints, devoting his life to the love of God.

Thus there grew up a school of mystics, including the great poet Chandidas and others, who devoted themselves to the cultivation of the spirituality of love and the deification of human love, and who thought that more could be learned through such efforts than through any other mode of worship. "There is no god or goddess in Heaven who can teach spiritual truths more than the person whom one loves with the whole heart." The goddess Basuli whom Chandidas worshipped is said to have admonished him to adhere to his love for the washerwoman Rami, saying that Rami would be able to teach him truths that no one else could, and to lead him to such bliss as not even the creator himself might do.

A somewhat similar idea of the purificatory power of intense human love is found in the Vishnupurana. In describing the illicit love of a cowherd girl for Krishna, the Vishnupurana says that at her separation from him she underwent so much suffering that all her sins were expiated, and that in thinking of him in her separation from him she had so much delight as would be equal to the collective culmination of all the happiness that she could enjoy as a reward of her virtuous actions. By the combination of the suffering and the bliss, she exhausted all the fruits of her bad and good deeds, and thus by her thoughts of Krishna she attained her liberation. Somewhat allied with the idea of human worship, though not of the man-and-women type just mentioned, is a certain attitude sometimes adopted toward man as a religious teacher. The latter was considered in many circles as the representative of God on earth, and self-surrender, love and devotion to him was considered to lead one to God. This sort of worship was prevalent among the Hindus and the Buddhists from pretty early times. One fact should be noted. It was associated with reverence and a sense of the religious teacher's superiority, whereas the other type of worship (through romantic love) raised the man and woman by their constancy and sufferings for each other and the happiness that each enjoys in the company and thought of the other.

In this latter case, love is religion, and all pain endured for the beloved, joy. With the exception of the phase of love-mysticism just mentioned, I have thus far confined myself to a description of different forms of mysticism as portrayed in Sanskrit writings. I shall now turn to the mysticism of divine love that found expression in the vernaculars of North India and of the South. But this is a vast subject and I can say only a few words.

Let me advert first to the Alvar saints of the South, the earliest of whom belonged to the second and the latest to the tenth century, A. D. They all wrote psalms or songs in Tamil, a Dravidian tongue of South India. They were inspired by the teachings of Vaishnavism when it travelled from the North to the South. Their doctrines were more or less similar to those touched upon in the preceding lecture in connection with the bhakti mysticism of the Bhagavata Purana and the Gita. They are embodied in psalms and not in any connected philosophical treatise. Describing his insatiable love of God, Nam Alvar says:

"As I dote on the Lord of Katkarai (God)
Whose streets with scarlet lily are perfumed
My heart for his wonderful graces melts
How then can I, my restless love suppress?"

With reference to Nam Alvar, Govindacharya has said: "Briefly, Saint Nam Alvar declares that when one is overcome by bhakti exaltation, trembling in every cell of his being, he must freely and passively allow this influence to penetrate his being, and carry him beyond all known states of consciousness; never from fear or shame that bystanders may take him for a madman, ought the exhibition of this bhakti-rapture that deluges his being, to be suppressed. The very madness is the means of distinguishing him from the ordinary mortals to whom such beatific vision is necessarily denied. The very madness is the bhakta's pride. In that very madness, the saint exhorts, "run, jump, cry, laugh and sing, and let every man witness it."

Let us now pass on to other saints of the South, Namdev and Tukaram. The bhakti school referred to in the last lecture, and most of the other branches of this school, developed under purely Brahminic traditions and in the shadow of Brahminic scriptures, the Puranas and the like. And though in the Bhagavata we find that even the foreign and aboriginal races of the Kiratas, Hunas, Andhras, Pulindas, Pukkasas, Abhiras, Suhmas, Yavanas, Khasas, etc., become pure if they are attached to God, yet the Brahminic civilization had such a hold over the country that the cult of bhakti grew up around the traditional cult of Rama, or Krishna, Shiva or Shakti.

Representation of God in images and their worship by the bhaktas, faith in the legends of Krishna and other inferior deities as told in the Puranas, preferential treatment of the Brahmin caste, respect to the Vedas, etc., became very intimately associated with the doctrine of bhakti preached in the Puranas and other Sanskrit scriptures. We know, of course, that the bhakti cult spread also among foreigners. Thus, in the second century B. C., the Greek king Heliodorus, son of Dios, dedicated to Vasudeva a flagstaff bearing an image of the bird Garuda, on which the God Vasudeva or Krishna was said to ride. Now, though the sons of some demons are also known to have been great bhaktas, as described in the Puranas, yet the latter all accepted the traditional God Vasudeva and they regarded the legends associated with Krishna or Vasudeva as real episodes of his life.

In the thirteenth century A. D., we find that Visoba Khecar, the teacher of the bhakta Namdev, denounced the worship of images as a substitute for the God Krishna or for any other god. He is said to have instructed Namdev to abandon image-worship, saying: "A stone god never speaks. What possibility then of his removing the disease of mundane existence? A stone image is regarded as God, but the true God is wholly different. If a stone god fulfils desires, how is it he breaks when struck? Those who adore a god made of stone, lose everything through their folly. Those who say and hear that a god of stone speaks to his devotees are both of them fools. Whether a holy place is small or large there is no god but stone or water. There is no place which is devoid of God. That God has shown Nama in his heart and thus Khecar conferred a blessing on him." 2 Namdev was a tailor by caste and he worshipped the idol at Pandharpur in the Maratha country in South India.

However, he had a full knowledge of the true nature of God, as had other bhaktas of Sanskritic traditions. Thus he says: "The Veda has to speak by Thy might and the Sun has to move round; such is the might of Thee, the Lord of the Universe. Knowing this essential truth I have surrendered myself to Thee. By Thy might it is that the clouds have to pour down rain, mountains to rest firm and the wind to blow." 3 Again: "Vows, fasts and austerities are not at all necessary; nor is it necessary for you to go on a pilgrimage. Be you watchful in your hearts and always sing the name of Hari.

It is not necessary to give up eating food or drinking water; fix your mind on the foot of Hari. Neither is it necessary for you to contemplate the one without attributes. Hold fast to the love of the name of Hari." "Recognize him alone to be a righteous man, who sees Vasudeva in all objects, eradicating all pride or egoism. The rest are entangled in the shackles of delusion. To him all wealth is like earth, and the nine gems are mere stones. The two, desire and anger, he has thrown out, and he cherishes in his heart quietude and forgiveness." 4 Again he says: "Firmly grasp the truth which is Narayana. Purity of conduct should not be abandoned; one should not be afraid of the censure of people and thus accomplish one's own purpose.

Surrender yourself to your loving friend (God) giving up all ostentation and pride. The censure of people should be regarded as praise and their praise not heeded. One should entertain no longing for being respected and honoured, but should nourish in oneself a liking for devotion. This should be rendered firm in the mind and the name of God should not be neglected even for a moment." The essence of the teachings of Namdev, as of almost all the other bhaktas of whom I shall now be speaking, is purity of mind, speech, and deed, utter disregard of castes, creeds and other social distinctions, a tendency to leave all for God, and in love and joy to live in God always, utterly ignoring all social, communal and religious prejudices, narrowness, dogmas and bigotry.

It is held that God is omnipotent and omnipresent and that He cannot be identified with any particular deity or his character properly narrated by any particular legendary or mythical ways of thinking. At the same time it is contended that we may call him by any name we like, for He is always the same in all.

Another great Maratha saint was Tukaram of the seventeenth century. Tukaram was a low class Hindu. His father was a petty trader. When his father, in his old age, wanted to give over his business to his eldest son Savji, the latter refused the task since he did not wish a worldly life. So the business was entrusted to Tukaram when he was at the age of thirteen. Four years later his father died. Then Tukaram was imposed upon by crafty persons and his business was wrecked. His wife, however, procured a loan; the business was restored and then he began to prosper. Once, however, while he was returning home, Tukaram met a man who was on the point of being dragged to prison for his debts. Tukaram at once gave all that he had to this debtor in order to achieve his release.

From that time on Tukaram renounced all worldly vocations and devoted his life to singing the glories of God and the dearness of our relations to Him. He employed a particular kind of verse which he often composed extempore and in which he frequently spoke. Thus Tukaram says: "God is ours, certainly ours, and is the soul of all souls. God is near to us, certainly near, outside and inside. God is benignant, certainly benignant, and fulfils every longing even of a longing nature." Again he says: "This thy nature is beyond the grasp of the mind or of words, and therefore I have made devoted love a measure, I measure the endless by the measure of love. He is not to be truly measured by any other means. Thou art not to be found by processes of concentration, sacrificial rites, practice of austerities, or any bodily exertions, or by knowledge. Oh Keshava, accept the service which we render to thee in the simplicity of our hearts." Still again: "The Endless is beyond, and between him and me there are lofty mountains of desire and anger. I am not able to ascend them, nor do I find any pass. Insurmountable is the ascent of my enemies. What possibility is there of my attaining my friend Narayana (God)?" He expresses his heart full of longing for God in the following words:

"As on the bank the poor fish lies
And gasps and writhes in pain,
Or, as a man with anxious eyes
Seeks hidden gold in vain,—
So is my heart distressed and cries
To come to thee again.
Thou knowest, Lord, the agony
Of the lost infant's wail
Yearning his mother's face to see.
How oft I tell this tale.)
O, at thy feet the mystery
Of the dark world unveil.
The fire of this harassing thought
Upon my bosom prays.
Why is it I am thus forgot?
(O, who can know thy ways?)
Nay, Lord, thou seest my hapless lot;
Have mercy, Tuka says."

Desolate and disconsolate for the love of God he prays at His door:

"A beggar at thy door,
Pleading I stand;
Give me an alms, O God,
Love from thy loving hand.
Spare me the barren task,

To come, and to come for nought.
A gift poor Tuka craves,
Unmerited, unbought."

Again:

"O save me, save me, Mightiest,
Save me and set me free.
O let the love that fills my breast
Cling to thee lovingly.
Grant me to taste how sweet thou art;
Grant me but this, I pray,
And never shall my love depart
Or turn from thee away.
Then I thy name shall magnify
And tell thy praise abroad,
For very love and gladness I
Shall dance before my God.
Grant to me, Vitthal, that I rest
Thy blessed feet beside;
Ah, give me this, the dearest, best,
And I am satisfied."

Leaving this bhakti movement of the South, which dates from the thirteenth to the seventeenth century, from Jnanesvar and Namdev to Tukaram, we pass to the bhakti movement of North India, represented by Kabir, Nanak and others. It followed the line traced by the Gita and the Bhagavata. Having been developed in the vernacular, however, it appealed directly to the masses. It largely dissociated itself from the complex entanglements of Hindu mythology which had enmeshed the devotional creed of spiritual loyalty to God in the legend of Krishna and his associates.

Kabir (1440-1518) was an abandoned child, probably because of the illegitimacy of his birth. He was brought up by a weaver, Niru, and his wife, Nina. Throughout his life he lived in Benares, probably himself following the profession of a weaver. He is said to have been a disciple of Ramananda, a disciple of

Ramanuja, the great Vaishnava teacher of the South. But he likewise came into touch with some Mohammedan Pirs and was also probably acquainted with certain forms of Sufism. His was a religion which derived its life from what was best among both the Hindus and the Mohammedans. However, he disliked the bigotry and superstitions of all formal religions and was consequently persecuted by both the Hindus and the Mohammedans.

With him and his followers, such as Ruidas and Dadu, we find a religion which shook off all the traditional limitations of formal religions, with their belief in revealed books and their acceptance of mythological stories, and of dogmas and creeds that often obscure the purity of the religious light and contact with God.

Kabir considered the practice of yoga, alms, and fasting, and the feeding of Brahmins, not only useless but improper without the repetition of God's name and love for Him. He discarded the Hindu ideas regarding purity, external ablutions and contact with so-called impure things with as much force as he rejected the Mohammedan belief in circumcision or the requirement that a Brahmin should wear a holy thread, or any other marks of caste. When Kabir's parents found that they could not subdue his Hindu tendencies they wanted to circumcise him, and at this he said:

> *"Whence have come the Hindus and Musalmans? Who hath put them in their different ways,*
>
> *Having thought and reflected in thy heart, answer this—who shall obtain Heaven and who Hell."*

Now we know that the doctrine of bhakti had a great levelling influence. Even according to the Gita and the Bhagavata Purana, bhakti removed all inequalities of caste and social status. We know that Haridas (his Mohammedan name is not known) was converted from Mohammedanism to Vaishnavism by Chaitanya and Nityananda. In lauding him Chaitanya once said: "Your holy thoughts are as the streams of the Ganges in which your soul bathes every hour. Your pious acts earn for you that virtue which the people seek in sacrificial rites prescribed in the scriptures. You are constantly in touch with the loftiest of ideals which give you the same merit as the study of the Vedas. What sadhu or Brahmin is there who is good and great as you are?" 8 In the Brihat Naradiya Purana we find that even a chandala (the lowest caste among the Hindus) becomes the greatest of all Brahmins if he loves God. So the new religious ideal of bhakti, in all its enthusiastic circles, dispensed with the considerations of caste, creed, and social status.

There was, therefore, nothing particularly novel in Kabir's insistence that the time-honoured distinctions of caste, creed and social status are absolutely valueless or in his emphasis upon the need of bhakti for all, as that which alone exalts a man. But in Kabir we find a reformatory zeal. He never tires of reiterating the worthlessness of all these superstitions of caste, creed, social status, external purity and impurity, penances, asceticism, and all sorts of formalities which passed by the name of religion though in fact having nothing to do with it. Thus Kabir says:

"If union with God be obtained by going about naked,
All the deer of the forest shall be saved.
What mattereth it whether man goeth naked or weareth a deerskin,
If he recognize not God in his heart?
If perfection be obtained by shaving the head,
Why should not sheep obtain salvation?
If, O brethren, the continent man is saved,
Why should not a eunuch obtain the supreme reward?
Saith Kabir, hear, O my brethren,
Who hath obtained salvation without God's name?"

Again he says:

"They who battle in the evening and the morning
Are like frogs in the water.
When men have no love for God's name,
They shall all go to the god of death.
They who love their persons and deck themselves out in various guises,
Feel not mercy even in their dreams.

Many leading religious men call them quadrupeds,

And say that only holy men shall obtain happiness in this ocean of trouble.

Saith Kabir, why perform so many ceremonies?

Forsaking all other essences quaff the great essence of God's name."

These allusions to bathing and other activities refer to religious practices followed by many Hindus but vigorously denounced by Kabir.

To a Yogin who said to Kabir that one could not attain deliverance without chastening his heart by the performance of yoga Kabir said:

"Without devotion the qualities of the heart cling to the heart,

Who secured perfection by merely chastening his heart?

What holy man has succeeded in chastening his heart?

Say who bath saved any one by merely chastening his heart.

Every one thinketh in his heart that he is going to chasten it,

But the heart is not chastened without devotion.

Saith Kabir, let him who knoweth this secret

Worship in his heart God, the lord of the three worlds."

Kabir in speaking of the search after God says:

"When I turned my thoughts toward God, I restrained my mind

and my senses, and my attention became lovingly fixed on Him.

O Bairagi, search for Him who neither cometh nor goeth, who neither dieth nor is.

My soul turning away from sin, is absorbed in the universal soul."

Describing the view that God is not confined to any mosque, church or temple, Kabir says:

"If God dwell only in the mosque, to whom belongeth the rest of the country?

They who are called Hindus say that God dwelleth in an idol:

I see not the truth in either sect.

O God, whether Allah or Ram, I live by Thy name,

O Lord, show kindness unto me.

Hari dwelleth in the south, Allah hath his place in the west.

Search in thy heart, search in thy heart of hearts; there is his place and abode.

The Brahmins yearly perform twenty-four fastings... the Musalmans fast in the month of Ramzan.

Kabir is a child of Ram and Allah and accepteth all gurus and Pirs."

Describing his great love and intoxication for God, Kabir says:

"I am not skilled in book knowledge, nor do I understand controversy:

I have grown mad reciting and hearing God's praises.

O father, I am mad; the whole world is sane; I am mad;

I am ruined; let not others be ruined likewise;

I have not grown mad out of my own will; God hath made me mad—

The true guru hath dispelled my doubts—

I am ruined, and have lost my intellect;

Let nobody be led astray in doubts like mine.

He who knoweth not himself is mad;

When one knoweth himself he knoweth the one God.

He who is not intoxicated with divine love in this human birth shall never be so.

Saith Kabir, I am dyed with the dye of God."

Thus, on the one hand, Kabir waged war against the prevailing superstitions, rituals and litanies of all religions and religious sects; and, on the other hand, he dived deep in the depth of God's love and he beheld nothing but God on all sides, becoming as it were one with Him in spiritual union. Thus, he says:

"With both mine eyes I look,
But I behold nothing save God;
Mine eyes gaze affectionately on Him."

The motto of his life was, as he often said, "Remember God, Remember God, Remember God, my brethren;" and in his own life he felt that he was absorbed in the Infinite.

Rui Das (also called Ravi Das), a shoe-maker by caste, was another great disciple of Ramananda. His songs and hymns are full of humility and devotion. However, he evidences none of the reformatory zeal that animated Kabir. I shall quote the translation of only one hymn which seems to me typical of Rui Das's attitude of love towards God. He says:

"There is none so poor as I, none so compassionate as Thou;
For this what further test is now necessary?
May my heart obey thy words, fill thy servant therewith.
I am a sacrifice to thee, O God;
Why art thou silent?
For many births have I been separated from Thee, O God;
This birth is on thine own account.
Saith Rui Das, putting my hopes in Thee, I live; it is long since I have seen thee."

Still another great saint of love was Mira Bai, a princess of Rajputana, who from her childhood (born about 1504 A. D.) was devoted to an image of Lord Krishna called Girdharlal. Her marriage proved unhappy. At the time of going to her husband's place she became very disconsolate. She wept until she became unconscious at the idea of leaving the image of Girdharlal behind. So her parents gave her the image as a part of her marriage dowry. It proved that Mira could not get on well with the family of her father-in-law, for she was always given to the adoration and worship of her little image, representing to her Lord Krishna, and it was this image that she considered as her husband. Her father-in-law made attempts to kill her, but she was miraculously saved. Ultimately she left his abode and went to Brindaban, the place of Lord Krishna's activities, to have her passion for Krishna realized. Here again, in the case of this princess saint who left her all for Krishna, we find the potency of the Krishna legend.

I shall quote here the translation of one of Mira Bai's hymns which show her great attachment for Krishna, in an image of whom, at Dvaraka, she was, as the tradition says, ultimately lost. Her soul was so full of deep longing for Lord Krishna, or Girdhar as she called him, that she proclaims:

> *"I have the god Girdhar and no other;*
>
> *He is my spouse on whose head is a crown of peacock feathers,*
>
> *Who carrieth a shell, discus, mace and lotus, and who weareth a necklace;*
>
> *I have forfeited the respect of the world by ever sitting near holy men.*
>
> *The matter is now public; everybody knoweth it.*
>
> *Having felt supreme devotion I die as I behold the world.*
>
> *I have no father, son, or relation with me.*
>
> *I laugh when I behold my beloved; people think I weep.*
>
> *I have planted the vine of love and irrigated it again*
>
> *and again with the water of tears,*
>
> *I have cast away my fear of the world, what can anyone do to me*
>
> *Mira's love for her god is fixed, come what may."*

India is a land of saints. There are hundreds of them of whom one could say much. But my time is limited and I have well-nigh exhausted your patience. Yet I cannot conclude without referring briefly to Tulsidas, the greatest Hindu poet of India and a great saint.

Tulsidas lived in the seventeenth century. He did not inaugurate any new faith, but accepted the Hindu mythology and the theory of the incarnation of God, the appearance of the attributeless God as a God of infinite attributes. In his view Rama was the incarnation of God, the saviour and father of mankind. An all-surrendering devotion to him, he believed, is our only duty and the sole legitimate passion of life. God is great not only in His greatness, but also in his mercy. He knows the sins and the frailties of men, and is always prepared to help them repel their temptations. To run counter to the will of God is sin, and it is only by acknowledging our sins and taking an all-surrendering refuge in Him, in love and faith, that we can be saved. Connected herewith was the doctrine of the brotherhood of man and of our duty toward our neighbours. Tulsidas is said to have been very much attached to his wife in his early life.

On one occasion he followed her to her father's place, much to her annoyance, and she said that if he had as much love for God Rama as he had for her he would be saved. This struck Tulsidas to the heart and he renounced the world. By his great strength of character, his remarkable poetic gifts which he applied to religious subjects, and by his strong faith, Tulsidas soon endeared himself to his countrymen. No one has exercised a greater influence than he over the Hindi-speaking people of North India. I have now described, though but briefly, some of the main types of Indian mysticism in their mutual relations; others could not be so much as touched upon owing to the limitations of time. I am fully alive to the imperfections of my treatment. Great as they are, they must have appeared to you even greater on account of the difficulty that you must have experienced in placing yourselves on the mental plane of these mystics. The subtle metaphysical and philosophical background of these different types of mysticism I have here been compelled to disregard.

But I have elsewhere undertaken an historical survey of all the different systems of Indian Philosophy. 9 Through oral instruction, tradition, and the example of great men who renounced the world in pursuance of the high ideals of philosophy, the essence of these different systems, with their spiritual longings and their yearnings after salvation and the cessation of rebirth, have gradually been filtering down into the minds of the masses of the population. The tiller of the soil and the grocer in the shop may be uneducated and often wholly illiterate, but even they, while tilling the ground, driving a bullock cart or resting after the work of the day, will be singing songs full of mystical meaning, and for the moment transporting themselves to regions beyond the touch of material gains and comforts:

"The sky and the earth are born of mine own eyes.

The hardness and softness, the cold and the heat are the products of my own body;

The sweet smell and the bad are of my own nose."

Or,

"Nobody can tell whence the bird unknown

Comes into the cage and goes out.

I would feign put round its feet the fetter of my mind

Could I but capture it."

A traveller in the village of Bengal or on board the steamers plying the rivers of the interior of rural Bengal, may often hear a middle-aged or old Mohammedan or a Hindu singing mystical, philosophical or mythical songs of the love of Krishna and Radha, or of the renouncement of the world by Chaitanya, while a large crowd of men is assembled around the singer listening to him with great reverence and feeling. The singer is probably describing the world as a mirage or a mere phantom show of *maya*, or is expressing the futility of his worldly life on account of his having lost his friendship with his own self.

"My hope of the world is all false,

What shall be my fate, O kind, good lord?

I am not in love with him (self) with whom

I have come to live in this house (body)

O kind, good lord."

So the sublime teachings of philosophy and the other-worldly aspirations of mysticism, with their soothing, plaintive and meditative tendencies, have watered the hearts of Bengal right into the thatched cottages of this land. Wealth and comfort they all appreciate as do people everywhere, but they all know that money is not everything, and that peace of mind and the ultimate good of man cannot be secured through it or any other worldly thing. They are immersed in the world; but still the wisdom of the ages and the teachings of the saints have not been in vain, and at times they are drawn away from the world—their souls unknowingly long for deliverance and find a mystic delight in it. It is only the educated or Anglicized Hindu who, dazzled by the gay colours of the West, sometimes turns a deaf ear to the old tune of his country—the flute of Krishna calling from afar through the rustling leaves of bamboos and the cocoanut groves of the village homes—and, in the name of patriotism and progress, installs a foreign god of money and luxury in the ancestral throne of the god of the Indian heart—the god of deliverance.

The thoughts and aspirations of the ages, our myths, our religions, our philosophies, our songs and poetry, have all interpenetrated and formed a whole which cannot be expressed through a portrayal of its elements. They represent a unique experience which I feel with my countrymen, but which is incommunicable to any one who is unable imaginatively to bring himself into tune with that spirit. The British in India have understood as much of the country as is necessary for policing it, but no foreigner has ever adequately understood our land. Those of you who see India through newspapers and the strange tales and stories of tourists who "do" India in a month, can hardly hope to go right to the place where the heart of India lies.

But, you may perhaps ask, what may I gain by knowing India as it really is at its heart? Well, that is a different matter. Perhaps you may derive gain, perhaps not. You may further ask what is it that one gains through such spiritual longing, realization, or mystical rapture. And I shall frankly confess that one certainly gains nothing that will show itself in one's bank account. But with all my appreciation and admiration of the great achievements of the West in science, politics and wealth, the Upanishad spirit in me may whisper from within: What have you gained if you have not gained yourself, the immortal, the infinite? What have you gained if you have never tasted in your life the deep longing for deliverance and supreme emancipation? And the spirit of the saints of ages whispers in my ears: What have you gained if you have not tasted the joys of self-surrender, if your heart has not longed to make of you a flute in the hands of Krishna, that master musician of the universe, and if you have not been able to sweeten all your miseries with a touch of God?

6

Hindu Dharma

Hinduism (known as Hindu Dharma in some modern Indian languages) is a religion that originated in the Indian subcontinent. In contemporary usage Hinduism is also referred to as Sanatana Dharma, a Sanskrit phrase meaning "eternal law". With its origins in the Vedic civilization it has no known founder, being itself a conglomerate of diverse beliefs and traditions. It is the world's oldest extant religion, and has approximately a billion adherents, of whom about 905 million live in India and Nepal, placing it as the world's third largest religion after Christianity and Islam. Other countries with large Hindu populations include Sri Lanka, Bangladesh, Indonesia, Malaysia, Fiji, Suriname, Guyana and Trinidad and Tobago.

Hinduism contains a vast body of scriptures. Divided as revealed and remembered and developed over millennia, these scriptures expound on a broad of range of theology, philosophy and mythology, providing spiritual insights and guidance on the practice of dharma (religious living). Among such texts, Hindus consider the *Vedas* and the *Upanishads* as being among the foremost in authority, importance and antiquity. Other major scriptures include the Tantras and the sectarian Agamas, the *Puranas* and the epic *Mahabharata* and *Ramayana*. The *Bhagwad Gita*, a treatise excerpted from the *Mahabharata*, is sometimes called a summary of the spiritual teachings of the *Vedas*.

Etymology

The Persian term *Hindu* comes from the Sanskrit *Sindhu*,

i.e. the Indus River. The Rig Veda mentions the land of the Indo-Aryans as *Sapta Sindhu* (the land of the seven rivers in northwestern South Asia, one of them being the Indus). This corresponds to *Hapta Hindu* in the *Avesta* (*Vendidad or Videvdad: Fargard* 1.18)—the sacred scripture of Zoroastrianism. The term was used for those who lived in the Indian subcontinent on or beyond the "Sindhu".

Beliefs

Core Concepts: Hinduism originates from the ancient Vedic tradition and other indigenous beliefs, incorporated over time. Due to its diversity Hinduism can only be defined in terms of peoples and places. It is possible to find Hindu groups whose beliefs have nothing in common and it is impossible to identify any universal belief of practice. Prominent themes in Hinduism include *Dharma* (ethics and duties), *Samsara* (The continuing cycle of birth, life, death and rebirth), *Karma* (action and subsequent reaction), and *Moksha* (liberation from the cycle of *samsara*). Buddhism, Jainism and Sikhism share traits with Hinduism, because these religions originated in India and focus on self-improvement with the general aim of attaining personal (first hand), spiritual experiences. They along with Hinduism are collectively known as *Dharmic* religions.

Concept of God

Hinduism is sometimes considered to be henotheistic, but such a view tends to oversimplify a diverse system of thought with beliefs spanning monotheism, polytheism, pantheism, monism and even atheism. For instance, the Advaita Vedanta school holds that there is only one causal entity (Brahman), which manifests itself to humans in multiple forms while many scholars consider the Samkhya school of thought to have had atheistic leanings.

Brahman

According to the monistic/panentheistic theologies of Hinduism, Brahman (the greater Self or God) is in the highest sense One and nondifferentiated from the world and its beings (hence 'nondualist'). In connoting Brahman's absolutely unparalleled nature, it is also called *Parambrahman*, where the Sanskrit prefix *param*-denotes "ultimate". Brahman is also sometimes seen as synonymous with the concept of *Paramatma* (Supreme Spirit).

Beyond time and space, both immanent and transcendent, *Brahman* is often described succinctly as *Sacchidananda*, meaning 'Truth-Consciousness-Bliss', not only possessing the qualities but also being their very essence. Advaita philosophy declares that ultimately Brahman (the impersonal God) is beyond mere intellectual description and can be understood only through direct spiritual experience, where the 'knower' and the 'known' are subsumed into the act of 'knowing'. The goal is to "wake up" and realize that one's *atman*, or soul, is really identical to Brahman, the uber-soul.

On the other hand, monotheistic (for example, Dvaita Vedanta) and other devotional (bhakti) schools, understand Brahman as a Supreme Being who possesses personality. In these conceptions, Brahman is associated with Vishnu, Shiva or Shakti depending on the sect. Brahman is seen as fundamentally separate from its reliant souls (humanity) so, in achieving liberation, individual beings experience God as an independent being, a living personality, and retain their individual identities.

Ishvara

When God is viewed as the supreme personal being (rather than as the infinite principle) God is called *Ishvara* ("The Lord";), *Bhagvan* ("The Auspicious One";), or *Parameshwara* ("The Supreme Lord"). *Ishvara* thus refers to the personal aspect of God in general; it is not specific to a particular deity. *Ishvara* transcends gender, yet can be looked upon as father, mother, friend, child, or even as sweetheart. Some schools of Hindu philosophy do not believe in *Ishvara*, while others interpret *Ishvara* in different ways. Some schools do not distinguish between *Ishvara* and *Brahman*. The Dvaita school holds that *Ishvara* is not incorporeal, but is infinite and a personal being.

Devas and Devis

The Hindu scriptures refer to many celestial entities, called *Devas* ("The heavenly or shining ones", also called *devatas*). *Devas* may be translated into English as gods, demigods, deities, celestial spirits or angels. The feminine of *deva* is *devi*. The *Vedas* and *Puranas* depict the devas in their mythological stories. The latter lauds the Trimurti of *Mahadevas* ("Great Gods"), which are the three aspects of God, Brahma, Vishnu and Shiva. Other devas have been worshipped throughout Hinduism's history. The *devas* are an integral part of Hindu culture and are depicted in art, architecture and through icons. Hindus can primarily worship one of these deities, known as their *isma devata*, or chosen ideal. The particular form of God worshipped as one's chosen ideal depends on individual preference and needs, influenced by regional and family traditions.

Avatars

Krishna (left), the eighth incarnation (avatar) of Vishnu, with his consort Radha. Many denominations of Hinduism teach that from time to time God descends to Earth in corporeal form to help humans along in their struggle towards liberation from rebirth (known as *moksha*) in the form of *bhakti* and restore dharma in society. Such an incarnation of God is an avatar. The most famous avatars are of Vishnu, the two most popular being Rama, whose life is depicted in the Ramayana, and Krishna, who is a central figure in the Mahabharata and whose life is depicted in the Srimad Bhagavatam.

Atheism

Mainstream Hindu philosophy talks about the existence of God, being heavily influenced by the Vedanta school, the dominant philosophical school of Hinduism. Nonetheless, there were earlier atheistic schools such as Samkhya, which did not acknowledge the existence of God.

Atman

Most Hindus believe that the spirit or soul, the true "self" of every person, called the atman, is eternal; as is Brahman, which may be seen as either the greater Self or as God, depending on the outlook. According to the Advaita (non-dualist) schools of philosophy, the individual self and greater Self are not fundamentally distinct. They argue that the core spirit, or "Self", of every individual person is identical with the greater Spirit. Referring to 'Brahman' unequivocally as God may reveal problems of semantics, where certain traditions understand God to be a motivating agency with personality and others that it is without personality and form, beyond any sort of definition and thus non-equivalent to the 'God' as understood by dualist schools of Hinduism or Abrahamic understandings of God.

According to the Upanishads, whoever gains insight into the depths of his own nature and becomes fully aware of the atman as the innermost core of his own Self will realize his identity with Brahman and will thereby reach Moksha. According to the Dvaita (dualist) school, (often associated with Vaishnavism), the atman is not identical with Brahman, which is seen as being God with personality (though not limited); instead, the atman is dependent on God. Moksha depends on love towards God and on God's grace.

Karma, Samsara and Moksha

Karma translates literally as action, work or deed and is often described as the "moral law of cause and effect". According to the Upanishads, an individual, known as the *jiva-atma*, develops samskaras (impressions) from actions, whether physical or mental. The "linga sharira", a body more subtle than the physical one, but less subtle than the soul, retains impressions, carrying them over into the next life, establishing a unique trajectory for the individual. Thus, the concept of a universal, neutral and never-failing karma intrinsically relates to reincarnation as well as one's personality, characteristics and family. Karma threads together the notions of free will and destiny.

This cycle of *action, reaction, birth, death, and rebirth* is a continuum called samsara. The notion of reincarnation and karma is a strong premise in Hindu thought. Thc Bhagwad Gita states that:

> *As a person puts on new clothes, discarding old and torn clothes, similarly an embodied soul enters new material bodies, leaving the old bodies.*

Samsara provides ephemeral pleasures, which lead people to desire rebirth to enjoy the pleasures of a perishable body. However, escaping the world of samsara through moksha (liberation) is believed to ensure lasting happiness and peace. It is thought that after several reincarnations, an *atman* eventually seeks unity with the cosmic spirit (Brahman/ Paramatman).

The ultimate goal of life, referred to as *moksha, nirvana* or *samadhi,* is described as the realization of one's union with God; realization of one's eternal relationship with God; realization of the unity of all existence; perfect unselfishness and knowledge of the Self; liberation from ignorance; attainment of perfect mental peace; or detachment from worldly desires. Such a realization liberates one from *samsara* and ends the cycle of rebirth.

The exact conceptualization of moksha differs among the various Hindu schools of thought. For example, Advaita Vedanta holds that after attaining moksha an atman no longer identifies itself with an individual but as part of Brahman. The followers of dualistic schools such as dvaita on the other hand, expect to spend eternity in a loka, or heaven, in the company of their chosen form of *Ishvara*. Thus, it is said, the followers of *dvaita* wish to "taste sugar," while the followers of Advaita wish to "become sugar."

Yoga

Hatha Yoga traditionally includes meditation, pranayama, and right action—unlike the popular modern approach in the West that emphasizes the physical aspect.

In whatever way a Hindu defines the goal of life, there are several methods (yogas) that sages have taught for reaching that goal. Someone who practices yoga is called a *yogi*. The chief texts dedicated to Yoga are the Bhagwad Gita, the Yoga Sutras, the Hatha Yoga Pradipika and, as their philosophical and historical basis, the Upanishads. Paths one can follow to achieve the spiritual goal of life (moksha, samadhi, or nirvana) include:

- Bhakti Yoga (the path of love and devotion),
- Karma Yoga (the path of right action),
- Raja Yoga (the path of meditation) and
- Jnana Yoga (the path of wisdom).

An individual may prefer one yoga over others according to his or her inclination and understanding. For instance some followers of the Dvaita school hold that Bhakti ("devotion") is the only practical path to achieve spiritual perfection for most people, based on their belief that the world is currently in the age of *Kaliyuga* (one of four epochs part of the Yuga cycle). Practice of one yoga does not exclude others. Many schools believe that the different yogas naturally blend into and aid other yogas. For example, the practice of *jnana yoga*, is thought to inevitably lead to pure love (the goal of *bhakti yoga*), and vice versa. Someone practicing deep meditation (such as in *raja yoga*) must embody the core principles of *karma yoga*, *jnana yoga* and *bhakti yoga*, whether directly or indirectly.

Bhakti Yoga

The bhakti traditions emphasize cultivation of love and devotion for God as the path to perfection. Followers of bhakti typically worship God as a divine personal being or avatar, such as Rama or Krishna. Followers of the bhakti path strive to purify their minds and activities through the chanting of God's names (japa), prayer, devotional hymns (bhajan) and treating all living creatures with compassion. Bhakti followers seek to enjoy a loving relationship with God, rather than to merge their consciousness with Brahman.

Karma Yoga

Swami Vivekananda, shown here practicing meditation, was a Hindu *guru* (teacher) recognized for his inspiring lectures on topics such as yoga.

Followers of karma yoga seek to achieve freedom by acting without attachment to the results of their actions. According to Hinduism, action is inevitable, and has one great disadvantage—any act done with attachment to its fruits generates karmic or psychological bondage. Followers of karma yoga follow the injunction in the Bhagwad Gita:

> *Without being attached to the fruits of action, one should act as a matter of duty; for by working without attachment, one attains the Supreme.*

Many followers of karma yoga offer the results of every action to God, thus combining karma yoga with bhakti yoga. Karma yoga is supposed to bring purification of the heart, freedom from bondage to the ego, humility, and the growing understanding that Brahman is in all people.

Raja Yoga

Followers of Raja yoga seek to experience the spiritual truth directly through meditation. Raja yoga is based on the Yoga Sutras of Patanjali, which has eight 'limbs' that describe the stages a yogi must pass through to reach the goal of *samadhi*. The eight limbs begin with right action (*yamas* and *niyamas*) and perfect meditative posture (*asana*), and continue with control of the body's life force (*pranayama*). From there, the yogi practices techniques of meditation that take him through the progressive stages of interiorization (*pratyahara*), concentration (*dharana*) and meditation (*dhyana*). The final goal of the raja yogi—and the eighth limb of Patanjali's Sutras—is *samadhi*, or oneness with Brahman.

Jnana Yoga

Jnana yoga is the path of wisdom, or true knowledge, and appeals to people with an intellectual nature. The jnana yogi typically practices the four interrelated means to liberation:

1. *Viveka*: discriminating between what is real (the immortal Atman, or true self), and unreal (the physical universe)
2. *Vairagya*, dispassion for material pleasures
3. *Shad-Sampat*, the *six virtues*, which bring about mental control and discipline.
4. *Mumukshutva*, intense desire for liberation.

These practices lead to the unfoldment of wisdom (intuitive perception), rather than mere intellectual knowledge. Through discrimination and introspection, the jnana yogi eventually realizes the highest truth, that "I am Brahman, the pure, all-pervading Consciousness."

HINDUISM

Hinduism, commonly called Sanatana Dharma by Hindus, is the oldest major world religion still practised today and first among Dharma faiths. Hinduism is characterized by a diverse array of belief systems, practices and scriptures. It has its origin in ancient Vedic culture at least as far back as 2000 BC. It is the third largest religion with approximately 890 million followers worldwide, 96% of whom live in the Indian subcontinent.

Perhaps the Hindu spirit, inspired by no one man or woman in particular, is best captured in a line from the ancient Rig Veda, the "oldest religious scripture in the world.":

"Truth is One, though the Sages know it as Many."

The Rig Veda (Book I, Hymn CLXIV, Verse 46)

Essentially, any kind of spiritual practice followed with faith, love and persistence will lead to the same ultimate state of self-realization. Thus, Hindu thought distinguishes itself by strongly encouraging tolerance for different beliefs since temporal systems cannot claim sole understanding of the one transcendental Truth.

To the Hindu, this idea has been an active force in defining the 'Eternal Dharma.' It has been for Hinduism what the infinite Divine Self of Advaita is to existence, remaining forever unchanged and self-luminous, central and pervasive, in spite of all the chaos and flux around it.

In general, Hindu views are broad and range from monism, dualism, pantheism, panentheism, alternatively called monistic theism by some scholars, and strict monotheism, but are not polytheistic as outsiders perceive the religion to be. Hinduism has often been confused to be polytheistic as many of Hinduism's adherents are monists, and view multiple manifestations of the one God or source of being. Hindu monists see one unity, with the personal Gods, different aspects of only One Supreme Being, like a single beam of light separated into colours by a prism, and are valid to worship.

Some of the Hindu aspects of God include Devi, Vishnu, Ganesha, and Shiva. One of the most prominent Hindu monists is the great saint, Ramakrishna whose preferred form of God is Devi and reiterated traditional Hindu beliefs, that aver devotees can invoke God, in whatever form a devotee prefers, (or as monists prefer to call, Ishta Devata, *i.e.*, the preferred form of God) and ask for God's grace in order to attain Moksha, end of the cycle of rebirth. However, like Judaeo-Christian religions which believe in angels, Hindus also believe in less powerful entities, such as devas.

Contemporary Hinduism is now divided into four major divisions:

- Vaishnavism,

- Shaivism,
- Shaktism,
- and Smartism.

Just as Jews, Christians, and Muslims all believe in the same one God but differ in their conceptions of Him, Hindus all believe in one God but differ in their conceptions. The two primary form of differences are between the two monotheistic religions of Vaishnavism which conceives God as Vishnu and Shaivism, which conceives God as Shiva. Other minor forms are aspects of Vishnu or Shiva.

Hinduism: A Brief Overview

Hinduism rests on the spiritual bedrock of the Vedas, hence Veda Dharma, and their mystic issue, the Upanishads, as well as the teachings of many great Hindu gurus through the ages. Many streams of thought flow from the six Vedic/Hindu schools, Bhakti sects and Tantra Agamic schools into the one ocean of Hinduism, the first of the Dharma religions.

The great debate between followers among the major Hindu philosophical school, Vedanta, from followers of Advaita philosophy on one hand and the strict theistic schools such as those of Ramanuja and Madhva on the other, focused on the true nature of Brahman, on whether Brahman was essentially attributeless or with attributes, *i.e.*, a personal Supreme Being.

The Eternal Way

"The Eternal Way", or the "Perennial Philosophy/Harmony/ Faith", is the one name that has represented Hinduism for many thousands of years. According to Hindus, it speaks to the idea that certain spiritual principles hold eternally true, transcending man-made constructs, representing a pure science of consciousness.

But this consciousness is not merely that of the body or mind and intellect, but of a supramental soul-state that exists within and beyond our existence, the unsullied Self of all. Religion to the Hindu is the native search for the divine within the Self, the search to find the One truth that in actuality never was lost. Truth sought with faith shall yield itself in blissful luminescence no matter the race or creed professed. Indeed, all existence, from vegetation and beasts to mankind, are subjects and objects of the eternal Dharma. This inherent faith, therefore, is also known as Arya/Noble Dharma, Veda/Knowledge Dharma, Yoga/Union Dharma, Hindu Dharma or, simply, the Dharma.

What can be said to be common to all Hindus is belief in Dharma, reincarnation, karma, and moksha (liberation) of every soul through a variety of moral, action-based, and meditative yogas. Still more fundamental principles include ahimsa (non-violence), the primacy of the Guru, the Divine Word of Aum and the power of mantras, love of Truth in many manifestations as Gods and Goddessess, and an understanding that the essential spark of the Divine (Atman/Brahman) is in every human and living being, thus allowing for many spiritual paths leading to the One Unitary Truth. An example of the pervasiveness of this paramount truth-seeking spirituality in daily life is the bindi (seen left), which is a common marker for Hindu women.

It symbolizes the need to cultivate supramental consciousness, which is achieved by opening the mystic "third eye." Hindus across the board stress meditative insight, an intuition beyond the mind and body, a trait that is often associated with the ascetic god Shiva. Men, too, will bear on their foreheads the equivalent tilak mark, usually on religious occasions, its shape often representing particular devotion to a certain main deity: a 'U' shape stands for Vishnu, a group of three horizantal lines for Shiva. It is not uncommon for some to meld both in an amalgam marker signifying Hari-Hara (Vishnu-Shiva indissoluble).

The Four Major Sects of Hinduism

Contemporary Hinduism is traditionally divided into four major divisions: Shaivism, Shaktism, Vaishnavism, and Smartism.

Hinduism is a very rich and complex religion. Each of its four sects shares rituals, beliefs, traditions and gods with one another, but each sect has a different philosophy on how to achieve life's ultimate goal (moksha, liberation) and on their views of the Gods. Each sect fundamentally believes in different methods of self-realization and in different aspects of the One Supreme God. However, each sect respects and accepts all others, and conflict of any kind is rare.

Some sects of Hinduism believe in a monotheistic ideal of Vishnu (often as Krishna), Shiva, or Devi; this view does not exclude other gods, as they are understood to be aspects of the chosen ideal (*e.g.*, to many devotees of Krishna, Shiva is seen as having sprung from Krishna's creative force). Often, the monad Brahman is seen as the one source, with all other gods emanating therefrom. Thus, with all Hindus, there is a strong belief in all paths being true religions that lead to one God or source, whatever one chooses to call the ultimate truth.

Shaivism: Also known as Shaivism, Shaivism is a branch of Hinduism that worships Shiva as the Supreme God. Followers of Shaivism are called Shaivites.

Shaivism is a monotheistic faith. Shaivites believe that there is only one God, who simultaneously permeates all creation and exists beyond it, being both immanent and transcendent. The concept is in contrast with many Semitic religious traditions, where God is seen as transcendent only. As all other Hindu denominations, Shaivism acknowledges the existence of many lower Gods under the Supreme One. These Gods are encompassed by Him, seen as either as manifestations of the Supreme Being or as powerful entities who are permeated by Him, as is all Creation. This type of Monotheism is called Panentheism or Monistic Theism.

Shaivism is a very deep, devotional and mystical sect of Hinduism. It is considered the oldest of the Hindu denominations, with a long lineage of sages and saints who have outlaid practices and paths aimed at self-realization and the ultimate goal of moksha, liberation. As a very broad religion, Shaivism encompasses philosophical systems, devotional rituals, legends, mysticism and varied yogic practices. It has both monistic and dualistic traditions.

Shaivites believe God transcends form, and devotees often worship Shiva in the form of a lingam, symbolizing all universe. God Shiva is also revered in Shaivism as the anthropomorphic manifestation of Shiva Nataraja.

Originated in India, Shaivism has appeal all over India and is particularly strong in South India (especially, Tamil Nadu) and the island of Sri Lanka. Some traditions credit the spreading of Shaivism into southern India by the great sage, Agastya, who is said to brought Vedic traditions as well as the Tamil language.

There can be found almost innumerable Saivite temples and shrines, with many shrines accompanied as well by murtis dedicated to Ganesha, Lord of the Ganas, followers of Shiva, and son of Shiva and Shakti.

Benares is considered the holiest city of all Hindus and Shaivites. A very revered Saivite temple is the ancient Chidambaram, in South India.

One of the most famous hymns to Shiva in the Vedas is Shri Rudram. The foremost Saivite Vedic Mantra is Aum Namah Shivaya.

Major theological schools of Shaivism include Kashmir Shaivism, Shaiva Siddhanta and Virashaivism.

Shaktism: Shaktism is a denomination of Hinduism that worships Shakti, the Divine Mother, in all of her forms whilst not rejecting the importance of masculine and neuter divinity.

Shaktism as we know it today developed between the 4th and the 7th centuries CE in India. It was during this development that the many religious texts, known as the Tantras, were written.

One may consider themselves a Shakta (a devotee of Shakti), a Shaiva (a devotee of Shiva), and a Vaishnava (a devotee of Vishnu) all at the same time.

This form of Hinduism, known as is strongly associated with Vedanta, Samkhya and Tantra Hindu philosophies and is ultimately monist, though there is a rich tradition of Bhakti yoga associated with it. The feminine energy (Shakti) is considered to be the motive force behind all action and existence in the phenomenal cosmos in Hinduism. The cosmos itself is Brahman, the concept of the unchanging, infinite, immanent and transcendent reality that is the Divine Ground of all being, the "world soul". Masculine potentiality is actualized by feminine dynamism, embodied in multitudinous goddesses who are ultimately reconciled in one.

The keystone text is the Devi Mahatmya which combines earlier Vedic theologies, emergent Upanishadic philosophies and developing tantric cultures in a laudatory exegesis of Shakti religion. Demons of ego, ignorance and desire bind the soul in maya (illusion) (also alternately ethereal or embodied) and it is Mother Maya, shakti, herself, who can free the bonded individual.

The immanent Mother, Devi, is for this reason focused on with intensity, love, and self-dissolving concentration in an effort to focus the shakta (as a Shakti worshipper is sometimes known) on the true reality underlying time, space and causation, thus freeing one from karmic cyclism. A common hymn describing the 1000 names of Devi is the Lalitha sahasranama.

Vaishnavism: Vaishnavism is the branch of Hinduism in which Vishnu or one of his avatars (*i.e.*, incarnations) is worshipped as the supreme God and is a monotheistic faith.

Major branches of Vaishnavism include Srivaishnavism, (espoused by Ramanuja) who advocated Vishishtadvaita, Dvaita (espoused by Shri Madhvacharya) and Gaudiya Vaishnavism (espoused by Shri Chaitanya Mahaprabhu adhered by ISKCON).

The distinction between this branch and others is made by those who study religion. However it may not always be clear to practising Hindus who often take freely from the practices of the different branches. It is likely that a majority (75-80%) of today's Hindus would consider themselves Vaishnava, if pressed to make a distinction. Of the remainder, most would probably consider themselves Shaivites.

Vishnu and Shiva are sometimes visualized as a single divinity named Harihara.

Smartism: Smartism is a denomination of the religion of Hinduism and is closely affiliated with the Advaita tradition. Smartism is monist in theological belief.

Smartas (followers of Smartism) accept and worship all major forms of God, (Ganesha, Shiva, Shakti, Vishnu, Surya and Skanda). Following a meditative, philosophical path, the denomination is generally considered to be liberal and non-sectarian.

In Smartism, devotees pray to whatever form of God a devotee prefers, (or as monists prefer to call, Ishta Devata, *i.e.*, the preferred form of God) and ask for God's grace in order to achieve Moksha, end of the cycle of rebirth.

Notably, Shakti is worshipped to reach Shiva, whom for Shaktas is the impersonal Absolute. Additionally, Shaivites and Vaishnavites often regard Surya as an aspect of Shiva and Vishnu, respectively. For example, the sun is called Surya Narayana by Vaishnavites. In Saivite theology, the sun is said to be one of eight forms of Shiva, the Astamurti. Additionally, Ganesha and Skanda for them, would be aspects of Shiva and Shakti. Hence, it appears to be the case that most Hindus worship Saguna Brahman as Vishnu or Shiva.

Hinduism Origins, Nomenclature and Society

In a 1966 ruling, the Supreme Court of India defined the Hindu faith as follows for legal purposes:

- Acceptance of the Vedas with reverence as the highest authority in religious and philosophic matters and acceptance with reverence of Vedas by Hindu thinkers and philosophers as the sole foundation of Hindu philosophy.
- Spirit of tolerance and willingness to understand and appreciate the opponent's point of view based on the realization that truth is manysided.
- Acceptance of great world rhythm—vast periods of creation, maintenance and dissolution follow each other in endless succession—by all six systems of Hindu philosophy.
- Acceptance by all systems of Hindu philosophy of the belief in rebirth and pre-existence.
- Recognition of the fact that the means or ways to salvation are many.
- Realization of the truth that numbers of Gods to be worshipped may be large, yet there are Hindus who do not believe in the worshipping of idols

DHARMA IN ORTHODOX HINDU CASTE SOCIETY

According to one view, the Caste system shows how strongly many have felt about each person following his or her dharma, or destined path. A perversion, according to many Hindus, of dharma's true meaning, caste still plays a significant role in Hindu society; however, post Independence, caste is rapidly losing favour in India and caste-based discrimination has been illegitimised. The British Raj and the subsequent governments have used the caste based politics effectively to divide and conquer for their own personal political gains. The Vedas do not condone discrimination of any sort. The four 'varna's (literally, 'colour') or castes, were based upon the duties to society and worked together towards the welfare of the society. They had equal standing in the society.

However over a period of time this division of labour was misunderstood and exploited. This became more ingrained over centuries until social mobility all but became a thing of the past. In spite of centuries of numerous reform movements, notably within Vedanta, bhakti yoga and Hindu streams of Tantra, and reformers, with recent stalwarts like Swami Vivekananda and Mahatma Gandhi, caste is so deeply ensconced in the Indian consciousness that even Christian converts have been known to separate church meetings for different castes. A number of Muslim communities have retained caste practices as well. What was first an injunction to living one's dharma in surrender to God became an oppressive mandate to surrender to Man. See caste for more.

THE SIX VEDIC SCHOOLS OF THOUGHT

Six Schools: The six Astika or orthodox (accepting the authority of the Vedas) schools of Hindu philosophy are Nyaya, Vaisheshika, Samkhya, Yoga, Purva Mimamsa (also called just 'Mimamsa'), and Uttara Mimamsa (also called 'Vedanta'). The non-Vedic schools are called Nastika, or heterodox, and refer to Buddhism, Jainism and Lokayata. The schools that continue to affect Hinduism today are Purva Mimamsa, Yoga, and Vedanta. See Hindu philosophy for a discussion of the historical significance of Samkhya, Nyaya, and Vaisheshika.

Purva Mimamsa: The main objective of the Purva ("earlier") Mimamsa school was to establish the authority of the Vedas. Consequently this school's most valuable contribution to Hinduism was its formulation of the rules of Vedic interpretation.

Its adherents believed that revelation must be proved by reasoning, that it should not be accepted blindly as dogma. This empirical and eminently sensible manner of religious application is key to the Sanatana/Hindu Dharma and was especially championed by rationalists like Adi Shankara and Swami Vivekananda. For greater depth, please see Purva Mimamsa.

Yoga: Sadhus (Hindu ascetic) are often seen meditating in padmasana (lotus pose). The Yoga system is generally considered to have arisen from the Samkhya philosophy. The yoga referred to here, however, is specifically Raja Yoga (or meditational union). It is based on the sage Patanjali's extremely influential text entitled the Yoga Sutra, which is essentially a compilation and systematization of meditational Yoga philosophy that came before. Upanishads and Bhagwad Gita are also indispensable literature in the study of Yoga.

The most significant difference from Samkhya is that the Yoga school not only incorporates the concept of Ishvara (a personal God) into its metaphysical worldview but also that it holds Ishvara as the ideal upon which to meditate. This is because Ishvara is the only aspect of purusha (the infinite Divine Ground) that has not become entangled with prakrti (the temporal creative forces). It also utilizes the Brahman/Atman terminology and concepts that are found in depth in the Upanishads, adopting Vedantic monist concepts. Realization of the goal of Yoga is known as moksha or samadhi. It, like the Upanishads, seeks realization of the Atman as being nothing other than the infinite Brahman through ethical (mind), physical (body) and meditational (soul) practices of one-pointedness on the 'one supreme truth.'

Uttara Mimamsa: The Three Schools of Vedanta: The Uttara ("later") Mimamsa school is perhaps one of the cornerstone movements of Hinduism and certainly was responsible for a new wave of philosophical and meditative inquiry, renewal of faith, and cultural reform. Primarily associated with the Upanishads and their commentary by Badarayana, the Vedanta Sutras, Vedanta thought split into three groups, initiated by the thinking and writing of Adi Shankara.

Most Hindu thought today in some way relates to changes affected by Vedantic thought, which focused on meditation, morality and centeredness on the one Self rather than on rituals and societal distinctions like caste. The great debate between followers among the major Hindu philosophical school, Vedanta, from followers of Advaita philosophy on one hand and the strict theistic schools such as those of Ramanuja and Madhva on the other, focused on the true nature of Brahman, on whether Brahman was essentially attributeless or with attributes, *i.e.*, a personal Supreme Being.

Pure Monism: Advaita

Advaita literally means "not two"; thus this is what we refer to as a monistic (or non-dualistic) system, which emphasises oneness. Its consolidator was Shankara (788?-820?). Shankara expounded his theories largely based on previous teachings of the Upanishads and his own guru Govinda Bhagwadpada. By analysis of experiential consciousness, he exposed the relative nature of the world and established the non-dual reality of Brahman in which Atman (the individual soul) and Brahman (the ultimate reality) are identified absolutely.

It is not merely philosophy, but a conscious system of applied ethics and meditation, all geared towards attaining peace and understanding of truth. Adi Shankara denounced caste and meaningless ritual as foolish, and in his own charismatic manner, exhorted the true devotee to meditate on God's love and apprehend truth.

To Advaitists (nondualists) Ultimate Truth is best expressed as Nirguna Brahman, or God without form, or God without personal attributes; indeed some might go so far as to say it is not 'God' but something beyond. However, even that definition can be limiting. Nirguna Brahman can never be described as that as It transcends all definitions. All personal forms of God such as Vishnu or Shiva are different aspects of God in personal form or God with attributes, Saguna Brahman.

God's energy is personified as Devi, the Divine Mother. For Vaishnvaites who follow Ramanuja's philosophy, Devi is Lakshmi, who is the Mother of all and who pleads with Vishnu for mankind who is entrenched in sin. For Shaivites, Devi is Parvati. For Shaktas, who worship Devi, Devi is the personal form of God to attain the impersonal Absolute, God, *i.e.*, Shiva. For them, Shiva is personified as God without attributes.

Qualified Monism: Vishistadvaita

Ramanuja (1040-1137) was the foremost proponent of the

concept of Sriman Narayana as the supreme Brahman. He taught that Ultimate reality had three aspects: Isvara (Vishnu), chit (soul) and achit (matter). Vishnu is the only independent reality, while souls and matter are dependent on God for their existence. Because of this qualification of Ultimate reality, Ramanuja's system is known as qualified non-dualism.

Dualism: Dvaita

Like Ramanuja, Madhva (1199-1278) identified God with Vishnu, but his view of reality was purely dualistic in that he understood a fundamental differentiation between the ultimate Godhead and the individual soul, and the system is therefore called Dvaita (dualistic) Vedanta.

Alternative Cultures of Worship

The Bhakti schools-The Bhakti (Devotional) school takes its name from the Hindu term that signifies a blissful, selfless and overwhelming love of God as the beloved Father, Mother, Child, or whatever relationship finds appeal in the devotee's heart. The philosophy of Bhakti seeks to tap into the universal divinity through personal form, which explains the proliferation of so many Gods and Goddesses in India, often reflecting the singular inclinations of small regions or groups of people. Seen as a form of Yoga, or union, it seeks to dissolve the ego in God, since consciousness of the body and limited mind as self is seen to be a divisive factor in spiritual realization. Essentially, it is God who effects all change, who is the source of all works, who acts through the devotee as love and light. 'Sins' and evildoings of the devotee are said to fall away of their own accord, the devotee shriven, limitedness even transcended, through the love of God.

The Bhakti movements rejuvenated Hinduism through their intense expression of faith and their responsiveness to the emotional and philosophical needs of India. They can rightly be said to have affected the greatest wave of change in Hindu prayer and ritual since ancient times.

The most popular means of expressing love for God in the Hindu tradition has been through puja, or ritual devotion, frequently using the aid of a murti (statue) in conjunction with the singing or chanting of meditational prayer in the form of mantras. Devotional songs called bhajans (written primarily from the 14th-17th centuries), kirtan (praise), and arti (a filtered down form of Vedic fire ritual) are sometimes sung in conjunction with performance of puja. This rather organic system of devotion attempts to aid the individual in connecting with God through symbolic medium. It is said, however, that the bhakta, through a growing connection with God, is eventually able to eschew all external form and is immersed entirely in the bliss of undifferentiated Love in Truth.

Shri Ganesha is the son of Shiva and Parvati; beloved by many Hindus, he is widely worshipped as Vignesh, the remover of obstacles. Altogether, bhakti resulted in a mass of devotional literature, music and art that has enriched the world and given India renewed spiritual impetus, one eschewing unnecessary ritual and artificial social boundaries.

Tantrism

According to the most famous Western Tantrik scholar, Sir John Woodroffe (pseudonym Arthur Avalon): "The Indian Tantras, which are numerous, constitute the Scripture (Shastra) of the Kaliyuga, and as such are the voluminous source of present and practical orthodox 'Hinduism'. The Tantra Shastra is, in fact, and whatever be its historical origin, a development of the Vaidika Karmakanda, promulgated to meet the needs of that age. Shiva says: 'For the benefit of men of the Kali age, men bereft of energy and dependent for existence on the food they eat, the Kaula doctrine, O auspicious one! is given' (Chap. IX., verse 12). To the Tantra we must therefore look if we would understand aright both ritual, yoga, and sadhana of all kinds, as also the general principles of which these practices are but the objective expression." (Introduction to Sir John Woodroffe's translation of "Mahanirvana Tantra.")

The word "tantra" means "treatise" or "continuum", and is applied to a variety of mystical, occult, medical and scientific works as well as to those which we would now regard as "tantric". Most tantras were written in the late middle ages and sprang from Hindu cosmology and Yoga.

History

Origins: The earliest evidence for certain (minor) elements of Hinduism date back as far as the late neolithic to the early Harappan period (ca. 5500–2600 BC). The beliefs and practices of the pre-classical era (ca. 1500-500 BC) are called the "Vedic religion". The oldest text of Hinduism is the Rigveda, which is dated to between 1700–1100 BC based on linguistic and philological evidence.

The Vedic Period

Sacred Mount Kailash in Tibet is regarded as the spiritual abode of Shiva.

Modern Hinduism grew out of the Vedas. The earliest of these, the *Rigveda*, centres on worship of deities such as *Indra*, *Varuna* and *Agni*, and on the *Soma* ritual. They performed fire-sacrifices, called *yajna* and chanted Vedic mantras but did not build temples or icons. Buddhist and Jain texts claim that animals were sacrificed in larger *yajnas*. The oldest Vedic traditions exhibit strong similarities to Zoroastrianism and with other Indo-European religions.

Epic and Puranic Periods

The epic poems Ramayana and Mahabharata were composed roughly from 400 BC to 200 CE but were transmitted orally for hundreds of years prior to this period. The Ramayana and Mahabharata contain secular and mythological stories of the rulers and wars of ancient India as well as on the avatars Rama and Krishna respectively.

They are interspersed with treatises on various Hindu philosophical concepts. These include the nature of the atma, karma, dharma, moksha, and the organisation of society and government. The later Puranas recount tales about devas and devis, their interactions with humans and their battles against demons.

The Age of Mahajanapadas

During the Iron Age in India, several schools of thought arose and developed in Hindu philosophy including Samkhya, Yoga, Nyaya, Vaisheshika, Purva-Mimamsa and Vedanta. Three key revolutions underpinned the nascence of a new epoch in Hindu thought.

These were the spiritual upheaval initiated by the

Upanishads, and the arrival of Mahavira (founder of Jainism) and the Buddha (founder of Buddhism). Charvaka, the leader of an atheistic materialist school, also came to the fore in North India in the sixth century BC. The Upanishads, Mahavira and Buddha taught that to achieve moksha or nirvana, one did not have to accept the authority of the Vedas or the caste system; the Buddha went a step further and claimed that the existence of a Self/soul or God was unnecessary.

In this intellectual ferment, many Hindus became Buddhists and Jains while others were influenced by their teachings. The arrival of new philosophies substantially changed the religion during the Maurya and Gupta periods.

Islam and Bhakti

From the last twelfth century successive waves of armies from Muslim kingdoms invaded and to varying degrees, gained control over North India. During this period Buddhism declined rapidly, and many Hindus converted to Islam. Some Muslim rulers such as Aurangzeb destroyed Hindu temples and otherwise persecuted non-Muslims, while others, such as Akbar, were more tolerant.

Hinduism underwent profound changes due in large part to the influence of the prominent teachers Ramanuja, Madhva, and Chaitanya. Followers of the Bhakti movement moved away from the abstract concept of Brahman, which the philosopher Adi Shankara consolidated a few centuries before, to a focus on the more accessible avataras, especially Krishna and Rama. A new attitude toward God—emotional, passionate love—replaced the old approaches of sacrificial rite and meditation on the formless Brahman.

Indology and Reform Movements

The 19th and 20th centuries saw an unprecedented interaction between Hindu and European thought (in the form of Abrahamic religions and Western Philosophy). This intercultural correspondence catalyzed developments in Indology, formations of new schools of Hindu thought, the global spread of Hinduism and changes within Hindu society. Meanwhile, traditional systems of Hinduism witnessed revivals and new developments that flourished independently.

Indology as an academic discipline of studying Indian culture from a European perspective was established in the 19th century, led by Max Muller and John Woodroffe. They brought much of the Vedic, Puranic and Tantric literature and philosophy to Europe and the United States. At the same time, societies such as the Brahmo Samaj and the Theosophical Society attempted to reconcile and fuse Abrahamic and Dharmic philosophies, endeavouring to institute societal reform.

This period also saw the emergence of movements which, while sometimes highly innovative, were rooted in indigenous tradition, sometimes based on the personalities and teachings of individuals, as with Shri Ramakrishna and Ramana Maharshi. Prominent Hindu philosophers, including Sri Aurobindo and Swami Prabhupada (founder of ISKCON) translated, reformulated and presented Hinduism's foundational texts for contemporary audiences in new iterations, attracting followers and attention in India and abroad. Others such as Swami Vivekananda, Paramahansa Yogananda, B.K.S. Iyengar and Swami Rama have been instrumental in raising the profiles of traditional Yoga and Vedanta in the West.

In the Indian subcontinent, Hinduism is still practised by the majority of India's inhabitants although the number in the areas of modern Pakistan and Bangladesh have dwindled after the Partition of India. Hinduism is the official religion in Nepal, which is the world's only Hindu state.

SCRIPTURES AND THEOLOGY

Hinduism is based on "the accumulated treasury of spiritual laws discovered by different persons in different times." The scriptures were transmitted orally, in verse form to aid memorization, for many centuries before they were written down. Over many centuries, sages refined the teachings and expanded the canon. The majority of the sacred texts are in the Sanskrit language. The texts are collectively referred to as *Shastras* and are classified into two classes: *Shruti* and *Smriti*.

Shruti

The *Rig Veda* is one of the oldest religious texts. This is a Rig Veda manuscript in Devanagari.

Shruti (lit: that which has been heard) refers to the *Vedas* which form the earliest record of the Hindu scriptures. While they have not been dated with much certainty, the most conservative estimates date their origin to 1200 BC or earlier.

Hindus revere the Vedas as eternal truths revealed to ancient sages (*Rishis*) through meditation. Many of these sages were women, called *Rishikas*. Many devotees do not associate the creation of the Vedas with a God or person. They are thought of as the laws of the spiritual world, which would still exist even if they were not revealed to the sages.

There are four Vedas (called *Rig-, Sama-Yajur-*and *Atharva*). The *Rigveda* is the first and most important Veda. Each Veda is divided into four parts: the primary one, the *Veda proper*, being the *Samhita*, which contains sacred *mantras*. The other three parts form a three-tier ensemble of commentaries, usually in prose and are believed to be slightly later in age than the *Samhita*. These are: the *Brahmanas*, *Aranyakas*, and the Upanishads. The first two parts were subsequently called the *Karmakanda* (the ritualistic portion), while the last two form the *Jnanakanda* (the knowledge portion).

While the Vedas focus on rituals, the Upanishads focus on spiritual insight and philosophical teachings. They constitute a major portion of the Jnana Kanda. The Upanishads discuss Brahman and reincarnation. While the *Vedas* are not read by most lay Hindus, they are revered as the eternal knowledge whose sacred sounds help bring spiritual and material benefits. Theologically, they take precedence over the *Smriti*, and local custom.

Smriti

The *Naradeya Purana* describes the mechanics of the cosmos. Depicted here are Vishnu with his consort Lakshmi resting on Shesha Nag. The sage Narada and Brahma are also pictured.

Hindu texts other than the *Shrutis* are collectively called the *Smritis* (memory). The most notable of the smritis are the *Itihasa* (epics), which consist of the *Mahabharata* and the *Ramayana*. *Bhagwad Gita* is an integral part of the *Mahabharata* and one of the most popular sacred texts of Hinduism. It contains philosophical teachings from *Krishna*, an incarnation of *Vishnu*, told to the prince Arjuna on the eve of a great war. The *Bhagwad Gita* is described as the essence of the *Vedas.*

The Smritis also include the *Purans*, which illustrate Hindu ideas through vivid mythological narratives. There are texts with a sectarian nature such as *Devi Mahatmya*, the *Tantras* as well as the *Mahanirvana Tantra, Tirumantiram, Shiva Sutras* and the *Hindu Agamas*. A more controversial text, the *Manusmriti*, is a prescriptive lawbook which epitomizes the societal codes of the caste system.

Most Hindu scriptures are not typically interpreted literally. More importance is attached to the ethics and metaphorical meanings derived from them. Hindu exegesis leans toward figurative interpretations of scriptures rather than the literal.

Many Scriptures, Many Paths

In contrast to the scriptural canons of some religions, the Hindu scriptural canon is not closed. Hindus believe that because the spiritual truths of the Vedas are eternal, they continue to be expressed in new ways. Some Hindus even venerate the scriptures of other religions. One much-quoted verse from the *Rigveda* that emphasizes the diversity of paths to the one goal is:

> *ekam sad vipra bahudha vadanty*
>
> *Truth is one, the wise call it in many different ways.*
> *—Rig Veda 1.164.46*

This openness means that there is little theological quarrel between Hindu denominations although these denominations may view God and their notions in a different form or sense.

Schools of Philosophy

The six *Astika* or orthodox schools of Hindu philosophy, which accept the authority of the Vedas, are *Nyaya, Vaisheshika, Samhya, Yoga, Purva Mimama* (also called *Mimama*), and *Uttara Mimama* (also called *Vedanta*). Although scholars mainly study these philosophies, they influence the beliefs of average Hindus.

Practices

Hindu practices generally involve seeking awareness of God and sometimes also seeking blessings from Devas.

Therefore, Hinduism has developed numerous practices meant to help one think of divinity in the midst of everyday life.

According to Swami Vivekananda: "The ideal of man is to see God in everything. But if you cannot see Him in everything, see Him in one thing, in that thing you like best, and then see Him in another. So on you go... Take your time and you will achieve your end."

Puja

Hindus can engage in formal worship (Sanskrit: puja, worship or veneration) either at home or at a temple. At home, Hindus often create a shrine with icons dedicated to the individual's chosen form(s) of God. Veneration may involve offering food, water, or flowers and may be expressed through the burning of incense, lighting of candles or oil-lamps, ringing a bell, waving a fan, or sounding a conch-shell. Other practices of Puja include meditation, chanting mantras, and reciting scriptures. Icons of *devas* and *devis* are an integral part of most Hindu temples. Shown here are icons of Ganesha and Lakshmi, heavily laden with garlands, taken during a Hindu prayer ceremony.

Devotional Singing

Devotional singing is an important part of *bhakti*. Devotional singing occurs in temples, ashrams, on the banks of holy rivers, at home and elsewhere. Hymns are in Sanskrit or in modern Indian languages. Musical instruments accompanying devotional singing include the manjeera, tanpura, harmonium, and tabla. Another form of community worship is Satsang, the practice of gathering for study or discussion of scriptures and religious topics as well as chanting *mantras*.

Yajna

Vedic rites of fire-oblation (yajna) are now only occasional practices although they are highly revered in theory. In a Hindu wedding ceremony however, the presence of sacred fire as the divine witness, the *yajna* and chanting of Vedic mantras is still the norm. The same applies to death rituals.

Worship of God Through Icons: Hindus may perform their worship through icons (murti), such as statues or paintings symbolic of God's power and glory. The icon serves as a tangible link between the worshipper and God. Another view is that the image is a manifestation of God, since God is immanent. The Padma Purana states that the *murti* is not to be thought of as mere stone or wood but as a manifest form of the Divinity. A few Hindu sects, such as the Arya Samaj, do not believe in worshipping God through icons.

Temples

Hindu temples are a place of worship for Hindus. They are usually dedicated to a primary deity along with associated subordinate deities though some commemorate multiple deities. Most temples are constructed as per the *agama shastras* and many are pilgrimage sites.

Visiting temples is not obligatory. Many Hindus only go during religious festivals but others visit more regularly. Temples are not used for funerals, or as social hubs but are sometimes used for weddings. Some view the four Shankaracharyas (the abbots of the monasteries in Joshimath, Puri, Shringeri and Dwarka) as the Patriarchs of Hinduism.

HINDU ICONOGRAPHY

Swastika: Hinduism has a developed system of symbolism and iconography to represent the sacred in art, architecture, literature and worship. These symbols gain their meaning from the scriptures, mythology, or cultural traditions. The symbols Om (which represents the *Parabrahman*), Swastika (which symbolizes auspiciousness) have grown to represent Hinduism itself, while other markings such as tilaka identify a follower of the faith.

Hinduism associates many symbols, which include the lotus, chakra and veena, with particular deities. These associations distinguish their physical representations in sculptures and pictures and are based on allegorical references in Hindu mythology. While most representations of deities are largely anthropomorphic there are exceptions. For instance the deity Shiva can be worshipped in the form of a pillar-like stone called a *lingam*.

The Guru-disciple Tradition

In many Hindu sects, spiritual aspirants adopt a personal spiritual teacher, called a guru. Traditionally, during brahmacharya a Guru taught a disciple all things necessary to lead a dharmic life. The student is expected to follow the instructions of the guru and to have a spiritual life.

Japa and Mantra

Mantras are prayers that through their meaning, sound, and chanting style help a person focus their mind on holy thoughts or to express devotion to God. Mantras are meant to give courage in exigent times and invoke one's inner spiritual strength.

After the pranava or "fundamental" mantra of "Aum", one of the most revered mantras is the Gayatri Mantra. Hindus are initiated into this most sacred mantra at the time of their Upanayanam (thread ceremony). Many Hindus perform morning ablutions at the bank of a sacred river while chanting the Gayatri or Mahamrityunjaya mantras.

Japa (ritualistic chanting) is extolled as the greatest duty for the Kali Yuga (what Hindus believe to be the current age) in the epic Mahabharata. Many Hindu traditions adopt Japa as their primary spiritual practice. The Gaudiya Vaishnava tradition chanting the Hare Krishna mantra is one such example.

Pilgrimage

Pilgrimage is not mandatory in Hinduism though many adherents undertake them. There are many Hindu holy places in India.

One of the most famous is the ancient city of Varanasi. Other holy places in India include Kedarnath and Badrinath in the Himalayas, the Jagannath temple at Puri, Rishikesh and Haridwar in the foothills of the Himalayas, Prayag, Rameshwaram in the South and Gaya in the east.

The largest single gathering of pilgrims is during the annual Kumbh Mela fair held in one of four different cities on a rotating basis. Another important "set" of pilgrimages are the 51 "Shakti Peethas," where the Mother Goddess is worshipped, the two principal ones being Kalighat and Kamakhya. Vaishno Devi, the Shakti temple near Katra, Jammu and Kashmir is the second most visited religious shrine in India, after Tirupati Balaji Mandir.

Hindu Festivals

Hinduism has many festivals throughout the year. Their dates are usually prescribed by the Hindu calendar and typically celebrate events from Hindu mythology, often coinciding with seasonal changes and occasions of importance in an agrarian society. There are festivals which are primarily celebrated by specific sects or in certain regions of the Indian subcontinent.

Some widely observed Hindu festivals are:

- Dusshera, or Durga Puja, celebrates events from Hindu mythology symbolizing the triumph of good over evil;
- Diwali, the festival of lights;
- Ganesha Chaturthi, the festival celebrating Ganesha;
- Maha Shivaratri, the festival dedicated to Shiva;
- Ram Navami, celebrates the birth of Rama, the seventh incarnation of Vishnu;
- Krishna Janmashtami, celebrates the birth of Krishna, the eighth incarnation of Vishnu;
- Holi, a spring festival of colours and light;
- Sankranti, a harvest festival of India

Cremation

On death, cremation is considered obligatory for all except *sanyasis*, *hijra*, and children under five. Cremation is typically performed by wrapping the corpse in cloth and burning it on a pyre. Manikarnika Ghat, in Varanasi, is a famous site where bodies are cremated by the side of the river, in full view of the public. Those not cremated may be simply wrapped in cloth, weighted with stones and cast into a river.

Hinduism obliges the closest male relative (son, father, husband, etc.) of the deceased to immerse the cremated remains in the holy river Ganga (Ganges), preferably at the holy city of Haridwar, India. The cremated remains may also be entombed, in case the deceased was a well-known person.

Society

Hinduism has no central doctrinal authority and many practising Hindus do not claim to belong to any particular denomination at all. However, academics categorize contemporary Hinduism into four major denominations:

Vaishnavism, Shaivism, Shaktism and Smartism. The denominations differ primarily in the God worshipped as the Supreme One and in the traditions that accompany worship of that God.

Vaishnavas worship *Vishnu*; Shaivites worship *Shiva*; Shaktas worship *Shakti* (power) personified through a female divinity or Mother Goddess, *Devi*; while Smartists believe in the essential sameness of all deities.

There are also many movements that are not easily placed in any of the above categories, such as Swami Dayananda Saraswati's *Arya Samaj*, which rejects image worship and veneration of multiple deities. It focuses on the *Vedas* and the Vedic fire sacrifices (*yajna*). The Tantric traditions in Hinduism have various sects, as Banerji writes in "*Tantra in Bengal*":

> *Tantras are also divided as* astika *or Vedic and* nastika *or non-Vedic. In accordance with the predominance of the deity the* astika *works are again divided as Shakta, Shaiva, Saura, Ganapatya and Vaishna.*

As in every religion, some view their own denomination as superior to others. However, many Hindus consider other denominations to be legitimate alternatives to their own. Heresy is therefore generally not an issue for Hindus.

Ashramas

Traditionally the life of a Hindu was divided into four *Ashramas* ("phases" or "stages"; unrelated meanings include "monastery").

The first part of one's life, *Brahmacharya,* the stage as a student, is spent in celibate, controlled, sober and pure contemplation under the guidance of a Guru, building up the mind for spiritual knowledge. *Grihastha* is the householder's stage, in which one marries and satisfies *kama* and *artha* within one's married and professional life respectively.

The moral obligations of a Hindu householder include supporting one's parents, children, guests and holy figures. *Vanaprastha,* the retirement stage, is gradual detachment from the material world. This may involve giving over duties to one's children, spending more time in religious practices and embarking on holy pilgrimages. Finally, in *Sanyasa*, the stage of asceticism, one renounces all worldly attachments to secludedly find the Divine through detachment from worldly life and peacefully shed the body for Moksha.

Monasticism

In their quest to attain the spiritual goal of life, some Hindus choose the path of monasticism (sanyasa). Monastics commit themselves to a life of simplicity, celibacy, detachment from worldly pursuits, and the contemplation of God. A Hindu monk is called a *sanyasi, sadhu*, or *swami*. A female renunciate is called a *sanyasini*. Renunciates receive high respect in Hindu society because their outward renunciation of selfishness and worldliness serves as an inspiration to householders who strive for *mental* renunciation. Some monastics live in monasteries, while others wander from place to place, trusting in God alone to provide for their needs. It is considered a highly meritorious act for a householder to provide sadhus with food or other necessaries. Sadhus strive to treat all with respect and compassion, whether a person may be poor or rich, good or wicked, and to be indifferent to praise, blame, pleasure, and pain.

VARNAS AND THE CASTE SYSTEM

Hindu society has traditionally been categorized into four classes, called *Varnas* (*Sanskrit*: "colour, form, appearance");

- the *Brahmins*: teachers and priests;
- the *Kshatriyas*: warriors, nobles, and kings;
- the *Vaishyas*: farmers, merchants, and businessmen; and
- the *Shudras*: servants and labourers.

Hindus and scholars debate whether the caste system is an integral part of Hinduism sanctioned by the scriptures or an outdated social custom. Although the scriptures contain passages that clearly sanction the *Varna* system, they contain indications that the caste system is not an essential part of the religion, and both sides in the debate can find scriptural support for their views.

The oldest scriptures, the *Vedas*, strongly sustain the division of society into four classes (varna) but place little emphasis on the caste system, mentioning it rarely and in a cursory manner. A verse from the Rig Veda indicates that a person's caste was not necessarily determined by that of his family:

> *"I am a bard, my father is a physician, my mother's job is to grind the corn." (Rig Veda 9.112.3)*

In the Vedic Era, there was no prohibition against the *Shudras* listening to the Vedas or participating in any religious rite, as was the case in the later times. Mobility and flexibility within the varnas challenge allegations of social discrimination in the caste system, as has been pointed out by several sociologists.

Many social reformers, including Mahatma Gandhi and B.R. Ambedkar, criticized caste discrimination. The religious teacher Sri Ramakrishna (1836-1886) taught that

"Lovers of God do not belong to any caste... A Brahmin without this love is no longer a Brahmin. And a pariah with the love of God is no longer a pariah. Through bhakti (devotion to God) an untouchable becomes pure and elevated."

Ahimsa and Vegetarianism

Hindus advocate the practice of *ahimsa* (non-violence) and respect for all life because divinity is believed to permeate all beings, including plants and non-human animals. The term *ahimsa* first appears in the Upanishads, and is the first of the five *Yamas* (eternal vows/restraints) in Raja Yoga.

In accordance with *ahimsa*, many Hindus embrace vegetarianism to respect higher forms of life. While vegetarianism is not a requirement of Hinduism, it is recommended for a *satvic* (purifying) lifestyle. Estimates of the number of lacto vegetarians in India (includes inhabitants of all religions) vary between 20% and 42%. The food habits usually vary with the community and region, with some castes having fewer vegetarians and coastal populations relying on seafood. Some Hindus avoid even onion and garlic, which are regarded as *rajasic* foods. Some avoid meat on specific holy days.

Observant Hindus who do eat meat almost always abstain from beef. The largely pastoral Vedic people and subsequent generations relied heavily on the cow for protein-rich milk and dairy products, tilling of fields and as a provider of fuel and fertilizer. Thus, it was identified as a caretaker and a maternal figure. Hindu society honours the cow as a symbol of unselfish giving. Cow-slaughter is legally banned in almost all states of India.

Conversion

Since the Hindu scriptures are essentially silent on the issue of religious conversion, the question of whether Hindus should evangelize is open to interpretation. Those who see Hinduism mainly as a philosophy, a set of beliefs, or a way of life generally believe that one can convert to Hinduism by incorporating Hindu beliefs into one's life and considering oneself a Hindu. Some view Hinduism as more of an ethnicity than a religion and believe being born a Hindu makes one a Hindu for life. These people tend to believe that there is an assumption that one is Hindu when they come from India. The Supreme Court of India has taken the former view, holding that the question of whether a person is a Hindu should be determined by the person's belief system, not by their ethnic or racial heritage.

There is no formal process for conversion to Hinduism, although in many traditions a ritual called *diksha* ("initiation") marks the beginning of spiritual life. Most Hindu sects do not actively recruit converts because they believe that the goals of spiritual life can be attained through any religion, as long as it is practiced sincerely. Nevertheless, Hindu "missionary" groups operate in various countries to provide spiritual guidance to persons of any religion. Examples include the Vedanta Society, Parisada Hindu Dharma, International Society for Krishna Consciousness, Arya Samaj and the Self-Realization Fellowship.

The History of Hinduism spans more than 9000 years. Hinduism is the world's oldest existing major religion. Worldwide religious tradition based on the Vedas and the beliefs and traditions of the various groups in India, Hinduism's origins include cultural elements of the Indus valley civilisation (c.3300 BC), and the Vedic religion of the Indo-Aryans, and other Indian civilizations. Being highly localised within India, Hinduism has seen many changes throughout the history of the Indian subcontinent. Over time, Hindu philosophy evolved into six schools: Samkhya, Yoga, Nyaya, Vaisheshika, Purva Mimamsa and Vedanta.

Earliest Records

The dates of Hinduism's origins are approximate, based on archaeological evidence and scriptural references:

- Archaeological evidence unearthed at Indus Valley Civilization sites has been dated to circa 3000 BC, suggesting that the Varnashrama system of four classes was adhered to no earlier than that. Seals depicting the deity Shiva in a Yogic posture of meditation also support that approximation. Philological evidence suggests that the earliest Hindu scripture, the Rig Veda, was composed around 1500-1300 BC.
- Astronomical interpretation of Hindu scriptures suggest a date of approximately 3102 BC. This date results from close examination of the Mahabharata, where the positions of the stars were noted at Sri Krishna's birth. Hindus believe Krishna was born 5000 years ago, and using the star locations in the Mahabharata, the exact year was 3228 BC. Sri Rama, according to the Ramayana, lived around 9000-5000 BC.

Analysis of Historic Sources

Early Hinduism is a term used to designate the religious development of India before written history. Two kinds of evidence are available: literature and archeology.

Literature

The earliest literature of Hinduism is made up of the four Vedas, namely the Rig-Veda, Sama-Veda, Yajur-Veda and the Atharva-Veda. Out of these, the Rig-Veda is considered to be the oldest surviving work of literature. Many Hindus believe that the Vedas were transmitted, via an oral tradition, for perhaps 8000 years (*Fisher*). {Hindus believe that Vedas were orally transmitted or revealed to the Saptha Rishis by the lord himself. We have to go by the Puranas written by the rishis and that is the oldest reference that is available. Puranas talk about various Kalpas and Manvantharas and Yugas as subdivision of each.

The total number of years that has elapsed since the creation of Earth will be in excess of a trillion billion years. Puranas talk about the creation and destruction (Pralaya) of many civilizations. Puranas also talk about life in other galaxies or planets and ability of some life forms to travel from one to the other. They talk about the ability of some Rishis to communicate or establish links between these different worlds or life forms. These cannot be thrown out as pure imagination. The oldest known civilization so far discovered through excavations in Indus valley, exhibits well planned cities with water supply and drainage.

The script used in the inscriptions has not been deciphered yet. This civilization is dating back to 2000 BC. Some bronze statues of Vedic/Hindu Gods (Rudra or Pasupathy) have been excavated from these sites. This indicates that Vedas precede this civilization. Maha Bhagavatham, which was written by Vyasa after completing all other Puranas is supposedly written soon after Swargarohana of Lord Krishna) Western commentators see this as an exaggeration, dating the earliest parts of the Veda, the Rig-Veda Samhita, to oral traditions reaching back to around 1800-1500 BC.

The earliest stage of the Vedas is the Rig-Veda, a collection of poetic hymns used in the sacrificial rites of the Aryan priests. (Rigveda does not prescribe any sacrificial rites. It prescribes worship) Most of the Rig-Veda concerns the offering of Soma-which is both an intoxicant and a god itself-to the gods. The gods in the Rig-Veda are mostly personified concepts, who fall into two categories: the devas, who were gods of nature, such as the weather deity Indra, Agni ("fire"), and Ushas ("dawn") and the asuras, gods of moral concepts, such as Mitra ("contract" or "friend"), Bhaga (guardian of marriage) and Varuna ("the rain god").

The Rigveda is verse narrated by over 12 main rishis. It has 10 Mandalas and there is significant variation in the language and style in the first 8 and the last two namely 9th, 10th mandalas. It is not correct to say that Indra or Varuna are the principal Gods. Rigveda talks about One God (Ekam Sathyam Vipra bahuda Vadanthi. Rigveda talks about the management organization as could be existing.

It assigns functions or roles to each Deva. There are verses in praise of Indra. But the puranas explain that Indra is the name of the post and many persons have occupied that post. Each Manvanthara has a different person as Indra. It is even said that in the next Manvanthara, the Indra will be the same person who was Asura King Mahabali. Hence it is a post with fixed tenure. Same case with other posts. (Veda says that God or Easwara or paramapurusha remains same and constant and has no beginning or end). Indra is head of Devas. Varuna has control over Water and its sources. Vayu has control over Air. There are also others like Agni, Mitra, Yama etc. with assigned roles.

For small or earthly requirements or satisfaction of senses, it is sufficient to pray to these Devas and appease them. Rigveda also talks about origin of sound and also Language. Veda itself says that it was revealed to the rishis by the lord. Rigveda also talks about Vishnu and also Rudra. Purushasooktham is totally in praise of Lord Vishnu and the supreme lord. The Rigveda does not talk about any rivalry between Devas or between Devas and Asuras.)

A rivalry between these two families was already apparent. *Asura* came to mean something like "demon" in later Hinduism, and it is already associated with mischief if not actual malice in the Rig-Veda. Compare this with Iranian Aryan religion, where ahura (*asura*) came to mean "god" and *daava* (cognate to deva) came to mean "evil demon". This theme can be found in other Indo-European religions outside of the Indo-Aryan branch, such as in Norse mythology in the war between the Aesir and the Vanir. The emerging deprecation of the asuras led to the creation of new categories of gods, such as the adityas. Indra is the king of the gods in the Rig-Veda, although some of the hymns (perhaps representing an older stage) have Varuna as the chief. (However there are no verses in Rig Veda to support this presumption.)

Archaeology

Early Hinduism comprises a period that is hazy in the eyes of archaeologists. The Vedic Aryans, although they left a rich body of hymns, left little material culture behind. The excavations of the pre-Vedic Indus Valley Civilization, has also not yielded much evidence of religious activity, for example communal temples. However, there is sufficient evidence that the civilization was certainly not purely secular. Only one Indus civilization graveyard has been found and excavated, and has yielded no elaborate royal burials, but the personal possessions buried with the bodies may indicate that these people believed in an afterlife in which they would need these things.

Many figurines of female deities have been discovered. These most probably signified creativity and the origin and continuity of life, and they may have been worshipped as symbolic embodiments of the female principle of creative Energy and Power. In modern Hinduism, the counterpart of these symbols is called Shakti. These "mother Goddess" figurines may have been worshipped in the home rather than in any major state cult, but scholars have seen ancient Dravidian feminine divinity sculptures in groups of seven that date back to the Harappan era which mirror the Hindu belief in a Mother Goddess (Devi) being represented in seven modes.

An Indus Valley seal with the seated figure termed *Pasupathy.*

Figures of a male deity with elaborate horns (or horned headgear) have also been uncovered. He is typically seen surrounded by cattle and is called Pasupathy, (the Protector of Animals), and is seen by some to be the prototype of Hinduism's ascetic God of Destruction, Shiva. Indeed, in modern-day Shaivism, Shiva has absorbed the names, stories and attributes of not only Pasupathy, by which name he is still commonly known, but also the Vedic 'Rudra.' Pasupathy is seen sitting in the meditative posture of yogis, suggesting that yoga or inner contemplation was one of their modes of discovering the secrets of life and creation.

To this day, the Tantric schools of Hinduism know Shiva to be Yogeshwara, Lord of Yoga, and he is said to be the master of Self-knowledge, meditating for centuries at a time. Others see Pasupathy as a form of Brahma.

It is noted by many that the Pasupathy figure is similar to sculptures, paintings and bas-reliefs of horned gods in Europe, stretching as far back as the Paleolithic painting of the "sorcerer" in the cave of Les Trois Frares in France. There exist, in addition, three-headed Pasupathy-statues that seem to resemble the Trimurti (Triple Form) of Brahma-Vishnu-Shiva (Creator-Sustainer-Destroyer) in contemporary Hinduism, and if nothing else, intimate the continuity of religious traditions that have morphed into Hinduism as we know it today from periods as far back as five thousand years ago.

Hindu Mythology

Apart from religious philosophy, mysticism and spiritualism and tales of superhuman heroes and events, Hindu mythology has a strong historical nature and character. It is perhaps the most extensive, although controversial and largely un-confirmable source for the history of ancient India and its peoples.

EARLY HINDUISM

Early Hinduism (the historical Vedic religion) consisted not only of aspects inherited from Indo-Iranian religion, but also inherited parts the religious system of the Dravidian peoples, and the Indus Valley Civilization.

Influences of the Indus Valley and Dravidian Peoples

Interestingly, the Rigvedic deities, like Indra, Agni, Vayu, etc., are not the principal gods of present day Hindus. Those Indo-Aryan gods have equivalents in other Indo-European gods worshipped by other Indo-European speaking peoples.

Those gods occupied the highest position until the advent of Christianity in those societies, with little discernible trace remaining of the Pre-Indo-European deities and traditions.

However in India the traditions of native groups such as the Dravidians seem to have mingled more fluently with those of the migrants. One view is that this unique mingling is what resulted in modern Hinduism.

Vedic Religion

At the height of the Vedic period, from ca. 800 BC, the inherited mantra texts of the Vedas were extensively commented upon in Brahman literature in many branches (shakhas) throughout India.

Evolution of Hindu Philosophy

From prehistoric times of Vedic civilization up to the Gupta Empire era, Hindu philosophy, theology and mythology were constantly evolving.

Socio-Religious Reform Movements

Many orders for religious reform, moksha and religious transformation arose across India.

Hinduism and Jainism

As opposed to Vedic tradition of Hinduism, Jainism follows shramanic tradition and is probably as old as Hinduism. The main disagreement today remains over the rejection of the Vedas, although Hindu society has to a large extent embraced ahimsa and vegetarianism.

Over several thousand years, Jain influence on Hindu philosophy and religion have been considerable, while Hindu influence on Jain temple worship and rituals can be observed in some Jain traditions. Jain scriptures are many and varied. Jain scripture rejects both the Hindu Vedas and non-Jain writings as sources of religious authority and practice. The Hindu Vedic (and generally theistic) concepts of divine creation, preservation and destruction are criticised in Jain scriptures such as the *Mahavira Charitam*.

Hinduism and Buddhism

When Mauryan Emperor Ashoka converted to Buddhism, he sponsored the growth of schools and monasteries, and sent missions to Sri Lanka, South East Asia, West Asia and Europe. Following the ascent of the Gupta Dynasty, many communities that had converted to Buddhism returned to Hinduism in India. Also, Hinduism was influenced by many of the teachings promoted by Buddhism and Jainism such as ahimsa and vegetarianism.

There was a substantial Buddhist community living in the Indus basin until the Islamic conquest. Later Hindu scriptures, such as the Bhagavata purana, describe the Buddha as an incarnation of Vishnu, effectively reincorporating Buddhism into the Hindu religion, and demonstrating the historical tendency of Hinduism to embrace and absorb many diverse beliefs and traditions. Buddhists themselves, of course, do not necessarily accept this view.

THE GOLDEN AGE

The Gupta dynasty ruled northern India (the north of the Vindhyas), between fourth and sixth centuries of the Common Era. Though not as vast as Mauryan Empire, Gupta rule has left a deep and wide cultural impact not only in the subcontinent but on the adjacent Asian countries as well. The practice of dedicating temples to different deities came into vogue followed by fine artistic temple architecture and sculpture. Books on medicine, veterinary science, mathematics, astronomy and astrophysics were written.

The famous Aryabhata and Varahamihira belong to this age. The Gupta established a strong central government which also allowed a degree of local control. Gupta society was ordered in accordance with Hindu beliefs. This included a strict caste system, or class system. The peace and prosperity created under Gupta leadership enabled the pursuit of scientific and artistic endeavours.

Adi Shankara and the Establishment of Vedanta

At the time of Adi Shankara's life (c. 788 AE "820 CE), Hinduism had began to decline because of the influence of Buddhism and Jainism. Hinduism had become divided into innumerable sects, each quarrelling with the others. The followers of Mimamsa and Sankhya philosophy were atheists; in so much that they did not believe in God as a unified being. Besides these atheists, there were numerous theistic sects also. Also there were those who rejected the Vedas, like the Charvakas.

Adi Shankara held debates with the leading scholars of all these sects and schools of philosophy to controvert their doctrines. He unified the theistic sects into a common framework of Shanmata system. In his works, Adi Shankara stressed the importance of the Vedas, and his efforts helped Hinduism regain strength and popularity. He travelled on foot to various parts of India to restore the study of the Vedas.

Even though he lived for only thirty-two years, his impact on India and on Hinduism cannot be stressed enough. He reintroduced a purer form of Vedic thought. His teachings and tradition form the basis of Smartism and have influenced Sant Mat lineages. He is the main figure in the tradition of Advaita Vedanta. He is the founder of the *Dashanami Sampradaya* of Hindu monasticism and *Shanmata* tradition of worship. He travelled all over India (Kerala to Kashmir and Nepal) three times over and was a major cause in the revival and integration of Sanatana Dharma. The mathas he founded are very much active today and form a major guiding force for Hinduism.

Adi Shankara, along with Madhva and Ramanuja, was instrumental in the revival of Hinduism. These three teachers formed the doctrines that are followed by their respective sects even today. They have been the most important figures in the recent history of Hindu philosophy. In their writings and debates, they provided polemics against the non-Vedantic schools of Sankhya, Vaisheshika etc. Thus they paved the way for Vedanta to be the dominant and most widely followed tradition among the schools of Hindu philosophy.

The Vedanta school stresses most on the Upanishads (which are themselves called Vedanta, *End or culmination of the Vedas*), unlike the other schools that gave importance to texts authored by their founders. The Vedanta schools have the belief that the Vedas, which include the Upanishads, are unauthored, forming a continuous tradition of wisdom transmitted orally. Thus the concept of *apaurusheyatva* (being unauthored) came to be the guiding force behind the Vedanta schools. However, along with stressing the importance of Vedic tradition, Adi Shankara gave equal importance to the personal experience of the student also. Logic, grammar, Mimamsa and allied subjects also form main areas of study in all the Vedanta schools.

Cultural Expansion in South-East Asia

During the 1st century, the trade on the overland Silk Road tended to be restricted by the rise in the Middle-East of the Parthian empire, an unvanquished enemy of Rome, just as Romans were becoming extremely wealthy and their demand for Asian luxury was rising. This demand revived the sea connections between the Mediterranean and China, with India as the intermediary of choice. From that time, through trade connection, commercial settlements, and even political interventions, India started to strongly influence Southeast Asian countries. Trade routes linked India with southern Burma, central and southern Siam, lower Cambodia and southern Vietnam, and numerous urbanized coastal settlements were established there.

For more than a thousand years, Indian influence was therefore the major factor that brought a certain level of cultural unity to the various countries of the region. The Pali and Sanskrit languages and the Indian script, together with Theravada and Mahayana Buddhism, Brahmanism, and Hinduism, were transmitted from direct contact and through sacred texts and Indian literature such as the Ramayana and the Mahabharata.

From the 5th to the 13th century, South-East Asia had very powerful empires and became extremely active in Buddhist architectural and artistic creation. The Sri Vijaya Empire to the south and the Khmer Empire to the north competed for influence.

Southeast Asian Hindu Kingdoms

Langkasuka (*-langkha* Sanskrit for "resplendent land"- *sukkha* of "bliss") was an ancient kingdom Hindu located in the Malay Peninsula. The kingdom along with Old Kedah are probably the earliest kingdom founded on the Malay Peninsula. According to tradition the founding of the kingdom happened in the 2nd century. Malay legends claim that Langkasuka was founded at Kedah, and later moved to Pattani.

Pan is a lost Hindu Kingdom believed to be exist around 3rd-5th Century CE somewhere in Kelantan or Terengganu, Malaysia.

Gangga Negara was believed to be a lost Hindu kingdom somewhere in the state of Perak, Malaysia, ruled by Raja Gangga Shah Johan. Researchers believed that the kingdom collapsed after an attack by King Rajendra Chola-I of Coromandel, South India, between 1025 and 1026.

From the 5th-15th centuries Sri Vijayan empire, a maritime empire centred on the island of Sumatra in Indonesia, had adopted Mahayana and Vajrayana Buddhism under a line of rulers named the Sailendras. The Empire of Sri Vijaya declined due to conflicts with the Chola rulers of India, before being destabilized by the Islamic invasion of India from the 13th century.

The Majapahit Empire succeeded the Singhasari Empire. It was one of the last and greatest Hindu empires in the Malay Archipelago.

Funan was a pre-Angkor Cambodian kingdom located around the Mekong delta, probably established by Mon-Khmer settlers speaking an Austro-Asiatic language. According to reports by two Chinese envoys, Kang Tai and Chu Ying, the state was established by an Indian Brahmin named Kaundinya, who in the first century CE, was given instruction in a dream to take a magic bow from a temple and defeat a Khmer queen, Soma. Soma, the daughter of the king of the Nagas, married Kaundinya and their lineage became the royal dynasty of Funan. The myth had the advantage of providing the legitimacy of both an Indian Brahmin and the divinity of the cobras, who at that time were held in religious regard by the inhabitants of the region.

The kingdom of Champa (or *Lin-yi* in Chinese records) controlled what is now south and central Vietnam from approximately 192 through 1697. The dominant religion of the Cham people was Hinduism and the culture was heavily influenced by India. Many Cham towers still stand in central Vietnam. The most significant example of Cham architecture is My Son near the Vietnamese city of Hoi An.

Later, from the 9th to the 13th century, the Mahayana Buddhist and Hindu Khmer Empire dominated much of the South-East Asian peninsula. Under the Khmer, more than 900 temples were built in Cambodia and in neighbouring Thailand. Angkor was at the centre of this development, with a temple complex and urban organization able to support around one million urban dwellers.

7

Hindu Religious Thought: Principles and Practices

Hindu religious thought embodies a variety of ideas, principles and practices, giving rise to various religious schools (*sampradayas*). Each school venerates the Supreme Deity, which represents a particular aspect of the Ultimate Reality (*Brahman*). Each school has temples, *guru* lineages, religious leaders, pilgrimage centres, monastic communities and sacred literature.

Some of these schools hold such divergent views that each appears to be a complete religion in itself. Yet, they all believe in the central doctrines of Hindu religion, such as *karma, dharma*, reincarnation, divinity of the *atman*, sacraments, deity worship, *guru-shishya* (teacher-disciple) tradition and the scriptural authority of the Vedas. None of these schools is in any way superior or inferior to the others. They simply represent different ways of approach to the same goal and are meant for various classes of people having different tastes, aptitudes, temperaments, and exhibiting various levels of spiritual development.

VEDANTA

The science of Vedanta is enshrined in the original spiritual texts of India. It is founded on the authority of the Upanishads, the *Bhagwad Gita* and the *Brahmasutram* of Badrayana Vyasa. Vedanta brings out the mystical, ethical and metaphysical aspects of philosophy. The abiding knowledge of Vedanta rests in the vision of the One Reality, a vision that transcends race, class, creed, gender and nationality. Vedanta is the one principle of truth encompassing all religions. There are three different philosophies on this concept. *Advaita* (non-duality) implies that there is an identity of Brahman and *Jiva atman* while *Dvaita* (duality) differs from *Advaita* and maintains an ultimate diversity between Brahman and *Jiva atman*. *Vishistadvaita* (qualified non-duality) maintains a crucial differentiation as well as a fundamental identity.

Advaita is the oldest extant school of Vedanta founded by Adi Shankaracharya. Advaita asserts that the real, essential identity of the *jiva*, the individual self, is nothing other than *Brahman* itself. It asserts that Brahman, the 'impersonal' God and the universal soul, is the Absolute Truth. Brahman has multiple roles to play: the creator, the maintainer, and the destroyer all in one. The teaching follows from the statements of the Upanishads (*Mahavakyas*) like *tat tvam asi* and *aham brahmasmi*. It is in this cardinal doctrine that *Advaita* differs from all other schools of Vedanta.

The *Vishishtadvaita* philosophy was expounded by Sri Ramanuja. According to this desirable qualities *viz.*, *satyam, jnanam* and *anandam*. The main exponent of the *Dvaita* philosophy was Sri Madhava (Purnaprajna). It says that the supreme goal of life is service of god.

Other systems which are not quite popular as the above mentioned philosophies include *Dvaitadvaita* (dual-non-dual doctrine), *Suddhadvaita* (pure non-dualism) and *Acinntyaa bhedabheda* (oneness and difference) were expounded by Nimbarka, Vallabha and Vidyabhusana respectively. All the above philosophers have written commentaries on the *Prasthana-traya* (triple canon) of the *Vedanta*, which are the *Upanishads*, *Brahma sutra* and the *Bhagwad Gita*.

The Hindu religious systems have been classified by Adi Shankaracharya into six major paths, called *Shad-maths*. These are *Shaivism*, *Vaishnavism*, *Shaktism*, *Ganapathyam*, *Kaumaram*, and *Sauram* or *Jyotiam*.

SHAIVISM

The followers of Shaivism venerate the Ultimate Reality as Lord Shiva. This tradition has been traced back by scholars to the Indus Valley Civilization. The archeologists have discovered the so-called proto-*Pasupathy* seals of this civilization, which depict Shiva as Lord *Pasupathy*, seated in a yogic pose. There are many schools of Shaivism, of which the six major systems are *Shaiva Siddhanta*, *Pashupata Shaivism*, Kashmir *Shaivism*, *Vira Shaivism*, *Siddha Siddhanta* and *Shiva Advaita*. These systems differ somewhat in their doctrines pertaining to the relationship between Shiva, the *Atman* and the world.

Most Hindus worship Lord Shiva as a member of the Hindu Trinity. However, the followers of Shaivism, called *Shaivas* or *Shaivites*, worship Him as the Ultimate Reality. The predominant philosophy of Shaivism is monistic-theism. According to this doctrine, Lord Shiva is both personal and impersonal. In the personal aspect, Shiva creates, controls and pervades all that exists. In this aspect, Shiva is what other religions call God. Shaivism declares that there is nothing outside Shiva and, thus, recognizes the oneness of *Pati-pau-pasa* (God-*Atman*-World). In the impersonal aspect, Shiva transcends all existence and in the liberated state the *Atman* is one with Shiva.

The main objects of Shiva worship are *shivalinga* and images of Shiva. The *linga* symbolizes both the creative and destructive power of the Lord and great sanctity is attached to it by the devotees. The *banalingas* are very sacred objects of worship to the followers of Shaivism. These are the elliptical stones of a special kind found in the bed of the river Narmada, one of the seven sacred rivers in India. Fresh flowers, pure water, young sprouts of *Kusha* (a holy grass) and *durva* (called bent or panic grass), fruit, *bilva* leaves and sun-dried rice are used in the ritual part of the Shiva worship.

According to tradition, offering leaves of the *bilva* tree (wood-apple) is considered very auspicious for the worship of Lord Shiva. *Mahashivaratri* (the great night of Shiva) is an annual festival that falls on the fourteenth day of the dark fortnight of *Phalguna* (February-March), and is dedicated to the worship of Lord Shiva. In mythology, Shiva is the husband of Parvati, the daughter of the Himalayas. They have two sons, Ganesha and Karttikeya and a daughter Jyoti. Their residence is the snow-clad mountain Kailash. The mythology depicts Shiva both as God of terror as well as benevolence. His five powers are revealment (offering grace to the devotees), concealment (obscuring by His power of *maya*), creation, preservation and dissolution. The major scriptures of Shaivism are Vedas, Shaiva Agamas and Shaiva Puranas.

VAISHNAVISM

Vaishnavism venerates the Ultimate Reality as Lord Vishnu. This tradition began during the Vedic period when its earliest schools *Pancharatra* and *Bhagavata* became popular around 300 BC. Modern day Vaishnavism includes five popular schools founded by Ramanuja, Madhva, Nimbarka, Vallabha and Chaitanya. Most Hindus worship Lord Vishnu as a member of the Hindu Trinity. However, the followers of Vaishnavism, called *Vaishnavas* or *Vaishnavites*, worship Lord Vishnu as the Ultimate Reality.

Although the philosophy of Vaishnavism includes dualism of Madhva, qualified dualism of Ramanuja, and nearly monistic views of Vallabha, the predominant philosophy of Vaishnavism is dualism. According to this doctrine, there are two categories of the Ultimate Reality. Lord Vishnu as personal God is the Absolute Reality, and the *Atmans* (individuals souls) are the relative realities, eternally distinct from each other and Lord Vishnu, but dependent on Him.

The doctrine of incarnation (*avatara*) is fundamental to all Hindus, especially to Vaishnavas. Lord Vishnu assumed each *avatara* for a particular end and as the situation demanded. The number of *avataras* of Lord Vishnu is generally accepted to be ten, with Rama and Krishna being the two most popular among Hindus.

Vaishnavism stresses on complete surrender (*prapatti*) to Lord Vishnu and His incarnations and advocates devotion (*bhakti*) as the highest spiritual discipline.

The objects of worship are the images of Lord Vishnu and His incarnations, and *salagramas*, small stones of different colours (predominantly black) recovered from the bed of the river Gandaki, one of the tributaries of the Ganges river in India. Fresh flowers, water, fruits and leaves of the *tulasi* plant are used in the ritual part of the worship of Lord Vishnu and His incarnations. One of the unique features of the Vaishnava worship is *kirtana*, which consists of choral singing of the names and deeds of Lord Vishnu and His incarnations, accompanied by drums and cymbals and synchronized with rhythmic bodily movements. The major scriptures of Vaishnavism are Vedas, Agamas, Puranas, Ramayana, Mahabharata and Bhagwad Gita.

SHAKTISM

Shakti means "creative energy," and *Shaktism* means "Doctrine of the Creative Energy." Shaktism venerates the Ultimate Reality as the Divine Mother-*Shakti* or *Devi*-of the universe.

Archeologists have recovered thousands of female statuettes at the Mehrgarh village in India, which indicate that Shakti worship existed in India as far back as 5500 BC. There are references to the female deities in the Rig Veda, including a popular Hymn to the Divine Mother, which holds special sanctity to Hindus in general and *Shaktas* (the followers of Shaktism) in particular.

Shaktism visualises the Ultimate Reality as having two aspects, transcendent and immanent. Shiva is the transcendent aspect, the supreme cosmic consciousness, and Shakti is the supreme creative energy. Shiva and Shakti are God and God's creative energy, which are inseparably connected. Metaphorically, Shiva and Shakti is an inseparable divine couple, representing the male and female principles in creation.

Shaktism greatly resembles Shaivism, but Shiva is considered solely transcendent and is not worshipped. Like Shaivism, the goal of Shaktism is to unite with Shiva. Such unity is possible only with the grace of the Divine Mother, who unfolds as *iccha shakti* (the power of desire, will and love), *kriya shakti* (the power of action), and *jnana shakti* (the power of knowledge and wisdom).

Within Shaktism, Shiva is the un-manifest Absolute and Shakti is the Divine Mother of the manifest creation. The Divine Mother is worshipped in both the fierce and benign forms. The fierce forms of Goddess include Kali, Durga, Chandi, Chamundi, Bhadrakali and Bhairavi. The benign forms of Goddess include Uma, Gauri, Ambika, Parvati, Maheshvari,

Lalita, Lakshmi, Saraswata and Annapurna. The major scriptures of Shaktism are *Vedas*, *Shakta agamas* and *Puranas*.

Ganapathyam

Ganesha, the elephant-headed deity, represents that aspect of the Ultimate Reality which removes obstacles. Hindus, therefore, invoke Lord Ganesha at the beginning of all undertakings, whether religious, spiritual or worldly, for Lord Ganesha removes obstacles and brings success to the enterprise. Ganesha is also called *Vighneshvara*, meaning "the Lord presiding over the obstacles." In the Rig Veda, Ganesha is the name of *Brihapati*, the Lord of prayer (the Holy Word). In mythology Ganesha is the first son of the divine couple Shiva and Parvati.

Ganapatyas, followers of Ganapathyam, venerate Lord Ganesha exclusively as the form of the Ultimate Reality (*Brahman*) that is accessible to the mind, senses and (through devotional practices) the heart. Ganapatyas regard Moraya Gosavi (1651 AD), the famous devotee of Ganesha, as their spiritual progenitor. Tradition holds that Moraya experienced a series of visions of Ganesha at a shrine at Moragaon, near Pune. An annual ten-day festival, *Ganesha Chaturthi*, is held in August-September to celebrate the birth of Ganesha. The major scriptures of this tradition are Vedas, Skanda Purana, and Mudgala Purana.

8

Rigveda

There are some words in the Rigveda which have been misinterpreted as names of Kings or Rishis (often because some of these words were also the names or epithets of Rishis in later parts of the text), thereby causing confusion in Rigvedic interpretation.

The exact nature of these words has, therefore, to be clarified. These words are:

A.Atri.

B.Kutsa.

C.Ausija.

D.Trksi.

E.Atithigva.

Atri: Atri is the name of a Rsi, the eponymous founder of the Atri family of Mandala V. His name is referred to in the following hymns (not counting references, to him, or to themselves, by the Atris):

I.45.3; 51.3; 139.9; 183.5; V.15.5; VIII.5.25; X.150.5

However, the word Atri existed *before* the period of this Rsi, *as a name or epithet of the Sun*, which was the original meaning of this word. The Rsi of this name came later.

We will be concerned here only with the references to this mythical Atri, the Sun. These references are found in 15 hymns:

I. 112.7, 16; 116.8; 117.3; 118.7; 119.6; 180.4; II. 8.5; V. 40.6-9; 78.4; VI. 50.10; VII. 68.5; 71.5; X. 39.9; 80.3; 143.1, 3.

The word in the above references is confused by scholars with the name of the Rsi Atri.

However, it is clear that there is a mythical Atri in the Rigveda distinct from the historical Atri, and, for that matter, a mythical Kutsa distinct from the historical Kutsa: Macdonell, in his Vedic Mythology, classifies Atri and Kutsa alongwith "Mythical Priests and Heroes" like Manu, Bhrgu, Atharvana, Dadhyanc, ANgiras, Navagvas, Dasagvas and Usana, whom he distinguishes from "several other ancient seers of a historical or semi-historical character... such (as) Gautama, Vishvamitra, Vamadeva, Bharadvaja and Vasishtha".

That this mythical Atri is distinct from the historical Atri, and the myth existed long before the birth of this historical Rishis confirmed by an examination of the references: we find that these references undergo a complete transformation in Mandala V, affected by Rishis of the Atri family in a deliberate attempt to try and appropriate the myth for themselves by identifying the mythical Atri with the eponymous Atri, their ancestor.

This, on the one hand, shows up an interesting aspect of the family psychology of the Rishis, and, on the other, confirms our chronological order of the Mandalas.

The references fall into three categories:

1. References in older Mandalas (VI, VII, II) where Atri is a name of the Sun.
2. References in Mandala V where Atri the Sun is deliberately transformed into Atri the Rsi, as part of two new myths.
3. References in later Mandalas (I, X) where the Rsi Atri is fully identified with the mythical Atri in a transformed myth.

To elaborate:

1. VI.50.10 and VII.71.5 refer to the Asvins rescuing Atri from "great darkness". As Griffith points out in his footnote to VII.71.5: "The reappearance, heralded by the Asvins or Gods of Twilight, of the departed Sun, appears to be symbolised in all these legends."

   VII.68.5 also refers to the same natural phenomenon,

the gradual appearance of the Sun at dawn, in a different way: it credits the Asvins with making Atri (the Sun) increasingly bright and glorious with food and nourishment from their rich store.

II.8.5 does not refer to the Asvins. It uses the word Atri as an epithet for Agni (who is literally the earthly representative of the Sun). The epithet is clearly a repetition of a simile in the previous verse, II.8.4, where also Agni is likened to the Sun (Bhanu).

2. Two references by the Atris bifurcate the original myth into two distinct myths, both connected up with their eponymous ancestor.

   In the original myth, the Asvins rescue Atri, the Sun, from "great darkness".

   In the two transformed myths:

   a. The Asvins rescue Atri, the Rsi, from a pit or cavern: V.78.4.
   b. Atri, the Rsi, rescues the Sun from "great darkness": V.40.6-9.

   In V.78.4, Atri, lying in a deep pit or cavern, calls out to the Asvins for help, and is rescued by them from his distress.

   In V.40.6-9, the Sun has been pierced "through and through with darkness" by a demon called Svarbhanu (literally "sky-sun"), and all creatures stand bewildered and frightened by the sight. Atri, however, by his Brahmanic powers, "discovered Surya concealed in gloom", and, with the same powers, "established the eye of Surya in the heavens". The hymn smugly concludes: "The Atris found the Sun again... This none besides had power to do."

3. All the eleven references (in nine hymns) in the later Mandalas (i.e. in late upa-mandalas of Mandala I, and in Mandala X) reflect one of the two transformed versions of the myth:

   They refer to the Rsi Atri being rescued (X.143.1, 3) from a fiery, burning pit (I.112.7, 16; 116.8; 11 8.7; 119.6; 180.4; X.39.9; 80.3), or simply a pit (I.117.3), by the Asvins.

> The "fiery, burning pit" of the transformed myth is clearly incompatible with the "great darkness" of the original nature-myth.

Kutsa: Kutsa is the name of a Rsi, the eponymous ancestor of the Kutsa Rishis of Mandala I. His name is referred to in the following hymns: VII.25.5; X.29.2; 38.5.

However, the word Kutsa existed before the period of this Rsi, *as a name or epithet of Vajra, the thunderbolt*, which was the original meaning of this word. The Rsi of this name came later.

We will, again, be concerned here only with the references to this mythical Kutsa, the thunderbolt. These references are found in 24 hymns:

I. 33.14; 51.6; 63.3; 106.6; 112.9, 23; 121.9; 174.5; 175.4;
II. 19.6;
IV. 16.10-12; 26.1; 30.4;
V. 29.9, 10; 31.8;
VI. 20.5; 26.3; 31.3;
VII. 19.2;
VIII. 1.11; 24.25;
X. 40.6; 49.3, 4; 99.9; 138.1.

The word in the above references is confused by the scholars with the name of the Rsi Kutsa. It is true that, in this case, there is more of an excuse for this confusion: while the mythical Atri is not a very personalized or anthropomorphised figure in the early references (before the Atris play their sleight of hand), the mythical Kutsa is a highly anthropomorphised form of the thunderbolt from the very beginning.

However, the confusion has been only in the minds of the interpreters of the hymns. The composers were under no delusions about the identity of this mythical Kutsa, and the evidence identifying this Kutsa with the thunderbolt is overwhelming:

1. The Naighantuka (2.20) gives *Kutsa* as one of the synonyms of *Vajra* (the thunderbolt).
2. Kutsa is given the epithet Arjuneya in four of the above hymns (I.112.23; IV.26.1; VII. 19.2; VIII.1.11). This is

wrongly interpreted as a patronymic of the Rsi Kutsa. Actually, this is an epithet signifying the white flash of the thunderbolt.

In another verse, III.44.5 (which does not refer to Kutsa), *arjunam*, "the Bright", is given as a synonym of *vajram*.

3. All the references to the mythical Kutsa (except the two by the Kutsas themselves: I.106.6; 112.9, 23) refer directly or indirectly to a celestial battle between Indra, the thunder-god, and Susna, the demon of drought whose other epithet is *kuyava*, "bad grain". (Two of the verses, IV.26.1 and X.40.6, only *mention* Kutsa, and do not refer to this battle, but other factors show that it is the mythical Kutsa who is being referred to.)

   The place of Kutsa in these references can be understood only on the basis of his identity as the personified form of Indra's thunderbolt:

   a. In three references, Indra kills the demon *with* Kutsa (*kutsena*) as with a weapon: IV.16.11; V.29.9; VI.31.3.

   b. In most of the references, however, Indra is represented as doing the deed of killing the demon *for* Kutsa, or *in aid* of Kutsa. There is, however, a coherent mythological explanation for the conversion of Kutsa from the *instrument* of the deed to its *beneficiary*:

      Six of the above references refer to the chariot-wheel of the Sun: I.174.5; 175.4; IV.16.12; 30.4; V.29.9; VI.31.3. In his footnote to I.175.4, Griffith explains that "Indra is said to have taken the wheel of the chariot of the Sun, and to have cast it like a quoit against the demon of drought". This was done, as per IV.30.4, "for... Kutsa, as he battled" (against the demon of drought).

      In another hymn (which does not refer to Kutsa), there is again a reference to this use of the chariot-wheel of the Sun. Here, in his footnote to I.130.9, Griffith provides the myth in greater detail, albeit in a later evolved form: *"He tore the Sun's wheel off*: according to Sayana, Brahma had promised the

Asuras or fiends that Indra's thunderbolt should never destroy them. Indra, accordingly cast at them the wheel of the Sun's chariot and slew them therewith." In short: as the thunderbolt (Kutsa) was proving to be ineffectual as it battled against the demon of drought, Indra despatched the chariot-wheel of the Sun to its aid.

c. In two of the references, Kutsa is even referred to as the charioteer of Indra: II.19.6; VI.20.5.

The connotation of Indra's "chariot" is clear in the Rigveda: Indra's chariot is the thunderbolt on which he streaks across the sky. The Bhrgus are credited in the Rigveda with the manufacture of Indra's thunderbolt: in IV. 16.20, they are described as the manufacturers of Indra's chariot.

The sense of Kutsa being Indra's charioteer is therefore clear: the thunderbolt is Indra's chariot, and the anthropomorphised form of the thunderbolt is Indra's charioteer.

4. The identity between the mythical Kutsa and Indra's thunderbolt should have been clear to the scholars:

Griffith, for example, describes Kutsa in his various footnotes as "the particular friend of Indra" (I.33.14); "a favourite of Indra" (I.112.23); "favourite of Indra" (II.19.6); "the favoured friend of Indra" (IV.16.10); "the special friend of Indra" (VI.31.3); "Indra's favourite companion" (X.29.2).

But, wherever there is a reference to Indra's "friend" within the hymns themselves, and no names are mentioned, Griffith, in his footnotes, has no doubt as to the identity of this friend: "*Thy friend*: probably the vajra or thunderbolt, which is Indra's inseparable associate and ally" (1.10.9); "*With thy friend*: the thunderbolt" (1.53.7); "*His friend*: his constant companion, the thunderbolt" (X 50.2).

Griffith's conclusion is based on a direct statement in VI.21.7: "With thy own ancient friend and companion, the thunderbolt..."

In the circumstance, it is strange that no scholar has

seen fit to think twice before deciding that the Kutsa, who is Indra's favourite friend and companion, could be a human Rsi.

5. The *only* other name in the Rigveda identified by Griffith in his footnotes as that of a friend of Indra, in a similar manner, is that of Usana Kavya: "the especial friend of Indra" (I.51.10; IV.16.2); "Indra's special friend" (V.29.9); "a favoured friend and companion of Indra" (X.22.6); "Indra's friend" (X.49.3).

   What is significant is that Usana is referred to five times in the same verse as Kutsa (VI.26.1; V.29.9; 31.8; X.49.3; 99.9) and five times in the same hymn (Kutsa: I.51.6; 121.9; IV. 16. 10-12; VI.20.5; X.40.6; Usana: I.51.10-11; 121.12; IV.16.2; VI.20.11; X.40.7).

   When we consider that there are 1028 hymns and 10552 verses in the Rigveda, and that the mythical Kutsa and Usana are referred to in only 29 verses and 19 verses respectively, the number of hymns and verses they share in common is too significant to be coincidental. Clearly, Kutsa and Usana share a close and special relationship. And what is this close and special relationship? The Rigveda is very clear at least about the nature of the close and special relationship between Indra and Usana: Usana Kavya is mythically credited with being the (Bhrgu) person who manufactured the *Vajra* or thunderbolt, and gave it to Indra for his weapon (I.51.10; 121.12; V.34.2).

   The nature of the close and special relationship between Usana, Indra and Kutsa is therefore clear: they are, respectively, the manufacturer, wielder, and personification of the thunderbolt.

6. Curiously, in a clear case of imitation of the Atris, we find here also a blatant attempt by the Kutsas to transform the myth so as to connect it up with their eponymous ancestor.

But while the transformation by the Atris is effected by bifurcating the original Atri myth into two different myths, the transformation by the Kutsas is effected by taking the original Kutsa myth, and the more successful of the two transformed

Atri myths, grafting them together, and then bifurcating them into two different myths:

In the original Kutsa myth, Indra aids the mythical Kutsa in a celestial battle.

In the transformed Atri myth, the Asvins rescue the Rsi Atri from a pit.

In the two transformed Kutsa myths:

a. Indra rescues the Rsi Kutsa *from a pit*: I.106.6 (which is also the only hymn which emphatically calls Kutsa a "Rsi").
b. The Asvins aid the Rsi Kutsa (in a battle? But this is not specified. Note: this is the only hymn in which Indra is replaced by the Asvins): I.112.9, 23.

This transformation of the original myth by the Kutsas is too clumsy, and too late in the day, to influence other references in the Rigveda, unlike the transformation of the Atri myth by the Atris, where the transformed myth becomes the basis for all subsequent references.

And the objective behind this transformation is far more modest than the objective of the Atris: while the Atris seek to glorify their eponymous ancestor by usurping the original deed of the Asvins and crediting their ancestor with supernatural powers, the Kutsas seem content merely with identifying their eponymous ancestor with the mythical Kutsa of earlier references.

But the transformation serves to underline the fact that the original mythical Kutsa originally had nothing to do with the Rsi Kutsa.

Besides the Rsi Kutsa and the mythical Kutsa, there is a third Kutsa in the Rigveda who is referred to in four hymns: I.53.10; II.14.7; VI.18.13; X.83.5.

We will examine these references in the course of our examination of the word Atithigva.

Ausija: Ausija is an epithet of the Rsi Kaksivan, who is called Kaksivan *Ausija* Dairghatamas in the Anukramanis, and whose descendants are considered as forming a third major branch of the Angiras family (after the Bharadvajas and Gotamas), the Ausijas.

In the Rigveda, however, this is neither the exclusive nor the original meaning of the word. In its original meaning, Ausija is *a name of the Sun.*

The word is referred to in the following hymns:

I.18.1; 112.11; 119.9; 122.4, 5; IV.21.6, 7; V.41.5; VI.4.6; X.99.11;

The references may be examined in three groups:

1. *The Family Mandalas:*
   a. VI.4.6: Agni is compared with the Sun. Agni spreads over both the worlds with splendour "like Surya with his fulgent rays", and dispels the darkness "like Ausija with clear flame swiftly flying".
   b. IV.21.6-8 (the word Ausija is not repeated in verse 8): Indra unbars the spaces of the mountains (i.e. the rain-clouds) and lets loose "his floods, the water-torrents" which are lying hidden in "Ausija's abode" (analogous to "Vivasvan's dwelling" in I.53.1; III.34.7; 51.3; X.75.1; aspecially X.75.1 which also refers to the Waters.)
   c. V.41.5: Atri is the priest of Ausija.

The meaning of Ausija is very clear from the above references. In the case of VI.4.6, Sayana recognizes Ausija as a name of the Sun. However, Griffith disagrees and feels instead that Ausija in VI.4.6 is "some contemporary priest who is regarded as bringing back the daylight by prayer and sacrifice". In the case of V.41.5, all scholars, from Sayana to Griffith, are in agreement that Atri is "the ministrant priest of Kaksivan, the son of Usij". According to these scholars, then, Ausija is a Rsi (Kaksivan) who dispels darkness with a clear flame flying in the sky, whose abode is the place (i.e. the sky) where rain-clouds store their water-torrents, and who has another Rsi, Atri, as his priest! The absurdity of the above ideas is self-evident. Clearly, it is the Sun being referred to in all the above references: V.40, as we have already seen, makes it very clear that the Atris consider themselves to be special priests of the Sun.

2. *Mandala I*

All the references to Ausija in Mandala I are in the

general and late upa-mandalas. Here, it is clear, the word is an epithet of Kaksivan: it is used in that sense in I.18.1; 119.9; 122.4, 5.

In I.112.11, it is used as an epithet of Dirghasravas, who is referred to as a merchant. However, Kaksivan is also referred to in the same verse, and it is natural to assume that the epithet applies to both of them.

3. *Mandala X*

On the basis of the references in Mandala 1, the scholars erroneously assume that Ausija is a patronymic of Kaksivan, rather than an epithet. Hence they presume the existence of an ancestor named Usij.

The single occurrence of this word in Mandala X disproves this presumption: in X.99.11, Ausija is an epithet of Rjisvan, who belongs to the Bharadvaja branch of the Angiras family.

Even Griffith realizes that the explanation of Ausija as a patronymic does not fit the case here: "*Ausija*: son of Usij. But as this patronymic does not properly belong to Rjisvan, the word here may perhaps mean 'vehement' 'eagerly desirous'."

What the scholars do not realize is that the explanation of Ausija as a patronymic does not fit the case anywhere: Ausija is the Sun in the Family Mandalas, and an epithet in later Mandalas: an epithet of Kaksivan in Mandala I and Rjisvan in (the single use of the word in) Mandala X.

Trksi: Trksi is the name of a tribe: the tribe to which Purukutsa and Trasadasyu belong, and hence equivalent to the Iksvakus of traditional history.

The word occurs only twice in the Rigveda: VI.46.8; VIII.22.7.

This name is wrongly interpreted as the name of a King on the basis of VIII.22.7, which is translated as: "Come to us, Lords of ample wealth, by paths of everlasting Law; Whereby to high dominion ye with mighty strength raised Trksi, Trasadasyu's son."

However, VI.46.8 makes it very clear that Trksi is the name of a *tribe* and not a person. The following is a translation of VI.46.7-8: "All strength and valour that is found, Indra, in tribes of Nahusas, and all the splendid fame that the Five tribes enjoy, bring all manly powers, at once. Or, Maghavan, what vigorous strength in Trksi lay, in Druhyus or in Puru's folk, fully bestow on us that, in the conquering fray, we may subdue our foes in fight."

On Trksi, Griffith comments: "*Trksi*: a King so named, says Sayana." However, it is clear that it is only tribes who are being referred to: the idea that the name of one King could be included in a list of tribes is based purely on the interpretation of VIII.22.7.

However, the interpretation of VIII.22.7 is wrong the phrase "Trksim... Trasadasyavam" is to be translated, *not* as "Trksi, Trasadasyu's son", but as "*the* Trksi, Trasadasyu's son". The name of the son is not specified, and he is referred to only by his patronymic, as in the case of so many other references in the Rigveda: eg. Pratardani (V1.26.8, son of Pratardana), Saryata (I.51.12; III.51.3, son of Saryata) and so on.

Atithigva: The word Atithigva is found in thirteen hymns in the Rigveda: I. 51.6; 53.8, 10; 112.14; 130.7; II. 14.7; IV. 26.3; VI. 18.13; 26.3; 47.22; VII. 19.8; VIII. 53.2; 68.16, 17; X. 48.8.

There is no general misinterpretation as such of this word. However, a clarification of the different meanings of the word will be in order here:

1. Atithigva is an epithet of Divodasa in five hymns: I.112.14; 130.7; IV.26.3; VI.26.3 (Divodasa 26.5); 47.22.

   This is also likely to be the case in one more hymn: I.51.6, which refers to Sambara (who is associated in numerous other references, including in four of the above ones, with Divodasa).
2. But in four hymns, Atithigva is an epithet of a *descendant* of Sudas (while Divodasa is an *ancestor* of Sudas: VII.18.25): I.53.8; VII.19.8: VIII.68.16, 17; X.48.8.

   Hymn VII.19 is a late hymn interpolated into Mandala VII, as we have seen in our earlier discussion on the Trksi interpolations, and it pertains to the late period of Mandala VIII. This hymn refers to Sudas as an ancient figure from the past, while it refers to the second Atithigva in the eighth verse as a contemporary figure. Griffith notes that this Atithigva is "probably a descendant of Sudas who must have lived long before the composition of this hymn".

In VIII.68.16, 17, as well, this Atithigva is a near contemporary figure: his son Indrota is the patron of the Rsi of this hymn.

I.53.8 and X.48.8 refer to the victory of this Atithigva over Karanja and Parnaya, who are not referred to elsewhere in the Rigveda.

The fact that Atithigva represents three different entities in the Rigveda is accepted by many scholars. Keith and Macdonell, in their *Vedic Index of Names and Subjects*, note that "Roth distinguishes three Atithigvas-the Atithigva Divodasa, the enemy of Pàrnaya and Karanja, and the enemy of Turvayana". Keith and Macdonell themselves appear to disagree: "But the various passages can be reconciled." However, actually, their own interpretation must also show three Atithigvas, since, even within the favourable references to Atithigva, they admit that while the word refers "in nearly all cases to the same king, otherwise called Divodasa", nevertheless "a different Atithigva appears to be referred to in a Danastuti ('Praise of Gifts') where his son Indrota is mentioned".

3. Finally, there is the third Atithigva who is referred to in four hymns: I.53.10; II.14.7; VI.18.13; VIII.53.2.

This Atithigva is clearly not the hero of the references. All the four references relate to the defeat of Kutsa, Ayu and Atithigva at the hands of (according to I.53.10 and VI.18.13) Turvayana.

These references, if taken at face value, are *absolutely incompatible* with *all* other information in the Rigveda: all the other references to both Atithigva and Kutsa are favourable ones, while these references are clearly hostile ones in their exultation at their defeat. What is more, I.53.8 exults in Atithigva's *victory* over Karanja and Parnaya, while two verses later, I.53.10 exults in Atithigva's *defeat* at the hands of Turvayana. Clearly, two different Atithigvas are being referred to. And this second Atithigva is compulsorily to be taken in combination with a Kutsa (obviously a different one from the Rsi Kutsa as well as the mythical Kutsa, the thunderbolt) and an Ayu (otherwise the name of an ancestral figure)

These references present an insoluble problem for all scholars engaged in a historical study of the Rigveda. Sayana, for example, tries to twist the meaning of the references in order to bring them in line with other references: Griffith notes, in his footnote to VI.18.13, that "Sayana represents the exploit as having been achieved *for* Kutsa, Ayu and Atithigva, but this is not the meaning of the words of the text".

Sayana's attempt to twist the meaning of the references is partly based on his knowledge of the identity of Turvayana: as Griffith notes, "according to Sayana, *Turvayana*, 'quickly going', is an epithet of Divodasa". But Atithigva is also an epithet of Divodasa.

Hence Sayana finds what he probably considers to be an internal contradiction within the references; and the only way he can resolve this contradiction is by assuming, *against* the actual meaning of the words of the text, that Kutsa, Ayu and Atithigva must be the heroes of the references.

We have the following rational (if speculative) solution to offer towards the elucidation of these seemingly senseless references:

a. Atithigva, as we have seen, is the epithet of an ancestor of Sudas (i.e. Divodasa), as well as of a descendant. A natural inference is that Atithigva was a common epithet of Kings of the Bharata dynasty.

b. The word Kutsa (apart from its identity as a synonym of the thunderbolt) is found in the Rigveda in the names of two persons: the King Purukutsa and the Rsi Kutsa. Purukutsa is a King of the Trksi (Iksvaku) dynasty; and the Rsi Kutsa, as per tradition (outside the Rigveda), was also the son of an Iksvaku king. On the analogy of Atithigva, Kutsa may then have been a common epithet of Kings of the Trksi dynasty.

c. There are many references in the Rigveda where tribes are named in combinations purely in a figurative sense, often with special reference to their geographical locations, in order to indicate generality or universality.

Thus, VIII. 10.5: "Whether ye Lords of ample wealth (Asvins) now linger in the east or west, with Druhyu, or with Anu, Yadu, Turvasa, I call you hither, come to me."

Or I.108.8: "If with the Yadus, Turvasas ye sojourn, with Druhyus, Anus, Purus, Indra-Agni! Even from thence, ye mighty Lords, come hither, and drink libations of the flowing Soma." However, the reference relevant to us is VI.46.7-8, which we have already seen earlier: "All strength and valour that is found, Indra, in tribes of Nahusas, and all the splendid fame that the Five tribes enjoy, bring all manly powers at once. Or, Maghavan, what vigorous strength in Trksi lay, in Druhyus or in Puru's folk, fully bestow on us, that, in the conquering fray, we may subdue our foes in fight."

The above is Griffith's translation. The meaning is: "Indra give us the strength and power of the tribes of Nahusas: the five tribes (Yadus, Turvasas, Druhyus, Anus, Purus). Give us the strength and power of all the tribes: the Trksis (in the east), the Druhyus (in the west) and the Purus (in the centre), that we may be invincible in battle." Here, clearly the Trksis in the east, the Druhyus in the west, and the Purus in the centre, when named together, signify "all the tribes".

The same symbolism is probably expressed in the naming together of Kutsa, Ayu and Atithigva. The three names probably represent the common epithets of the Kings of the Trksis, the Druhyus and the Purus (i.e. Bharatas); and when taken in combination, they mean "all the tribes".

Therefore, what the four references mean is: "Indra is the Lord of all peoples and lands"; or, in two of them: "Indra made Turvayana (Divodasa) the sovereign of all the tribes.".

In conclusion: we have conducted a full examination and analysis of the Rigveda from all the relevant angles, namely:

1. The interrelationships among the composers.
2. The references to composers within the hymns.
3. The references to Kings and Rishis.
4. The family structure of the Mandalas.
5. The system of ascription of hymns in the Mandalas.

The chronological picture that we obtain, jointly and severally, in other words unanimously, from all these angles is that the chronological order of the Mandalas is: VI, III, VII, IV, II, V, VIII, IX, X (The upa-mandalas of Mandala I covering the periods of Mandalas IV, II, V, VIII).

THE GEOGRAPHY OF THE RIGVEDA

The internal chronology of the Rigveda being firmly established, the next step in our historical analysis of the Rigveda is the establishment of the geography of the text.

The geography of the Rigveda has been the most misrepresented aspect of the text in the hands of the scholars: the geographical information in the Rigveda, to put it in a nutshell, more or less pertains to the area from Uttar Pradesh in the east to Afghanistan in the west, the easternmost river mentioned in the text being the Ganga, and the westernmost being the western tributaries of the Indus.

This geographical information is treated in a simplistic manner by the scholars, and the result is a completely distorted picture of Rigvedic geography:

1. Firstly, taking the, Rigveda as one monolithic unit, the information is interpreted to mean that the area of the Rigveda extended from western Uttar Pradesh to Afghanistan.

   It is further assumed that the habitat of the Vedic Aryans, during the period of composition of the Rigveda, was the central part of this area: the Saptasindhu or Punjab, the Land of the Five Rivers bounded on the east by the Saraswati and on the west by the Indus. Their eastern horizon was western Uttar Pradesh and their western horizon was Afghanistan.

   The consensus on this point is so general that even in our *own* earlier book dealing with the Aryan invasion theory, where we have *not* yet analysed the Rigveda in detail, we have automatically assumed the Punjab to be the habitat of the Vedic Aryans during the period of the Rigveda.

   However, as we shall see in the course of our analysis, the habitat of the Vedic Aryans during the period was considerably to the *east* of the Punjab.

2. Secondly, after taking the Punjab to be the habitat of the Rigvedic Aryans, the matter is not left at that. A further slant is introduced into the interpretation of the geographical data in the Rigveda: it is automatically assumed, on the basis of an extraneous theory based on

a misinterpretation of linguistic data, and without any basis within the Rigvedic data itself, that a movement from west to east is to be discerned in the Rigveda.

Thus, western places within the horizon of the Rigveda are treated as places old and familiar to the Vedic Aryans, being their "early habitats"; while eastern places within the horizon of the Rigveda are treated as new and unfamiliar places with which the Vedic Aryans are "becoming acquainted".

The same goes for places *outside* the horizon of the Rigveda (i.e. places *not* named in the Rigveda): places to the west of Afghanistan, not named in the Rigveda, are treated as places which have been "forgotten" by the Vedic Aryans; while places to the east of western Uttar Pradesh, not named in the Rigveda, are treated as places "still unknown" to the Vedic Aryans.

3. Thirdly, and as a direct corollary to the above, it is automatically assumed that there was a movement of place-names as well from west to east.

   There are three rivers named in the Rigveda to which this applies: the Saraswati, Gomati and Sarayu. The Saraswati in the Rigveda is the river to the *east* of the Punjab (flowing through Haryana) and the Gomati and Sarayu in the Rigveda are rivers to the west of the Punjab (western tributaries of the Indus). This is the general consensus, and it is confirmed by an examination of the references in the Rigveda.

   But a Saraswati (Haraxvaiti) and a Sarayu (Haroiiu) are also found in Afghanistan; and a Gomati and a Sarayu are found in northeastern Uttar Pradesh. Clearly, there has been a transfer of name, in the case of these three river-names, from one river to another.

   The logical procedure would be to suspend judgement, till further evidence is forthcoming, as to the locations of the rivers which originally bore these three names.

   A second, and slightly less logical, procedure, would be to automatically assume that the Rigvedic rivers originally bore all the three names, since the oldest recorded occurrence of the three names is in the Rigveda.

However, a west-to-east movement is assumed in respect of all three names, and consequently, the westernmost rivers bearing the three names are taken to be the original bearers of those names.

4. Thus far, the distortion in interpretation and presentation of the geographical data in the Rigveda is still relatively mild. It is in fact too mild for some extremist scholars who would like to present a more definitive picture of a west-to-east movement into India.

Some of these scholars attempt to connect stray words in the Rigveda, *often words not even having any geographical context*, with places far to the west of the horizon of the Rigveda: an extreme example of this is the attempt to suggest that a root word *rip*-in the Rigveda indicates a subdued memory of the Rhipaean mountains: the Urals.

Some scholars, not satisfied with the idea that the Vedic Aryans *came* from the west, attempt to show that they were *still* in the west even during the period of composition of the Rigveda: the Saptasindhu, it is suggested by some, refers to seven rivers in Central Asia, and the Saraswati in the Rigveda is *not* the river of Haryana, but the river of Afghanistan.

There is even an extreme lunatic fringe which would like to suggest that the Ganga and Yamuna of the Rigveda are rivers in Afghanistan. A political "scholar", Rajesh Kochhar, as part of a concerted campaign to show that the events in the Ramayana took place in Afghanistan, transfers the entire locale of the epic to Afghanistan: "Ravana's Lanka can be a small island in the midst of river Indus... by Vindhyas is meant Baluch hills, and by sea the Lower Indus." He does this under cover of examining the geography of the Rigveda, in his book, *The Vedic People: Their History and Geography* (Orient Longman, New Delhi, 1999), where he decides that in the Ramayana (which he examines for the geography of the Rigveda), Saraswati is identified with Helmand and Ganga and Yamuna as its tributaries in the hilly areas of Afghanistan. He makes this revolutionary discovery on the basis of a verse in the Valmiki Ramayana (2.65.6) where "Yamuna is described as surrounded by mountains".

This is the level to which "scholarship" can stoop, stumble

and fall. In this book, we will examine the geography of the Rigveda, *not* on the basis of interpretations of verses from the Valmiki Ramayana or the Hanuman Calisa, but on the basis of the actual geographical data within the hymns and verses of the Rigveda itself, under the following heads:

I. The Rigvedic Rivers.
II. The Evidence of River-names.
III. The Evidence of Place-names.
IV. The Evidence of Animal-names.
Appendix: The So-called Negative Evidence.

THE RIGVEDIC RIVERS

The rivers named in the Rigveda can be classified into five geographical categories:

1. *The Northwestern Rivers (i.e. western tributaries of the Indus, flowing through Afghanistan and the north):*
   Trstama (Gilgit)
   Susartu
   Anitabha
   Rasa
   Sveti
   Kubha (Kabul)
   Krumu (Kurrum)
   Gomati (Gomal)
   Sarayu (Siritoi)
   Mehatnu
   Svetyavarai
   Prayiyu (Bara)
   Vayiyu
   Suvastu (Swat)
   Gauri (Panjkora)
   Kusava (Kunar)
2. *The Indus and its minor eastern tributaries:*
   Sindhu (Indus)
   Susoma (Sohan)
   Arjikiya (Haro)

3. *The Central Rivers (i.e. rivers of the Punjab):*
   Vitasta (Jhelum)
   Asikni (Chenab)
   Parusni (Ravi)
   Vipas (Beas)
   Suturi (Satlaj)
   Marudvrdha (Maruvardhvan)
4. *The East-central Rivers (i.e. rivers of Haryana):*
   Saraswati
   DRSadvatI/Hariyupiya/Yavyavati
   Apaya
5. *The Eastern Rivers:*
   Asmanvati (Assan, a tributary of the Yamuna)
   Yamuna/Amsumati
   Ganga/Jahnnvi

A few words of clarification will be necessary in the case of the identities of some of these rivers:

1. *Hariyupiya / Yavyavati*: Hariyupiya is another name of the Drsadvati: the river is known as Raupya in the Mahabharata, and the name is clearly a derivative of Hariyupiya.

   The Yavyavati is named in the same hymn and context as the Hariyupiya, and almost all the scholars agree that both the names refers to the same river.

   It is also possible that Yavyavati may be another name of the Yamuna. M.L. Bhargava, in his study of Rigvedic Geography, incidentally (i.e. without making such an identification) makes the following remarks: "The old beds of the ancient Drsadvati and the Yamuna... ran very close to each other... the two rivers appear to have come close at a place about three miles southwest of Chacharauli town, but diverged again immediately after... the Yamuna... then again ran southwestwards almost parallel to the Drsadvati, the two again coming about two miles close to each other near old Srughna......"

The battle described on the Hariyupiya-Yavyavati may therefore have taken place in the area between these rivers.

However, pending further evidence (of this identity of Yavyavati with the Yamuna), we must assume, with the scholars, that the Yavyavati is the same as the Hariyupiya.

2. *Jahnnvi*: Jahnnvi, which is clearly another name of the Ganga, is named in two hymns; and in both of them, it is translated by the scholars as something other than the name of a river: Griffith translates it as "Jahnu's children" (I.116.19) and "the house of Jahnu" (III.58.6).

   The evidence, however, admits of only one interpretation:

   a. Jahnnvi is clearly the earlier Rigvedic form of the later word Jahnavi: the former word is not found after the Rigveda, and the latter word is not found in the Rigveda.

      The word clearly belongs to a class of words in the Rigveda which underwent a particular phonetic change in the course of time: *Jahnavi* in the Rigveda becomes *Jahnavi after* the Rigveda; *Brahmana* becomes *Brahmana* in the Rigveda itself (both words are found in the Rigveda while only the latter is found after the Rigveda); and the word *Pavaka* has already become *Pavaka* in the course of compilation of the Rigveda (only the latter form is found in the Rigveda, but according to B.K. Ghosh, "the evidence of the metres... clearly proves that the actual pronunciation of the word *Pavaka* must have been *Pavaka* in the Rigvedic age").

   b. The word Jahnavi (and therefore also the word Jahnavi which has no independent existence, and for which there is no alternative source of information since it is found only twice in the Rigveda and nowhere outside it) literally means "daughter of Jahnu", and not "Jahnu's children" or "the house of Jahnu".

      And the word Jahnavi (and therefore also Jahnavi as well) has only one connotation in the entire length and breadth of Sanskrit literature: it is a name of the Ganga.

c. One of the two references to the Jahnavi in the Rigveda provides a strong clue to the identity of this word: JahndvI (I. 116.19) is associated with the *Simsumara* (I.116.18) or the Gangetic dolphin. The dolphin is not referred to anywhere else in the Rigveda.

The Mandala-wise distribution of the names of the rivers in the Rigveda is as follows:

Early Mandala I

Saraswati: I.3.10-12.

Middle Mandala I

Saraswati: I.89.3.

Sindhu: I.83.1.

General and Late Mandala I

Gauri: I.164.4.

Rasa: I. 112.12.

Sindhu: I.44.12; 122.6; 126.1; 186.5

(plus the references to the Sindhu in the refrain of the Kutsas in the last verses of I.94-96, 98, 100-103, 105-115).

Saraswati: I.13.9; 142.9; 164.49, 52; 188.8

Jahnavi: I.116.19.

Mandala II

Saraswati: II.1.11; 3.8; 30.8; 32.8; 41.16-18.

Mandala III

Vipas: III.33.1.

Sutudri: III.33.1.

Saraswati: III.4.8; 23.4; 54.13.

Drsadvati: III.23.4,

Apaya: III.23.4.

Jahnavi: III.58.6.

Mandala IV

Sarayu: IV.30.18.

Kusava: IV.18.8.

Sindhu: IV.30.12; 54.6; 55.3.

Parusni: IV.22.2.

Vipas: IV.30.11.

Rasa: IV.43.6.

Mandala V

Sarayu: V.53.9.

Kubha: V.53.9.

Krumu: V.53.9.

Anitabha: V.53.9.

Rasa: V.41.15; 53.9.

Sindhu: V.53.9.

Parusni: V.52.9.

Saraswati: V.5.8; 42.12; 43.11; 46.2,

Yamuna: V.52.17.

Mandala VI

Saraswati: VI.49.7; 50.12. 52.6; 61.1-7, 10-11, 13-14

Hariyupiya: VI.27.5.

Yavyavati: VI.27.6.

Ganga: VI.45.31.

Mandala VII

Asikni: VII.5.3.

Parusni: VII.18.8, 9.

Saraswati: VII.2.8; 9.5; 35.11; 36.6; 39.5; 40.3; 95.1-2, 4-6; 96.1, 3-6.

Yamuna: VII.18.19.

Mandala VIII

Gomati: VIII.24.30.

Svetyavarai: VIII.26.18.

Suvastu: VIII.19.37.

Prayiyu: VIII.19.37.

Vayiyu: VIII.19.37.

Sindhu: VIII.12.3; 20.24, 25; 25.14; 26.18, 72.7.

Arjikiya: VIII.7.29; 64.11.

Susoma: VIII.7.29; 64.11.

Asikni: VIII.20.25.

Parusni: VIII.75.15.

Saraswati: VIII.21.17, 18; 38.10; 54.4

Amsumati: VIII.96.13.

Rasa: VIII.72.13.

Mandala IX

Sindhu: IX.97.58.

Arjikiya: IX.65.23.

Saraswati: IX.5.8; 67.32; 81.4.

Rasa: IX.41.6.

Mandala X

Sarayu: X.64.9.

Gomati: X.75.6.

Mehatnu: X.75.6.

Kubha: X.75.6.

Krumu: X.75.6.

Sveti: X.75.6.

Rasa: X.75.6; 108.1, 2; 121.4.

Susartu: X.75.6.

Trstama: X.75.6.

Sindhu: X.64.9; 65.13; 66.11; 75.1, 3-4, 6-9.

Arjikiya: X.75.5.

Susoma: X.75.5.

Vitasta: X.75.5.

Marudvrdha: X.75.5.

Asikni: X.75.5.

Parusni: X.75.5.

Sutudri: X.75.5.

Saraswati: X.17.7-9; 30.12; 64.9; 65.1,13; 66.5; 75.5; 110.8; 131.5; 141.5; 184.2

Asmanvati: X.53.8.

Yamuna: X.75.5.

Ganga: X.75.5.

THE EVIDENCE OF RIVER NAMES

The names of the rivers in the Rigveda have always formed the basis for any analysis of Rigvedic geography.

Let us examine the geographical picture presented by these river-names when the Mandalas are arranged in their chronological order (click on the link).

As the Chinese put it, one picture is worth a thousand words. The graph gives us the entire geographical picture in a nutshell: (click on the link)

1. In the pre-Rigvedic period and the early part of the Early Period (Mandala VI), the Vedic Aryans were inhabitants of an area to the east of the Saraswati.
2. In the course of the Early Period (Mandalas III and VII), and the early part of the Middle Period (Mandala IV and the middle upa-mandalas), there was a steady expansion westwards.
3. Though there was an expansion westwards, the basic area of the Vedic Aryans was still restricted to the east in the Middle Period (Mandala II), and even in the early parts of the Late Period: Mandala V knows the western rivers from the Kubha (Kabul) in the north to the Sarayu (Siritoi) in the south, but its base is still in the east. Saraswati is still the most important river in the Mandala: it is referred to by the eponymous Rsi Atri (V.42.12; 43.11) who also refers to the Rasa (V.41.15). All the other references to the western rivers (Sarayu, Kubha, Krumu, Anitabha, Rasa, Sindhu) occur in a single verse (V.53.9) by a single Rsi Syavasva, obviously a very mobile Rsi who also refers elsewhere to the Parusni (V.52.9) and even the Yamuna (V.52.17)
4. In the later part of the Late Period (Mandalas VIII, IX, X, and the general and late upa-mandalas) the Vedic Aryans were spread out over the entire geographical horizon of the Rigveda.

Let us examine the evidence of the river-names in greater detail under the following heads:

A. The Westward Expansion in the Bharata Period.

B. The Evidence of Some Key Rivers.

***The Westward Expansion in the Bharata Period*:** The graph of the rivers clearly shows that there was a *westward* expansion of the Vedic Aryans from the time of Sudas onwards.

In the Early period, right from pre-Rigvedic times to the time of Sudas, the Vedic Aryans were settled in the area to the *east* of the Punjab: Mandala VI knows of no river to the west of the Saraswati.

However, in the Mandalas and upa-mandalas following Mandala VI, we find a steady movement westwards:

a. Mandala III refers to the *first two* rivers of the Punjab *from the east*: the Sutudri and the Vipas.

b. Mandala VII refers to the next two rivers of the Punjab *from the east*: the Parusni and Asikni.

c. The middle upa-mandalas of Mandala I contain the first reference to the Indus, but none to the rivers *west* of the Indus.

d. Mandala IV contains the first references to rivers *west* of the Indus.

If the case for the westward expansion is strong enough even merely from the evidence of the *names* of the rivers, it becomes unimpeachable when we examine the *context* in which these names appear in the hymns:

1. The Sutudri and Vipas are not referred to in a casual vein. They are referred to in a special context: hymn III.33 is a special ode to these two rivers by Vishvamitra in commemoration of a historical movement of the warrior bands of the Bharatas led by Sudas and himself, across the billowing waters of these rivers.

   What is important is that this hymn is characterized *by the Western scholars themselves* as a historical hymn commemorating the migratory movement of the Vedic Aryans across the Punjab.,

   But the Western scholars depict it as a movement from the west to the east: Griffith calls the hymn "a relic of the traditions of the Aryans regarding their progress eastward in the land of the Five Rivers".

However, an examination of the facts leaves no doubt that the direction of this historical movement was *from the east to the west*: the very distribution of the river-names in the Rigveda, as apparent from our graph of the rivers, makes this clear.

But there is more specific evidence within the hymns to show that this movement was from the east to the west:

Sudas is a descendant of Divodasa (VII.18.25), Divodasa is a descendant of Srnjaya (VI.47.22 and Griffith's footnotes to it) and Srnjaya is a descendant of Devavata (IV.15.4): Sudas is therefore clearly a remote descendant of Devavata.

Devavata established the sacrificial fire on the banks of the Apaya between the Saraswati and the Drsadvati (III.23.3-4) The Saraswati is to the *east* of the Vipas and Sutudri, and the Apaya and Drsadvati are *even further east*. No ancestor of Sudas is associated with any river to the west of the Saraswati.

The historical movement of the Vedic Aryans across the Sutudri and the Vipas, at the time of Sudas, can only be a *westward* movement.

2. The Parusni and Asikni, also, are not referred to in a casual vein: they also are referred to in a special context. The context is a major battle fought on the Parusni by the Bharatas under Sudas and Vasishtha (who replaced Vishvamitra as the priest of Sudas).

   The direction of the movement is crystal clear in this case as well: Sudas with his *earlier* priest Vishvamitra is associated with the Sutudri and Vipas, and with his *later* priest Vasishtha is associated with the Parusni which is to the west of the two other rivers. But there is more specific evidence in Mandala VII about the direction of movement in this battle, which is the subject of various references throughout the Mandala:

   a. The battle is fought on the Parusni and the enemies of Sudas (who is referred to here as the Puru) are described in VII.5.3 as the people of the Asikni. The Asikni is to the west of the Parusni hence it is clear that the enemies of Sudas are fighting from the *west* of the Parusni while Sudas is fighting from the *east*. Curiously, Griffith mistranslates the name of the river Asikni as "dark-hued", thereby killing two birds with one stone: the people of the Asikni become "the dark-hued races", thereby wiping out the sense of direction inherent in the reference, while at the same time introducing the racial motif

b. In VII.83.1, two of the tribes fighting against Sudas, the Prthus and the Parsus, are described as marching *eastwards* (*praca*) towards him.

   Griffith again mistranslates the names of the tribes as "armed with broad axes" and the word praca as "forward".

c. VII.6.5 refers indirectly to this battle by talking of the defeat of the tribes of Nahus (i.e. the tribes of the Anus and Druhyus who fought against Sudas) as follows: "Far, far away hath Agni chased the Dasyus, and, in the east, *hath turned the godless westward*". Sudas is therefore clearly pressing forward from the east.

3. The first references to the Indus are in the middle upa-mandalas (I.83.1) and in Mandala IV (IV.30.12; 54.6; 55.3). There is, perhaps, a westward movement indicated even in the very identity of the composers of the hymns which contain these references: I.83 is composed by Gautama Rahugana *who does not refer to any river west of the Indus*, while the references in Mandala IV are by his *descendants*, the Vamadeva Gautamas, who also refer to two rivers to the west of the Indus (IV.18.8; 30.18).

   Thus, we have a clear picture of the westward movement of the Vedic Aryans from their homeland in the east of the Saraswati to the area to the west of the Indus, towards the end of the Early Period of the Rigveda: IV.30.18 refers to what is clearly the westermnost point in this movement, a battle fought in southern Afghanistan "on yonder side of Sarayu".

The Evidence of Some Key Rivers: The key rivers in the Rigveda are:

a. The Indus to the west of the Five Rivers of the Punjab.
b. The Saraswati to the east of the Five Rivers of the Punjab.
c. The Ganga and Yamuna, the easternmost rivers named in the Rigveda.

The evidence of these key rivers is extremely significant:

1. *The Indus and the Saraswati:* The word Sindhu in the Rigveda primarily means "river" or even "sea"; it is only secondarily a name of the Indus river: thus Saptasindhava can mean "seven rivers" but not "seven Induses".

   The relative insignificance of the Indus in the Rigveda is demonstrated by the fact that *the Indus is not mentioned even once in the three oldest Mandalas of the Rigveda*.

   Since the word Sindhu, in its meaning of "river", occurs frequently throughout the Rigveda, scholars are able to juggle with the word, often mistranslating the word Sindhu as "the Indus" even when it means "river".

   However, *even this sophistry is not possible in the case of the three oldest Mandalas (VI, III and VII)*: the word Sindhu, except in eight verses, occurs only in the plural, and can be translated only as "rivers".

   In seven of the eight references, in which the word occurs in the singular, it clearly refers to some other "river" which is specified within the context of the reference itself:

   a. III.33.3, 5; 53.9: Vipas.
   b. VII.18.5: Parusni.
   c. VII.33.3: Yamuna.
   d. VII.36.6; 95.1: Saraswati.

In the eighth reference (VII.87.6) the word means "sea": the verse talks of the sun setting in the sea.

In sharp contrast, the Saraswati is referred to many times in the three oldest Mandalas. In fact, there are three whole hymns dedicated to it in these Mandalas: VI.61; VII.95, 96.

All in all, the Saraswati is referred to in nine Mandalas out of ten in the Rigveda (i.e. in all except Mandala IV, which represents the westernmost thrust in the westward movement of the Vedic Aryans).

The Indus is referred to in only six Mandalas (I, IV, V, VIII, IX, X); and in three of these (V, IX, X), the references to the Saraswati far outnumber the references to the Indus.

It is only in the *latest* parts of the Rigveda that the Indus overshadows the Saraswati:

a. In Mandala VIII, the references to the Indus outnumber the references to the Saraswati (by six verses to four).
b. In the general and late upa-mandalas of Mandala I, the Indus, but not the Saraswati, is enumerated with other deities in the refrain of the Kutsas which forms the last verse of nineteen out of their twenty-one hymns.
c. In Mandala X, although there are more references to the Saraswati, it is the Indus, and not the Saraswati, which is the main river lauded in the *nadIstuti* (X.75), the hynm in Praise of the Rivers.

The Saraswati is so important in the *whole* of the Rigveda that it is worshipped as one of the Three Great Goddesses in the Apri-suktas of all the ten families of composers (being named in nine of them and implied in the tenth). The Indus finds no place in these Apri-suktas.

The contrast between the overwhelming importance of the Saraswati and the relative unimportance of the Indus is so striking, and so incongruous with the theory of an Aryan invasion from the northwest, that many scholars resort to desperate explanations to account for it: Griffith, in his footnote to VI.61.2, suggests that perhaps "Saraswati is also another name of Sindhu or the Indus".

2. *The Eastern Rivers*: The Ganga and the Yamuna are the two easternmost rivers named in the Rigveda. One or the other of these two rivers (either by these names, or by their other names, Jahnavi and Amsumati respectively) is named in seven of the ten Mandalas of the Rigveda, *including the three oldest Mandalas* (VI, III and VII).

By contrast, the Indus and its western tributaries, as we saw, are named in only six Mandalas, which do *not* include the three oldest Mandalas of the Rigveda.

But even more significant than these bare statistics is the particular nature of the four references to the Ganga, the easternmost river of them all:

a. The *nadIstuti* begins its enumeration of the rivers with the Ganga and moves westwards.

   Whether this circumstance in itself is a significant one or not is debatable; but while many scholars, without necessarily having arrived at any specific ideas about Rigvedic chronology or geography, find it important, certain others seek to deflect its importance, and even to dismiss the importance of the Ganga itself in the Rigveda:

   Griffith, in his footnote to X.75.5, takes pains to suggest that "the poet addresses first the most distant rivers. *Ganga*: the Ganges is mentioned, indirectly, in only one other verse of the *Rigveda*, and even there, the word is said by some to be the name of a woman. See VI.45.31."

b. The reference in VI.45.31 is definitely significant: the composer compares the height of a patron's generosity to the height of the wide bushes on the banks of the Ganga.

   This makes it clear that even in the oldest Mandala in the Rigveda, the Ganga is a familiar geographical landmark, whose features conjure up images which are very much a part of traditional idiomatic expression.

c. The reference in III.58.6. is infinitely more significant. Griffith translates the verse as follows: "Ancient your home, auspicious is your friendship: Heroes, your wealth is with the house of Jahnu."

   Here, not only does Griffith mistranslate Jahnavi as "the house of Jahnu", he compounds it with a further misinterpretation of the grammatical form:

   Jahnavyam is clearly "on (the banks of) the Jahnavi" on the lines of similar translations by Griffith himself in respect of other rivers: *Parusnyam* (V.52.9: on the banks of the Parusni), *Yamunayam* (V.52.17: on the banks of the Yamuna), *Drsadvatyam... Apayayam Sarasvatyam* (III.23.4: on the banks of the Drsadvati, Apaya and Saraswati).

The correct translation of III.58.6, addressed to the Asvins, is: "Your ancient home, your auspicious friendship, O Heroes, your wealth is on (the banks of the Jahnavi." What is noteworthy is that the phrase *Puranamokah* "ancient home" is used in the second oldest Mandala in the Rigveda, in reference to the banks of the Ganga.

d. The reference in I.116.19 associates the Jahnavi with Bharadvaja, Divodasa and the Gangetic dolphin (all of whom are referred to in the earlier verse I.116.18). It is clear, therefore, that the river is specially associated with the oldest period of the Rigveda, the period of Mandala VI (which is also the only place, outside the *nadistuti*, where the Ganga is referred to by that name).

The evidence of the rivers in the Rigveda is therefore unanimous in identifying the area to the east of the Saraswati as the original homeland of the Vedic Aryans.

9

The Golden Thread of Vedanta

The Divine Life Society was founded by worshipful Guru Maharaj Swami Sivanandaji, in order to proclaim to the whole world of the modern times, the way of living one's life so as to be able to attain, experience and become established in the Divine Perfection which is inherent in each one of the human being, as his unalienable, true, eternal nature. All of you have an apparent human personality which is only the external facade of your Reality.

This human personality is not the Reality according to the Vedanta. You have to know this because you are participants in the Yoga Vedanta Academy Course. So you must know what Vedanta has to say about your life, about this world and about everything pertaining to life in this world.

You have come here as *jijnasus. Jijnasus* are those who are keenly eager for attaining *jnana,* the Knowledge. *Jijnasus* attending this course have a special uniqueness, a special distinction. You are *jijnasus* with a difference.

Apara-vidya: What is that difference? The difference is: All other seekers of knowledge are trying to acquire *apara-vidya,* the worldly knowledge; whereas you seek to acquire *Para-vidya.* This is a basic, fundamental difference. *Apara-vidya* enables you to get, keep, possess and enjoy objects of this world. But Vedanta says, this world is only a temporary dream. *Apara-vidya* enables you to get distinction, name and fame, and the objects you can possess, keep and enjoy.

The World is Transitory: But all these only for a brief while; because the whole world is transitory, subject to decay, subject to ultimate dissolution. Everything here is unstable, nothing here endures, nothing here is lasting, nothing here is permanent. Therefore this world is not having any permanent validity.

What is the meaning of everything? *Aabrahmaa sthoola paryantam*. From a blade of a grass up to the position of *Brahmaa*, the creator; *Brahma-loka*, the greatest, the biggest status in the cosmic scheme of things—everything is worthless, valueless. This is what has been declared by the great sages who have known the impermanence of all the things. So I have said that your outer personality is not the reality according to the *Vedanta*.

The Reality: Why did I say according to the Vedanta? Vedanta gives a specific definition for Reality. What is truly, authentically and genuinely Real? You have to try to understand with a very subtle intellect, what Vedanta wants to convey to you. That alone can be called Sat, really true, the Reality which is beginningless and endless, which is ever present, ever *is*, in all the three periods of time. It always existed in the past, It does exist in the present and will always exist in the future as well. It never will cease to be. There is a further qualification: That is the Reality which abides always, in all the three periods of time without undergoing any change, It always remains the same. Nothing can alter It, nothing can change It. That is something which is always in Its Fullness, in Its Perfection.

This is the classical specific definition of *Sat*, the Reality: It is always present in all the three periods of time, past, present and future and It is never subject to any change, It is unalterable, unchangeable. If you apply this test to anything in this world, you will find that all the things fail to fulfil this requirement. All the things change right from the beginning. Your body changes right from the birth, so it cannot be the Reality. Your human personality did not exist before you were born. The duration of its existence here on the earth plane is for a limited time. One day, everyone who is born has to go. Everyone knows this. It does not require any study of any big philosophy.

Death the Leveller: Gurudev used to sing: *Time sweeps away kings and barons*. Even the big people who wield great deal of power, were powerless before old age, disease, decay and death. The glories of our personality are shadows only, they are not substantial things. There is no power against fate. Death lays its icy hands on kings and barons. Even the biggest sceptre and crown must tumble down in the dust one day. An emperor may be holding a sceptre as a symbol of royal power and may be wearing a crown as a symbol of the royal status, but all these must go in dust and become as worthless as the dust.

The title of Gurudev's poem is "Death the Leveller." Death makes everyone equal, whether he is a beggar on the street-side or a great king, a president of a big state or an ordinary labourer breaking stones on the road-side or cutting wood in a forest. When death comes they all become the same, either they turn into a little ash or become food for the worms under the earth! This is a common human experience.

So Gurudev says:

Time sweeps away kings and barons!

Where is Yudhishthira? Where is Ashoka?

Where is Shivaji? Where is Napoleon?

Where is Valmiki? Where is Shakespeare?

Where are those mighty people? Where are Yudhishthira and Ashoka? One is the greatest from the point of view of Dharma, the righteousness, and the other is great from the point of view of vastness of the empire. The empire of Ashoka stretched from South India and went beyond the North India and covered Pakistan, Afghanistan, Kabul and Gandhar. Archaeologists find his coins and Ashoka's inscription carved on rocks and stone pillars and in all these areas. All the great warriors, great poets have disappeared.

Lord Krishna who is the creator, preserver and dissolver of countless billions of universes, who is the supreme Lord Himself, He opens the wisdom teachings of Srimad-Bhagavad-Gita and right in the beginning of His teachings says; "*Jatasya hi dhruvo mrityuh.* [Certain is the death for the born]." For one who is born, death is certain. That is the only certain thing, other things may be uncertain. Therefore, this human personality which did not have any existence before we were born, will come to an end one day. One may live very long, say a hundred years, hundred and ten years, but ultimately this life has to end. If it does not end, you yourself will pray to God: 'O God! Please take me away from here. It is painful to live here; I cannot stand, I cannot even sit, I cannot eat. Every moment is painful. Please relieve me from the burden of this body.'

Where do you go after death? The human personality is not there. That means the human personality is *asat*. Anything which is changing is *asat*. You were something in infancy, something different in your childhood, adolescent, youth and old age. Everyday there is a change in your mood, change in your attitude, change in your health condition. Everything changes. Instability is the second name of this body. This body is changeful, it has a beginning and an end. It is temporary in time. Therefore, it cannot be the Reality.

Your Essential Nature: Which is the unreal aspect of your being? What is *anitya, asat,* non-real and changeful? The Reality is always present, always unchanging; It is without a beginning and an end. Why? Because It is a part of the Cosmic Principle that is eternal, infinite, unchanging, permanent, imperishable. That Cosmic Being is called the Universal Soul or Paramatma. They call It God, they call It Allah, they call It Almighty Father in the Heaven, or Ahura Mazda or Tao or the Supreme Reality. They may call It by any number of different names, but It is the same One, the same Universal Essence who is the source, the support and the fulfilment of all the existence. That is Perfect, That is Full, That is Divinity. You are a part of That in your inner Reality, in your essential Nature.

That Divinity is inherent in you. It is your true identity, essential identity, eternal identity. That eternal identity is immortal Spirit, That eternal identity is perfectly Divine.

This Reality is the very central Principle on which Gurudev has focused his message. He says: "You are immortal Atman; you are perfectly Divine. This life is a rare gift, a golden chance, a unique opportunity given to you. You should always make use of this life to become awakened within. Unfold this slumbering Divinity. Your endeavour should be to transform yourself into a Divine personality, into a Perfect Being." You are not just a human personality with all the drawbacks and weaknesses; you are simultaneously a Divine personality. You are the Divinity on the earth. "Awaken the sleeping God within you," says Swami Vivekananda. This is the great task of your life. Live your life in such a way, make your thinking, feeling and actions in such a way, that all these become a great help for bringing about an inner process in this direction; so that they become a wonderful support for the specific techniques and practices for bringing about this unfoldment.

Gurudev gave his message as a message of Divine Life, living the life in such a way that the Divinity within you becomes awakened through Bhakti-Yoga, Jnana-Yoga, Raja-Yoga and various other Yoga systems and constant practice. If your inner life and spiritual practices are supported by a helpful, and become supplementary and complementary to your outer life which also partakes of the same quality of divinity, then your whole life becomes a unified process of trying to attain one single objective of the Divine Perfection.

That is the great objective with which Gurudev founded this institution; and to initiate you into the ways and means of bringing about this more rapidly, more effectively, he set up this Yoga Vedanta Forest Academy. His objective was to initiate you into the inner skills, the secrets of *sadhana* and practical spiritual life so that you can live actively an inner spiritual life.

The Vedanta Doctrines: All the Upanishads taken together are called Vedanta, because they comprise the Jnana-kanda, the end portion of the Vedas. Vedanta literally means the end portion of the Vedas. These Upanishads are the culminating portion of Vedas; it is pure *jnana*. So Vedanta means *jnana*. The Jnana-kanda of the Vedas is the record of transcendental Experiences and the ways and means of attaining It. So the contents of the Upanishads is about the nature of that transcendental Experience and about what happens to the person when he attains that Experience.

How many kinds of Vedanta are there? Innumerable. Because, unfortunately the learned scholars who study the Upanishads deeply, reflect over them and try to understand them, have understood them in various ways. So each one gives his own interpretation of what he thinks is the correct interpretation of the Upanishads. According to the interpretation given by that particular person who understood it in a particular way, a school of thought of Vedanta arises.

All the human beings are not the same. They have different intellects and different ways of understanding things, different approaches and different ways of looking at things, both physically, as well as, through the intellect. Later on, the scholars started to interpret the structure of the words of Vedanta. One school says: *'Tattvam-asi'*, the other tries to prove that it is *'Atattvam-asi'*. Due to such varied interpretations, certain well recognised systems have come into existence. The amazing part of it is that all these systems form valid parts of the total body of *Sanatana Dharma*. *Sanatana Dharma* does not take any side or validate any particular system. These are merely interpretations of the scholars and have become part of it and it tolerates them and treats as valid. So all these schools are called Vedanta.

The Absolute Monism of Sankaracharya (788-820) is called Kevala Advaita Vedanta Siddhanta, a little modification of which is known as Vishishta-Advaita Vedanta or Qualified Non-dualism of Ramanujacharya (11th century). Sankaracharya said *jiva* and *Brahma* are one. Ramanujacharya agrees with this oneness but interprets that it is so in a specific way only. In the Absolute Monism, *jiva*-hood is considered as a myth or an imaginary existence only; there is no real existence of *jiva*. *Ekameva-advitiyam Brahma, Neha naanaasti kinchit*. One and only One exists, there is not many. There is only One without a second. He is uncompromising about this and as though to emphasise it, he says: 'If you think anything else exists, it is not real but it is your *bhranti* only.' You may argue: 'How do you explain *jiva*?' he says: 'What do you mean? There is no *jiva* to be explained. *Jiva*-hood is a myth, it is non-existent, it is a non-entity.' What he was trying to prove was his own *Aparoksha-anubhuti*, his direct Experience of the Reality, his Advaitic Experience of non-dual Consciousness.

Nimbarkacharya (1162) gave another interpretation known as Dvaita-Advaita Vedanta Siddhanta, the Dual-Nondual Doctrine of Vedanta. He says: "It is inexplicable thing! There is *dvaita* as well as *Advaita*.

Then came Madhvacharya (1199) who propounded Dualism or the Dvaita Vedanta Siddhanta. Individual soul and the Supreme Soul are proved by him to be different and separate entities. They can never become one. In essence the individual soul may be like the Supreme Soul, but it is a *jiva's* status, can never be the same, it can never have the same power or glory as that of the Supreme. He is Supreme, individual is under Him. The distinction, the *bheda*, is eternal and so they remain two, as *jivatma* and *Paramatma*.

Then came another Acharya called Vallabhacharya (1479) who gave Shuddha-Advaita Siddhanta, the Pure Non-dualism, which is also known as the Pushti Marga.

Five hundred years after Sankaracharya, another great scholar, great grammarian and a brilliant intellectual took his birth in Mayapuri, Nabadweep. He is known as Sri Krishna Chaitanya (1486). He expounded a certain school of thought of philosophy and mysticism, known as Achintya Bheda-Abheda Doctrine. He says:

'The nature of the absolute Reality is impossible for us to grasp. Our mind is a petty, finite instrument. How can it comprehend That which is supernal and infinite? How can it grasp that Being which existed before the mind had come into existence? How can the mind go to that Realm, because it did not exist when That alone existed? That is beyond the mind, It transcends the mind; the mind cannot reach That. The mind cannot even think of That. Whenever the mind thinks that it is thinking about That, it is only a thought or an imagination; it is not That. That Being is *achintya*, unthinkable. So the relationship between That and Its creation, including we all, the *jivatma*, cannot be thought about; it is both, oneness, as well as, *bheda,* the difference.

When a river ultimately merges with the ocean, you cannot distinguish the river from the ocean. There is no more any river, there is only the ocean. But you cannot say that the river water does not exist at all. It is continuously flowing and the river water forms a part of the ocean water, no matter even if it has got mixed up with it. The river water will be different from the water of the ocean at the centre. The river water cannot reach there. So long as the river has lost its separate existence, there is oneness or non-dualism between the river and the ocean. But so long as we cannot completely deny or entirely ignore the existence of the river water, there is *bheda,* a difference, there is duality.'

All these doctrines are having the same origin, the Upanishads or the Jnana-kanda of the Vedas. So all of them are known as Vedanta Doctrines. All these Acharyas were highly learned scholars. Each one of them gave his own interpretation of the Vedanta and proved his system, his view point, to be valid, using arguments, logic and all that. Our great people are so large-hearted that they recognised all these systems to be valid part of our Satya Sanatana Vedic Dharma. All of them are given a place in it and we study all of them. What is the height of generosity is that even Charvaka Doctrine is studied! It is a school of philosophy that does not at all recognise the existence of God. Ours is a great democracy of spiritual thought with complete freedom of speech and expression. The highest spiritual Experience is interpreted by different sages from different points of view, ability and depth. So have come different doctrines.

Veda accepts such divergence by saying; *Ekam Sad-vipra bahudha vadanti.* [There is only one Truth which the scholars describe differently.] It is also said: *Shrutir-vibhinnaa smritayopi vibhinnaa; tathaa muninaam matayo vibhinnaa.* [Vedas are many, other Scriptures are many; so also the views of the sages.] The views of scriptures also vary; there are different views. So also the opinions of sages and saints are different. This is to be expected in human beings as each human being is different. In Hindi it is said: 'All the five fingers are different.' Similarly, the siblings of the same parents are all having different temperaments, different nature. But the parents accept them all. Similarly, all the different doctrines are accepted by the parental Sanatana Dharma. The same one Being is termed differently, viewed differently by the sages.

There is one common Golden Thread in all these various schools of Vedanta. Whatever may be the nature of your relationship with the eternal divine Reality, one thing is certain. And all of them recognise that: '*You are Divine; and you ale inseparably related to the supreme Being.* That is the origin from which you have come; you are of That; and within you there is something of That.' All the Doctrines agree about this; no one disputes this. There is no disagreement; there is no difference of opinion.

This is the most important thing and Gurudev focused hundred per cent on this. This one thing is enough, you need not worry about other things. Let the scholars quarrel and disagree with each other; let them prove one thing and disprove another. You may not bother about all those things if you remember this one thing that *you are Divine*. Beyond your passing, temporary, apparent, imperfect human personality which is non-real according to the Vedantic Doctrines, there is hidden within you the unchanging, eternal Reality, Divine Perfection, All-auspiciousness, All-blessedness. It is the Beauty of beauties, incomparable and unimaginable. It is full of light, full of purity, full of everything. It is glorious and grand, radiant and shining. *That is you*. That is your real nature.

Awaken Your Divinity: When you are That, why should you be content in making your life merely a process of petty, little expressions of imperfect qualities of your mind, intellect and all that? When you have the potential, when you have the capacity to become glorious, perfect, pure radiant Being, why do you not opt for That? Why should you remain content at a much lower level? Why should you remain sometimes loving, sometimes hating, sometimes liking, sometimes disliking, sometimes very friendly, sometimes quarreling and fighting? This is foolishness. So our sages say: 'Come! Come! Wake up from this slumber of imperfect life. Awaken yourself to your Divinity. Unfold your Divinity. Attain that All-perfection. Do not opt for anything but the highest and the best. Do all that is necessary to attain your real Nature. Do not compromise.'

That is the ideal of Divine Life. That is the fulfilment of the fundamental discovery of the Truth within as expounded by the Vedanta. The discovery and declaration of the Vedanta about Divinity within you is: 'Within each one of you is the Divinity.' These are the words prompted by Gurudev. This is the declaration coming from the Vedic era. When the ancient sages discovered It, they declared this and they have made a wonderful device to preserve this highest wealth of the humanity, by setting up a system of unbroken succession of a lineage of master and disciple, of *Guru-shishya parampara*.

This invaluable treasure should not be lost. So a disciple should make him fit and worthy of that, so that the wisdom of the scriptures may be imparted to him. He can thus be inspired by the Guru to attain It during this very life. If he chooses ten such worthy disciples and imparts them the wisdom of the scriptures and even if two or even one disciple experiences It, it is enough. Even if we have a single candle lit, we can have from it another, from it another, from it yet another, and the chain continues and the Light will perpetuate perennially. This is the wonderful device of an unbroken lineage of master and disciple. This *Guru-shishya parampara* has succeeded marvellously and most effectively in preserving this great flame of living spirituality from the ancient times till now, so that even now, towards the end of the twentieth century, you are in a position to be told:

"You are Divine. Divinity is your birth-right. Divinity is your true identity. Divinity is your essential, true, unchangeable, eternal, real nature. That is your super, greater and real personality. Human personality is a subordinate personality. You have a dual personality; the Divine and the humane. In spite of all the drawbacks, defects and weaknesses of your human personality, you are still the Pure and Perfect; nothing can touch your this aspect; nothing can alter it. Even though, you are now subject to imperfections of your temporary, passing human personality, you are fully Perfect. Recognise this and rejoice. Tell yourself: 'I am always the radiant Divine within. I will not lose a single day, a single chance of trying to bring about the great inner awakening and unfoldment. In this very body, in this very birth, I must succeed in fully awakening my Divinity, experiencing That, becoming established in That.'

> *"That is the Goal, becoming liberated by attaining the full experience of your Divinity. That is the ideal of your life. That is to be attained right now, while living in this body; not in some unknown state after death, after the body is buried or burnt."*

Divinity is Your Birth-right: Is this possible? Yes, certainly. The history of our great country shows that in every generation, there have been such great *jeevan-muktas*, the liberated ones, who say: 'I have attained It. Why don't you attain It? It is your birth-right. You have been given this human birth to attain It, that is the purpose of your life.' The human birth throws wide open the portal to this blessed state of Divine Consciousness, the Cosmic Consciousness. It is only the human personality which has power to think, reason, reflect, ask, probe, analyse, and discriminate. The very fact that you have been endowed with this rare gift of human personality is sufficient for you to fix the goal of attaining the fullest Blessedness; and that should always be your endeavour.

This is the declaration of the Vedanta: *Uttishthata jaagrata, praapya varaannibodhata.* [Arise! Awake! having reached the great (teachers) attain that Atman. Katha Upanishad 1-3-14.] Become awakened! Approach knowledgeable persons; they are there waiting for you. Come and ask, they are waiting for you to give the highest Knowledge. They expect nothing from you; they have got everything. They are Full and this Fullness spontaneously enriches the whole world; just as the spring season without any reason, spontaneously brings about abundance of flowers and fruits and turns the earth into beautiful greenery, makes all the lives to flourish. The saints are like that spring. So *Jagad-Guru Adi* Sankaracharya says: 'They are there; go to them. Become fully awakened as they have become. Attain Bodhi, the full awakening.'

That is what you are. You are fully awakened but you are in the sleep state and you are dreaming. You are *"Nitya shuddha, nitya Buddha." Buddha* means awakened. This is the eternal call of Vedanta. This is the Vedanta in nutshell for you. You must respond to this great call of Vedanta. You should never forget it. Vedanta is not to be stored in the books and lectures. Vedanta is to be actively lived for awakening. You must respond to the great call *'Uttishthata jaagrata, praapya varaannibodhata'* and say: 'Yes, I shall now wake up and attain Illumination. I am prepared to do anything for It.' This should become inseparable part of very breath of your life, every cell of your life.

10

Upanishads Associated with 'Esoteric Knowledge'

In approaching the question of the esoteric nature of the Upanishads I intend to give a brief explanation of the meaning of the word Upanishad and to place the Upanishads within their context as part of the Vedas. I will then move on to discuss issues surrounding the authorship of the Upanishads and the social context within which they arose especially with reference to the Srmana or renounciant movements that took place between 800-400BC a time contemporary with the composition of the Upanishads (sometime between 600-300BC.) Then I will be looking at new ideas the Upanishads introduce into the Vedas. I shall briefly discuss the esoteric concept of correspondences and the internalisation of the ritual, followed by an exploration of the central concept of Brahman and atman. I will then focus on the idea of rebirth and karma as they first appear in the Brihadanyaka Upanishad before moving on to my conclusion.

The word Upanishad literally means 'to sit near' and is derived from the Sanskrit roots *upa,* near *ni,* down and *sad,* to sit. The association is of groups of students sitting around a wise teacher in order to here spiritual truths. This in itself implies a certain sense of something esoteric which is passed from teacher to student. An alternative meaning is it is itself a word which means 'connection' or 'equivalence', from the word *bandhu* which means kin. This idea of correspondences is itself a central plank of esoteric thought as I shall explore below.

The Upanishads are a part of the collection of texts referred to as the Vedas. They appear as the final part of the Vedic collection and are often referred to as Vedanta which literally means coming at the end of the Veda.

Although there are a wide variety and number of texts within the broad Hindu tradition which are referred to as Upanishads, there are fourteen major texts that are more or less closely incorporated into the Veda. This collection of early Upanishads are the texts which I will be referring to as Upanishads throughout this essay.

There are four collections of Vedas: *Rig Veda, Yajurveda* (which itself has two sub divisions the Black and the White), *Samaveda* and the *Atharthaveda*. In General each of these collections is divided into four categories: Samitas, which are ritual/ liturgical texts, concerned mainly with the ritual formulas which are to be performed by the priests; *Bramanas,* explanatory material relating to the *Samitas; Aranyakas,* ritual texts for forest hermits which also contain commentaries on the Samitas and Bramanas and the Upanishads which are also commentaries upon the Samitas and the Brahmans. There is not necessarily a clear distinction between the Aranyakas and the Upanishads. In many places they blend into each other. The Upanishads are however later than the Aranyakas and generally place metaphysical and cosmological questions to a more central position.

In general the Vedic rituals and commentaries within the first two divisions are concerned with gaining rewards in this life. Vedic rites in the early period where based around the idea of a ritual sacrifice, as Gombrich has pointed out:

> *'The early parts of the Rig Veda offer no evidence that at the beginning there was any elaborate theory of the sacrifice: it was a matter of giving things to the gods and getting sons, cattle and long life in return.'*

On the other hand the Upanishads, and to a lesser degree the *Aranyakas,* begin to raise questions of a more 'transcendental' nature. They are concerned primarily with understanding the existential questions relating to life and death, and ultimately with the attainment of spiritual knowledge rather than with ritual action.

In examining the Upanishads however it is I feel important to point out that they do not represent one single unified theory or approach to the religious problems they address. They are texts written over a period of several centuries across a wide variety of regions. Further more even within the collections of the early Upanishads there is a distinct movement from pantheistic monism through monism to monotheism. This is not necessarily a linear progression however. Rather than one set of ideas superseding the next they seem to interact and overlap in a wide variety of ways.

The Upanishads present many new ideas into the Indian religious milieu. The content of the Upanishads and the nature of the ideas they present will be examined below. First however I would like to look at how these texts and the ideas they contain arose.

Issues of the authorship of the Upanishads are difficult to establish as they are anonymous documents. Furthermore the earliest Upanishads are compilations of texts that may have had an earlier independent existence and where compiled by a series of editors. If we look to the internal evidence of the Upanishads for authorship then many references to kings and other members of the Kshatriya (warrior) class appear.

Indeed Brockington argues that the passages containing the greatest innovations are those associated with the Kshatriyas. On the surface therefore it is possible to assume that the ideas exposed in the Upanishads are those of the Kshatriyas, however as Olivelle points out the relationship between the Brahmins and the Kshatriyas was extremely complex, with both groups being dependent upon each other and simultaneously in conflict with each other for social influence.

It may well be the case that some Brahmins put forward the ideas contained within the Upanishads but disguised the authorship by putting words into the mouths of Kshatriyas. On this basis then the new ideas which appear within the Upanishads may have arisen from within the Brahmanical tradition. Indeed this idea has been put forward by Heesterman in his 'orthogenetic theory' which suggests a gradual development of thought within Vedic culture.

Another idea which has been put forward is that the 'new' ideas of the Upanishads have non-Vedic origins and in fact represent a totally new development that may have initially challenged Vedic orthodoxy. Indeed Bronkhorst has argued this point and puts great emphasis on the Srmana (renouncer) tradition as having it's roots outside of the Brahmanical Orthodoxy.

These Srmana traditions are of two kinds orthodox (astika) and heterodox (nastika). The heterodox movements rejected Brahmanical and Vedic authority completely. These movements include Buddhism, Jainism and the Aryajivikas, it is possible that there where many more similar movements at the time which were not so successful and so have left no mark, indeed the Aryajivikas have not survived into the present time at all.

These new religions where closely associated with the Kshatriyas and Romilla Thapar points out that the heterodox and the orthodox movements where mutually hostile. Olivelle however presents a third position,. He argues that the development of these new ideas comes about as a result of changes within the Brahmin community and arises due to a conflict between those who continue to support the sacrifice and those who are moving in the direction of support for the idea of renunciation and the ideas that go along with it. He sees the movement which gave rise to new religious ideas as being '...either non-Aryan or even non-Brahmanical.'

The growing trend towards renunciation, represented by the Srmana movements and the new ideas they where developing happened at a time contemporus with the composition of the early Upanishads. It has been argued that these movements represent a turn within society away from the early Vedic religion of a predominantly agrarian society and arise at a time of increased urbanisation and trade. Developments which themselves inevitably lead to a large increase in the movement of people, allowing more cross fertilisation of ideas, along with an increased sense of individuality and individual freedom.

As Ollivelle says:

'What is important, however, is not whether a particular doctrine originated among the Kshatriyas,

but that the new religious climate in northern India, of which the Upanishads were a part, was created through the intellectual interaction among 'new thinkers' within both groups.'

So what are the new ideas presented within the Upanishads? As has already been pointed out above the Upanishads form part of the Vedas, as such they are regarded as orthodox (*astika*). Whilst Brahminism rejects the Srmana traditions the Upanishads elaborate ideas that are very close to those of the heterodox movements. These ideas as Gombrich points out are ones which today are commonly excepted as part and parcel of Hinduism. They are rebirth, karma and liberation (*moksha*). There are also two more ideas that are found within the Upanishads which have great bearing on how it is possible to think of the Upanishads as esoteric texts, these are the internalisation of the ritual and the concept of Brahman and Atman.

The Brahmans and Aranyakas aim to interpret the meaning of the Vedic rituals. These texts become increasingly concerned with the importance of the knowledge of correspondences based on the ritual actions. The knowledge of the correspondences seem to take greater precedence over the ritual actions. The Brahmans maintained that knowledge of the correspondences between the cosmos and the ritual is a source of power.

This knowledge however is hidden and so is not available to ordinary people. Whilst the Brahmans and the Araṅyakas are concerned with the correspondences between the ritual and cosmic spheres, the Upanishads shift the emphasis to the person, the correspondences sought are now interpreted as being between the cosmic reality and the parts of the human organism. It is this search for secret hidden correspondences which is one of the features that make the Upanishads esoteric. Only that which is carried out with this knowledge is powerful:

'Those who know this and those who do not both perform these rites using this syllable. But knowledge and ignorance are two very different things. Only what is performed with knowledge, with faith, and with an awareness of the hidden connections (upanishad) becomes truly potent.'

Furthermore it seems that many of these correspondences are established through a process of phonetic similarities between two words within the Sanskrit language, or two words that have the same number of syllables.

Internalisation of the ritual is the way in which the Upanishads realise this idea of human/cosmic correspondence. By identifying aspects of the ritual practice to both the human being and the cosmos the Upanishads point to an underlying principle that is the essence of the ritual, the cosmos and the self. This essence is called Brahman.

As Olivelle points out the Brahman principle is not easy to pin down and in translation and discussion of the Upanishads the Sanskrit word is often kept as it is difficult to translate, indeed it has a number of meanings. In the earliest Upanishads the Brahman principle is identified variously from a materialistic point of view as either food or breath or both. From this early speculation however Brahman comes to be seen as the inner essence of the world and the world as manifesting from Brahman. Brahman therefore is the ultimate reality.

If the Brahman is the essence in the world then this essence must also appear in man. This essence is the atman. Atman while having many meanings within the Upanishads can broadly be identified with the 'self'. For the early Upanishadic thinkers then the aim is to realise the self (Brahman) in the self (atman), the macrocosm and the microcosm are identified as one:

> *'In the beginning this world was only brahman, and it knew only itself (atman), thinking: 'I am brahman.' As a result, it became the Whole. Among the gods, likewise, whosoever realized this, only they became the Whole. It was the same also among the seers and among the humans. Upon seeing this very point, the seer Vamadeva proclaimed: 'I was Manu, and I was the sun.' This is true even now. If a man knows 'I am brahman' in this way, he becomes this whole world. Not even the gods are able to prevent it, for he becomes their very self (atman). So when a man venerates another deity, thinking, 'he is one, and I am another', he does not understand.'*

This realisation of the self leads to liberation (*moksha*) one of the central ideas that arises around the same time as the composition of the Upanishads in the Srmana traditions. Whilst these traditions disagreed on points of doctrine and practice they all accepted the basic idea that the world is suffering (*duhka*) and that the only way out of this suffering is through liberation (*moksha*). This liberation is a form of gnosis or direct spiritual knowledge (*jnana*). For the Upanishads this gnosis is the realisation of the unity of atman and Brahman.

The world however is not just suffering, it is the constant repetition of suffering an endless cycle of birth and death (samsara). Within this cycle our actions determine the type of rewards we will reap in the next life and the actions of our last life are influencing us in this life. This in essence is the doctrine of Karma.

It is unclear if the doctrine of Karma originally comes from within the Srmana traditions, both Buddhism and Jainism have developed sophisticated ideas about karma and the transmigration of the self from one life to another, or emerged from with in the earlier Vedic texts. Gombrich points out that the term karman was used as a term for a religious act. In Brahmanical literature it refers specifically to significant acts, especially rituals. Therefore the idea of causality, inherent within the early Brahmanical idea of the sacrifice, may easily have been widened to includ certain moral qualities and applied to the new modes of thought within the Upanishads. Another possibility is that the transmigration theory may have it's roots in the tribal religions of the Ganges valley or in the Dravidian culture of south India.

The one thing that does seem fairly certain is that the earliest textual mention of the law of karma appears in Brihadaranyaka Upanishad. Here is also another point where the Upanishads are esoteric. Artabhaga after questioning the sage Yajnavalkya about the fate of someone after death, is lead away by Yajnavalkya and told the secret of karma in a secluded place:

> *Yajnavalkya replied: 'my friend we cannot talk about this in public. Take my hand, Artabhaga lets go and discuss this in private.'*

So they left and talked about it. And what did they talk about?-they talked about nothing but action. And what did they praise?-they praised nothing but action. Yalnavalkya told him: ' a man turns into something good by good action and into something bad through bad action.' Thereupon, Jaratkarava Artabhaga fell silent.'

Here it appears that Yajnavalkya cannot publicly tell Artabhaga about the law of Karma, and when the later finally hears this teaching he is lost for words. This information is clearly secret and only to be shared amongst a few.

In conclusion then it is possible to see that the Upanishads have developed at a time of great cultural upheaval. Within this period it has been necessary to develop ideas that have religious significance and meaning for people finding themselves in a new situation. Within this context there are a variety of movements which are challenging the established order of the Brahmins, and the beginnings of a number of new religious movements.

Within this context, a number of Brahmins, perhaps interacting with non-Aryan trends, may have began to question the validity of the ritual sacrifice and in trying to answer the new religious questions they are faced with (and possibly in light of religious experiences) begin to develop a world view sees the sacrifice as symbolic of a greater truth. The truth of Brahman a universal essence which permeates every thing in the world. In trying to return to this original state the emphasis shifts from ritual action to knowledge and indeed gnosis as a path towards the realisation of the truth. The world now seen as a fetter, is a constant source of suffering to be escaped from. This ideas are original kept secret and circulated only amongst a few people until they are formulated into the text that are now known as the Upanishads.

Hindu Gods and Goddesses

What is called 'Hinduism' in the present day could not be destroyed by an invader or foreigner or practicing Hindu could explore Hinduism in depth. Its roots are embedded in mysterious sources. Its branches have invaded space. Hinduism is all-pervasive, all-inclusive and penetrating into depths. Hinduism is supposed to be *apauruseya*, *i.e.* of impersonal origin and therefore it is devoid of errors of instrument and cognition. Even if the three prasthanas (authorities) namely, the Upanishads, the Brahma sutras and the Bhagavad Gita did not exist, that could have hardly done any harm to Hinduism.

Even so are the gods of Hinduism. They are eternal, undecaying and undying. Some Gods are prominent in the Vedas and some in later Vedic literature, itihasas and puranas. The Vedic dictum 'Truth is one. Sages call it by different names' set the tune in the orchestra of Hinduism. This idea disproves the notion that Hinduism is polytheistic.

The Greeks had many gods and goddesses in their pantheon. They would take sides in battles or wars, hating or loving some human being. Other ancient religions and mysteries had their own gods and goddesses. In Hinduism gods and goddesses do not take sides prominently. We may ask, 'What is the need to have so many gods in religion? Are they personifications of nature or conceptual symbols?' According to some scholars gods represent forces of nature. Agni represents fire. Vayu represents the wind. Indra is the thunderbolt. Soma is the god of plants and liquor and on. Here we find one tendency in the prayers of Vedic Aryans. When Varuna or Indra is glorified, that particular god has all the attributes of the Highest. This view also disproves the multiplicity of the gods.

Hinduism has not turned its back on Vedic beliefs. On the contrary it is a continuation of Vedic tradition. Veda in its embryonic state has all the characteristics which developed in course of time. It has already been stated that each god was praised as the Highest. Naturally there was no absolute sovereign but still some gods permanently occupied a lasting place. For instance Indra is a great warrior who drove back darkness, killed the demon Vrtra and protected the votaries.

Towards the end of the Vedic age, *i.e.* towards the end of the 5th century BC, there appeared the Upanishads. Without giving up the Vedic modes of thought, the texts revealed a sort of philosophico-gnosticism which established the relation between Atman and Brahman. Towards the end of the Upanishadic period, popular Hinduism comes out in bold relief. Here we see a religion fighting against some tendencies, open to some tendencies and making the Upanishadic ideas more popular. In Brihadaranyaka Upanishad we find Vidagdha Sakalya questioning Yagnavalkya thus: How many gods are there? He answered in accord with the Nivid: "Three hundred and three, and three thousand and three." By a process of regress the gods are reduced to one, the unitary Brahman.

The Anglo-Saxon word 'god' hardly gives the sense of the Sanskrit term 'deva'. While god is pantheistic in Western poetry and mysticism, there is a tendency for transcendentalism in Hinduism. Nevertheless though one Godhead is emphasized, again and again a sort of trinity is recognised in Brahma, Vishnu and Shiva. While Brahma is the principle of creation, Vishnu preserves and Shiva destroys. Among the Vedic Gods Vishnu and Shiva is nothing. Ultimately by a series of developments Vishnu and Shiva are identified with the Brahman of the Upanishads.

There is a remarkable passage in Brihadaranyaka Upanishad: 'The gods are fond of the cryptic, as it were, and dislike the evident' (*paroksapriya iva hi devah pratyaksadvisah*). Many a scholar has overlooked this esoteric sentence. The meaning is, we are not to take every sentence in an etymological sense. The names of the gods, their raiment, and their instruments have symbolic and psychological significance. For instance, the Astrabhusanaadhyaya of Vishu Purana (1.22) is a great authority on the subject.

The ornaments and weapons which adorn the body of the divine Figure, symbolically represent the principals of the universe. It is thus: the living principle is in the form of Kaustubha, Prakrti Srivasta, Mahat the club, Sattvikaaharikara the conch, Tamasa ahanikara the bow, knowledge the sword, ignorance its sheath, the mind the discus, sense and motor organs the arrows, and the subtle and gross elements the garland. Similarly we have to understand the Vedic language and the subsequent literature symbolically.

Subrahmanya

If Ganapati is universally revered by almost all the Hindus, Buddhists and Jains, and has even succeeded in going abroad to many countries of Southeast Asia, China, Japan and Afghanistan, his brother Subrahmanya has somehow remained confined to South India. Historically speaking, Subrahmanya is a much older deity, being mentioned in stone inscriptions and shown on coins (1 Cent. to 5 Cent. AD), and was well-known in North India. The sixth day of a lunar month (sashti) is considered sacred to him (as with serpent deities). He is said to have been married to a forest maid Valli Amma. The peacock is his carrier mount. His temples are usually found on hilltops.

All these factors may indicate that he was a sylvan deity connected with serpent-worship and tree worship, and hence was more popular among the people of lower strata in society. Now, however, all sections of Hinduism have accepted him and venerate him.

Subrahmanya is stated to have been born in a forest of arrow-like grass (hence the name Saravanabhava) and reared by the six divine mothers of the constellation Krittika (Pleiades), hence the names 'Karttikeya' and 'Sanmatura'. It seems he assumed six faces to suckle the milk of the six mothers and so got the appellation 'Sadanana or Sanmukha'.

He was appointed the commander-in-chief of the gods and thus became "Devasenapati'. With his matchless weapon, the shakti or lance shining brilliantly like fire, he easily destroyed Tarakusara thus becoming 'Shaktidhara' and 'Tarakari'. Being very young and virile he is 'Kumara' or 'Sanatkumara'. A forceful attacker in war, he is known as 'Skanda'. 'Skanda' also means one who has accumulated the power of chastity.

He likes holy people (Brahmans) and is always good to them. Hence he is 'Subramanya'. Once he broke down the Krauncha-parvata (a mountain) earning the name Kraunchabhetta. At the time he exposed Brahma's ignorance of the Vedas and hence got the name Brahma-Sasta.

His other names are Guha (the secret one), Gangeya (son of Ganga) and Swaminatha (the preceptor of his own father)

In icons, Subrahmanya is shown as a boy either with one head and two arms or with six heads and twelve arms. His lance and his peacock are also prominently displayed. A fowl adorns his banner. Subramanya, the son of Shiva and Shakti, represents the greatest state to which spiritual aspirants can evolve. Etymologically the word 'Subramanya' means 'one who tends the spiritual growth of the aspirants'. It is only he who reached the summit of the spiritual perfection in this life that is capable of tending the spiritual growth of others. Mythology describes him as the Son of God begotten to save the world from tyranny of the fiend Tarakasura. This is more true in the spiritual sense.

Subramanya, the Sanmukha, is depicted with six heads and twelve hands, all of them being attached to one trunk resting on two feet. Of course, even a boy knows that biologically this is impossible even as an angel with wings is! But a concept like this can be conceded if it fits into useful philosophical postulations. His six heads represent the five sense organs and the mind, which co-ordinates their activities. When these are controlled, refined and sublimated, man becomes a Superman. This is the implication of the symbology.

According to Yoga psychology, there are six centres of psychic energy, of consciousness, in the human body, designated as chakras. They are: Muladhara (at the anus), Svadhisthana (at the root of the sex organ), Manipura (at the naval) Anantha (at the region of the heart), Visudda at the throat) Ajna (between the eyebrows) and Sahasrara at the top of the head which is the destination for this energy. When the Yogi successfully raises his psychic energy to this topmost centre he has a vision of Shiva-Shakti.

Though it is the same energy that flows through all the six centres, in the case of an ordinary being it is concentrated in the three lower centres. In a perfect being the flow is so refined and uniform, that practically all the centres have been elevated to the highest level. Subramanya represents this perfected state of spiritual consciousness.

Man has only two hands. But, his superior intellect has enabled him to invent so many tools and instruments through which he can accomplish manual tasks, symbolically represents this power and capacity of man.

The combination of the six heads and twelve hands teaches us that the ideal of humanity is the perfected being who is not only a great Yogi but also a great worker!

Subramanya has two consorts: Valli and Devasena. The former is the daughter of a humble chieftain of a race given to agriculture and woodcraft. The latter is the daughter of Indra, the king of Gods.

This is just to show that God does not make any distinction between the humble folk and the elite. He loves both equally.

Alternatively, this can also mean that the true leader of a society will espouse agriculture and industry on the one hand, and the armed forces on the other, in order to develop the society as also to protect it.

The lance of dazzling brightness is the weapon with which the Devasenapati vanquished many an enemy. It actually stands for knowledge and wisdom with which all the ugly demons of ignorance can be destroyed.

The peacock is Subrahmanya's mount. It is shown as belabouring a snake with one of its legs. The snake stands for time. The peacock that kills it stands for what is opposed to it. By riding the peacock he is showing that he is beyond what is within time and outside it. He is beyond all dualities.

If the snake represents lust, as it often does in the symbology of psychology, the peacock signifies the power of celibacy. As Skanda, he is the very personification of the powers of chastity and hence is shown as riding on the peacock.

Lastly, the peacock, with its beautiful plumage, represents creation in all its glory. Hence he that rides it is the Supreme Lord, the Master of creation.

11

The Puranas

The *Puranas* are of the same class as the *Itihasas* (the Ramayana, Mahabharata, etc.). They have five characteristics (*Pancha Lakshana*), *viz.*, history, cosmology (with various symbolical illustrations of philosophical principles), secondary creation, genealogy of kings, and of Manvantaras (the period of Manu's rule consisting of 71 celestial Yugas or 308, 448, 000 years). All the Puranas belong to the class of *Suhrit-Sammitas*, or the Friendly Treatises, while the Vedas are called the *Prabhu-Sammitas* or the Commanding Treatises with great authority. Vyasa is the compiler of the Puranas from age to age; and for this age, he is Krishna-Dvaipayana, the son of Parasara.

The Puranas were written to popularise the religion of the Vedas. They contain the essence of the Vedas. The aim of the Puranas is to impress on the minds of the masses the teachings of the Vedas and to generate in them devotion to God, through concrete examples, myths, stories, legends, lives of saints, kings and great men, allegories and chronicles of great historical events. The sages made use of these things to illustrate the eternal principles of religion. The Puranas were meant, not for the scholars, but for the ordinary people who could not understand high philosophy and who could not study the Vedas.

The Darsanas or schools of philosophy are very stiff. They are meant only for the learned few. The Puranas are meant for the masses with inferior intellect. Religion is taught in a very easy and interesting way through the Puranas. Even to this day, the Puranas are popular. The Puranas contain the history of remote times. They also give a description of the regions of the universe not visible to the ordinary physical eye. They are very interesting to read and are full of information of all kinds. Children hear the stories from their grandmothers. Pundits and Purohits hold *Kathas* or religious discourses in temples, on banks of rivers and in other important places. Agriculturists, labourers and bazaar people hear the stories.

Eighteen Puranas: There are eighteen main Puranas and an equal number of subsidiary Puranas or Upa-Puranas. The main Puranas are: Vishnu Purana, Naradiya Purana, Srimad Bhagavata Purana, Garuda (Suparna) Purana, Padma Purana, Varaha Purana, Brahma Purana, Brahmanda Purana, Brahma Vaivarta Purana, Markandeya Purana, Bhavishya Purana, Vamana Purana, Matsya Purana, Kurma Purana, Linga Purana, Shiva Purana, Skanda Purana and Agni Purana. Of these, six are Sattvic Puranas and glorify Vishnu; six are Rajasic and glorify Brahma; six are Tamasic and they glorify Shiva.

Neophytes or beginners in the spiritual path are puzzled when they go through Shiva Purana and Vishnu Purana. In Shiva Purana, Lord Shiva is highly eulogised and an inferior position is given to Lord Vishnu. Sometimes Vishnu is belittled. In Vishnu Purana, Lord Hari is highly eulogised and an inferior status is given to Lord Shiva. Sometimes Lord Shiva is belittled. This is only to increase the faith of the devotees in their particular Ishta-Devata. Lord Shiva and Lord Vishnu are one.

The best among the Puranas are the Srimad Bhagavata and the Vishnu Purana. The most popular is the Srimad Bhagavata Purana. Next comes Vishnu Purana. A portion of the Markandeya Purana is well known to all Hindus as *Chandi*, or *Devimahatmya*. Worship of God as the Divine Mother is its theme. Chandi is read widely by the Hindus on sacred days and Navaratri (Durga Puja) days.

Ten Avataras and their Purpose

The Srimad Bhagavata Purana is a chronicle of the various Avataras of Lord Vishnu. There are ten Avataras of Vishnu. The aim of every Avatara is to save the world from some great danger, to destroy the wicked and protect the virtuous. The ten Avataras are: *Matsya* (The Fish), Kurma (The Tortoise), Varaha (The Boar), *Narasimha* (The Man-Lion), *Vamana* (The Dwarf), *Parasurama* (Rama with the axe, the destroyer of the Kshatriya race), *Ramachandra* (the hero of the Ramayana—the son of Dasharatha, who destroyed Ravana), *Sri Krishna,* the teacher of the Gita, *Buddha* (the prince-ascetic, founder of Buddhism), and *Kalki* (the hero riding on a white horse, who is to come at the end of the Kali-Yuga).

The object of the Matsya Avatara was to save Vaivasvata Manu from destruction by a deluge. The object of Kurma Avatara was to enable the world to recover some precious things which were lost in the deluge. The Kurma gave its back for keeping the churning rod when the Gods and the Asuras churned the ocean of milk. The purpose of Varaha Avatara was to rescue, from the waters, the earth which had been dragged down by a demon named Hiranyaksha. The purpose of Narasimha Avatara, half-lion and half-man, was to free the world from the oppression of Hiranyakasipu, a demon, the father of Bhakta Prahlada. The object of Vamana Avatara was to restore the power of the gods which had been eclipsed by the penance and devotion of King Bali. The object of Parasurama Avatara was to deliver the country from the oppression of the Kshatriya rulers. Parasurama destroyed the Kshatriya race twenty-one times. The object of Rama Avatara was to destroy the wicked Ravana. The object of Sri Krishna Avatara was to destroy Kamsa and other demons, to deliver His wonderful message of the Gita in the Mahabharata war, and to become the centre of the Bhakti schools of India. The object of Buddha Avatara was to prohibit animal sacrifices and teach piety. The object of the Kalki Avatara is the destruction of the wicked and the re-establishment of virtue.

Lilas of Lord Shiva

Lord Shiva incarnated himself in the form of Dakshinamurti to impart knowledge to the four Kumaras. He took human form to initiate Sambandhar, Manikkavasagar, Pattinathar. He appeared in flesh and blood to help his devotees and relieve their sufferings. The divine *Lilas* or sports of Lord Shiva are recorded in the Tamil Puranas like Shiva Purana, Periya Purana, Shiva Parakramam and Tiruvilayadal Purana.

The eighteen Upa-Puranas are: Sanatkumara, Narasimha, Brihannaradiya, Shivarahasya, Durvasa, Kapila, Vamana, Bhargava, Varuna, Kalika, Samba, Nandi, Surya, Parasara,

Vasishtha, Devi-Bhagavata, Ganesha and Hamsa. Study of the Puranas, listening to sacred recitals of scriptures, describing and expounding of the transcendent Lilas of the Blessed Lord—these form an important part of Sadhana of the Lord's devotees. It is most pleasing to the Lord. *Sravana* is a part of *Navavidha-Bhakti*. *Kathas* and *Upanyasas* open the springs of devotion in the hearts of hearers and develop *Prema-Bhakti* which confers immortality on the Jiva.

The language of the Vedas is archaic, and the subtle philosophy of Vedanta and the Upanishads is extremely difficult to grasp and assimilate. Hence, the Puranas are of special value as they present philosophical truths and precious teachings in an easier manner. They give ready access to the mysteries of life and the key to bliss. Imbibe their teachings. Start a new life of *Dharma-Nishtha* and *Adhyatmic Sadhana* from this very day, and attain Immortality.

Purana is the name of a genre (or a group of related genres) of Indian written literature (as distinct from oral literature). Its general themes are history, tradition and religion. It is usually written in the form of stories related by one person to another.

There are many texts designated as 'Purana.' The most important are:

- *Mahapuragas and Upapuragas:* Written in Sanskrit. They usually adhere to the 'Panca-laksana' typology. They tell of the creation of the universe and the human race, narrate the genealogies of kings and saints, and contain assorted narratives, stories, and philosophical and religious topics.

  Included among the texts of distinctly lesser importance that also bear the name Puranas are
- *Sthala Puragas*: Scriptures usually extolling the virtues of a certain Hindu temple. They narrate stories of the temple's creation and spiritual history.
- *Kula Puragas*: Scriptures that deal with the origin and legends of a particular caste.

The designation 'Purana' implicitly confers on a text a kind of factual aura, somewhat similar to the designation 'History' in Western discourse.

Mahapuranas and Upapuranas

Structure and Content: Maha-(Sanskrit 'great', 'mighty') and Upa-(Sanskrit 'lower', 'additional') Puranas are written in Sanskrit. Traditionally they are said to narrate five subjects, called Panca-laksana (Sanskrit 'five distinguishing marks'), which are:

1. *Sarga:* The creation of the universe.
2. *Pratisarga:* Secondary creations, mostly recreations after dissolution.
3. *Vamcea:* Genealogy of gods and sages.
4. *Manvantara:* The creation of the human race and the first human beings.
5. *Vamuanucaritam:* Dynastic histories.

Most Mahapuranas and Upapuranas deal with these subject matters, although the bulk of their text consists of historical and religious narratives. Some scholars have suggested that these 'distinguishing marks' are shared by other traditional religious scriptures of the world (e. g. the Bible). A Purana usually gives prominence to a certain deity—(Shiva, Vishnu or Krishna, Durga)—and depicts the other gods as subservient. Most use an abundance of religious and philosophical concepts in their narration, from Bhakti to Samkhya.

Classification: Traditionally it is said that there are eighteen Mahapuranas and eighteen Upapuranas. Of the Mahapuranas it is said that six belong to the quality (*guna*) of goodness, six to passion, and six to ignorance. According to the *Padma Purana,* these are the Mahapuranas and their corresponding qualities.

- *Goodness (Sattva):* Vishnu Purana, Bhagavata Purana, Naradeya Purana, Garuda Purana, Padma Purana, Varaha Purana
- *Passion (Rajas):* Brahmanda Purana, Brahma Vaivarta Purana, Markandeya Purana, Bhavishya Purana, Vamana Purana, Brahma Purana
- *Ignorance (Tamas):* Matsya Purana, Kurma Purana, Linga Purana, Shiva Purana, Skanda Purana, Agni Purana.

Some Upapuranas are: Sanat-kumara, Narasimha, Brihannaradiya, Shiva-rahasya, Durvasa, Kapila, Vamana, Bhargava, Varuna, Kalika, Samba, Nandi, Surya, Parasara, Vasishtha, Devi-Bhagavata, Ganesha, and Hamsa. Most of these have not been critically edited yet, and are available mostly through devotional publications, in multiple versions and recensions.

Special Purana : Adhata Purana

Apart from the system of classification above mentioned, the Puranas are enumerated and classified in multiple ways. The canonical lists of Puranas vary from place to place and from time to time.

Author and Disemmination: Traditionally, the Puranas are said to have been composed by the sage Vyasa, the narrator of the Mahabharata epic. Vyasa in Sanskrit means 'Divider,' and some scholars therefore take this simply as a term meaning 'Editor'. The texts, these scholars say, were probably written all over India and are being rewritten and re-edited to the present day all over the world. The Puranas, being in Sanskrit, are usually not directly accessible to the common man as read texts. They are, however, available in vernacular translations and are disseminated by Brahmin scholars, who read from them and tell their stories, usually in Katha sessions (in which a travelling Brahmin settles for a few weeks in a temple and narrates parts of a Purana, usually with a Bhakti perspective).

Chronology: The Itihasa-Purana is mentioned in the Chandogya Upanishad. There are also references to the Puranas in the Atharvaveda 11. 7. 24 and the Satapatha Brahmana 11. 5. 6. 8. and 13. 4. 3. 13. There are probably also references to the Itihasa in the Nirukta. The Itihasa-Purana was considered to be almost as sacred and ancient as the Vedas, *i.e.* the "fifth Veda" according to the Brihad-aranyaka Upanishad. However, the ancient Itihasa-Purana was probably not exactly the same as the text of the Puranas that we know today. Scholars argue that some contents of the Puranas may date to an earlier period. According to Pargiter, the original Purana may date to the time of the final redaction of the Vedas. Pargiter has argued that in the Puranas, the Puranic Krta Yuga "ended with the destruction of the Haihayas [by Rama Jamadagnya]; the Treta began approximately with Sagara and ended with Rama Dasarathi's destruction of the Raksasas; and the Dvapara began with his reinstatement at Ayodhya and ended with the Bharata battle".

Vedic and Puranic Genealogies: The Puranas also lay emphasis on keeping a record of genealogies, thus Vayu Purana says: "As seen by good people in the ancient times the suta's duty was to preserve the genealogies of gods, rsis and glorious kings and the traditions of great men." (Vayu P. 1. 31-2)

The Vedic and Puranic genealogies indicate a greater antiquity of the Vedic culture. The Puranas themselves state that these lists are incomplete. But the accuracy of these lists is disputed. In Arrian's Indica, Megasthenes is quoted as stating that the Indians counted from Shiva (Dionysos) to Chandragupta Maurya (Sandracottus) "a hundred and fifty-three kings over six thousand and forty-three years." The Brhadaranyaka Upanishad (4. 6.), ca. 8th century BCE, mentions 57 links in the Guru-Parampara ("succession of teachers"). This would mean that this Guru-Parampara would go back about 1400 years, although the accuracy of this list is disputed. The list of kings in Kalhana's Rajatarangini goes back to the 19th century BCE. The Puranic genealogies indicate that Manu Vaivasvata lived 95 generations before the Bharata War.

Notable Puranas

- *The Bhagavata Purana*: It is concerned with Vishnu Bhakti, telling of the exploits and deeds of Vishnu's Avataras. Its tenth canto (its longest) narrates the deeds of Krishna and, probably for the first time in Sanskrit, tells of his exploits as a child, a theme later elaborated by many Bhakti movements.
- *The Devi-bhagavata Purana*: An Upapurana extolling the virtues of the goddess Durga as the supreme being. It has become (along with the Devi Mahatmya of the Markandeya Purana) a basic text for Devi worshippers.
- *The Skanda Purana*: Probably the longest of all. A vast storehouse of parables, legends and stories, with multiple versions and recensions. Many untraced quotes from a Purana are conveniently attributed to this Purana.

Sthala Puranas: This corpus of texts narrates the virtues and stories connected with a certain temple or shrine (the word 'Sthala' means 'Place' in Sanskrit). There are numerous Sthala

Puranas, most written in vernaculars, some with Sanskrit versions as well. Most claim to have a Sanskrit origin, and some of the Sanskrit versions also appear in a Mahapurana or an Upapurana. Some Tamil Sthala Puranas have been researched by David Dean Shulman.

Kula Puranas: These are mostly caste focused Puranas (the word 'Kula' means 'Family' or 'Tribe' in Sanskrit). They deal with a caste's origin myth, stories and legends. The caste Purana is an important source for caste identity and is usually contested by other, rival, castes. This subgenre is usually in the vernacular and might at times be oral.

This subgenre has been little researched. But it is rather well documented in the caste section of the British Census of India Report and the various Gazzeteers.

Other Puranas: There are many other narratives that go by the name of Purana. Most are written in vernaculars and are usually concerned with mythical and historical narrations. These texts, such as the Padma Purana of Bengal and Assam (narrating the story of the goddess Manasa), are vast in number and scattered all over the Indian subcontinent.

Non-Hindu Puranas: There are many Jaina Puranas, dealing with Jaina myths, history and legends. Studies and translations of this particular genre are meagre. Arguably, some Buddhist Mahay:na Sutras seem to have some characteristics of Puranas.

12

Lord Shiva

Of all the Hindu Gods, none appealed to the emotions of a Hindu mind as much as Lord Shiva, the dweller of the mountains and the bearer of the trident, who with His third eye symbolizes the all knowing awareness of the universe.

Description of Shiva: Unlike Vishnu who is depicted as dark blue, Shiva is white in colour, except for his neck, which is dark blue. His neck became dark blue when he swallowed the poison emanated from the sea in the process of churning the amutham. He took the whole poison by himself to protect the cosmos from destruction and thus the images of him are prevailing in dark blue colour here and there.

He leads a life of severe austerities. But in the images we find him tall and well built. His body is usually besmeared with ashes, denoting his frequent rounds to the cremation grounds and highlighting his fondness for Thiruneeru, a white sacred ash. He has three eyes. The third eye rests between his eyebrows. It is the eye of wisdom, by opening which he destroys the evil to maintain the cosmic harmony.

Though he is described in the scriptures as god of anger, he is, in fact, the god of love and he always bestows all kinds of wealth and power to the devotees and this is the reason for which we generally find him in his cheerful and jovial mood in the images.

Ravana and Surapathma were blessed with immortal powers by Lord Shiva which gave a room for the birth of Rama and Skanda. Sometimes he is depicted with a lot of innocence in his demeanour as Bholenath. He is generally shown sitting cross-legged in a yogic posture, with his eyes closed and deep in meditation. When he is shown with his eyes open, his face expresses love and compassion. The images of Shiva evoke us in deep emotions. Those who are inclined to worship god are naturally drawn to him as they hold him in their minds and this is the reason for which the Saint Thirumular used to name him as Anbe Shivam, the lord of love.

Shiva is the god of simplicity, exemplary humility and austerity. A tiger skin and an elephant skin serve as his garments. His long matted hair is normally tied into a knot or left flowing. He has four arms. With one he holds his weapon the trident. With another, he holds Damaru, a small drum. The remaining two is held in abhaya and varada mudras (postures).

THE TRIDENT AND THE SNAKES

The trident is the weapon of Shiva with which he destroys evils and restores order. The trident stands for the triple qualities of nature, namely, sattva, rajas and tamas. Shiva is the master of maya and thereby master of these three qualities with which he controls the universe.

The trident symbolically represents the fact that Shiva is the controller of the universe and the controller of all illusion. The trident also represents the three aspects of time, the past, the present and the future.

Shiva is master of Time, Kala Bhairava who determines the progress of the universe according to his will. The trident represents the three paths to self-realization, namely the path of knowledge, the path of action and the path of devotion.

With these three paths, Shiva transforms his devotees and destroys the evil in them. The trident stands for the three primary evils which need to be destroyed in order to make progress towards the divine. They are the evil of anger, the evil of lust and the evil of pride

The damaru denotes his connection with the primal sound AUM, the creation of alphabets, languages, grammar and music. His long matted hair denotes his spiritual life and his great powers. The crescent moon adorns his hair like a silver diadem.

Symbolism of Snakes: He wears a garland of snakes around his neck. Sometimes we see more snakes; one across his body like a sacred thread and two acting as bracelets around his muscular hands. The snakes symbolically represent his control over desire and sensuality. Sometimes in his ferocious aspects, he is shown wearing a garland of skulls.

There is a deep symbolism hidden behind this. The snake stands for all the evil and demoniacal nature in the world. By wearing the snake around his neck, Lord Shiva gives us the assurance that no evil can touch us or destroy us once we surrender to him, seek his protection and worship him with deep devotion.

The snake also stands for the power of kundalini, which is described as a coiled serpent lying dormant in the muladhara chakra of all human beings and descends upwards when one starts ones spiritual journey and becomes increasingly divine oriented.

The snake around the neck of Shiva conveys the meaning that in him the kundalini not only has arisen fully but is also actively involved in the divine activity by keeping an eye on all the devotees who approach Shiva with their individual problems.

The snake also stands for all passions and desires. By wearing the snakes around his neck, Lord Shiva conveys the message to all his devotees that He has overcome all desires and is in full control of Prakriti, or maya and its various machinations.

The Ganges: And the Ganges flows from his head down into the world below.

The river Ganges is very sacred to the Hindus. Those who take a dip in the river are said to be ridden of all their sins and attain immortality.

It is believed that the river used to flow in the heavens till the sage, Bhageerath, made severe penances and directed its flow towards the earth to save his 60000 ancestors who were lying in the nether world (patala) in a heap of ashes due to a curse delivered by sage Kapila.

Since earth was not yet prepared to withstand the impact of its downward descent, Lord Shiva came forward to allow it to fall on His head first and then flow down towards the earth.

He also made the Ganges His permanent companion. Three of them flowed west and three east. The remaining seventh stream followed Bhageerath to the nether worlds and helped all his ancestors from damnation. The river is eternal and said to reward immortality to those who come into contact with it.

Symbolically, on the earth plane, the river stands for divine consciousness. It descended into the earth consciousness through the efforts of sage Bhageerath.

Being divine consciousness, who ever immerses himself in it becomes immortal. It is eternal because it is the highest consciousness, which human beings are capable of attaining during their spiritual endeavour.

In the body plane, the story of Ganga reveals the divine origin of kundalini and its descent through the various chakras of the body into the lowest chakra, the muladhara corresponding to the patala regions of the world, where it remains coiled like a serpent till it ascends again into the higher chakras during ones spiritual sadhana.

If we interpret the word Bhageerath as "bhaga"+"rathi" it means he who rides bhaga (the reproductive organ) which is the place where the kundalini ordinarily remains in a coiled state. Probably the sons of Sagara whom sage Bhagirath rescued correspond to the various nerve centres in that region.

The divine consciousness thus entering into earth plane (human body) through Lord Shiva made spiritual evolution possible on earth as well in human body.

The second interpretation is that Ganga symbolically represents a particular branch of divine and esoteric knowledge with the powers to elevate the dead as well as the living towards heavens, with the strength of its purity and illumination, which was probably not available to the mankind, till sage Bhagirath tried to bring it down into human awareness through his devotion and surrender to Lord Shiva, who ultimately helped him to receive it and help his ancestors attain immortality.

Shiva and His Family: Though Shiva is an ascetic, he lives with his family. He is very fond of his consort, Parvathi, whom he married after subjecting her to a lot of tests. Shiva treats his wife as his equal and shares his seat with her. She is literally his better half and occupies half of his body. This earned him the title ardhanarishwara (half female, half male). Normally we find Parvathi always by his side, especially when he is seated in Kailash, sharing with her all the honours that he receives.

His beloved children are Skanda or Kumara and Lord Ganesha or Vinayaka. The Bull Nandi is his vehicle. Nandiswara is humility personified. He is very knowledgeable also. Nandi taught universe the secrets of Vedas and lessons in humility! Hanuman is a form of representation of the powers of Lord Shiva. Another important member of his pariwar is Bhringi, the zealous devotee who was not inclined to worship anyone other than Shiva and refused to worship even Parvathi, till he was made to realize his mistake. Although a mountain dweller, Shiva is not attached to anything and true to his ascetic nature, keeps wandering from place to place. Mount Kailash is his abode, where live his family, his devotees who attained liberation and his great army of goblins, imps and ghosts.

Symbolism: Shiva symbolically represents the tamasic quality. Because of this, he is called pasupathi, (the lord of the animals). His body colour, which is white, denotes his purity (Shivam) and association with the snowy mountains. His three eyes represent the sun, the moon and the earth, the three paths of liberation and the triple nature of creation.

The third eye is actually the eye of wisdom or occult knowledge. The moon that adorns his head represents the movement of time and also his cosmic proportions. With the moon there, his head becomes the night sky, for which he earned the name Vyomakesa (one who has the sky or space as his hair). The moon also symbolizes his association with the occult and the tantras.

Shiva is generally seated in yogic posture with which most Hindus are familiar. However we also come across Shiva as nataraja or tandavamurthi in a dance posture. With his hair flying in all directions and hands and feet in dynamic motion, the image of nataraja is a symbol of harmony and rhythm. Among the objects, which are associated with him popularly, apart from the trident and the Damaru, are battle-axe (parasu), rosary (aksamala), pasa (noose), khatvanga (magic wand) and khadga (sword). Lord Shiva is know as Pasupathinath, the lord of all creatures. Being a lord of the animals he has complete control on their behaviour. Since a snake is one of the most feared and dangerous animals in the world, the garland of snakes around the neck firmly establish the fact that he is a lover of animals and the animals always remain under his control.

Although universally acknowledged as one of the trinity gods of Hinduism, to His followers, He is Maheswara, representing the Trinity all by Himself, His different aspects manifesting themselves as the creator, preserver and destroyer of the worlds He creates. Symbolically He is worshipped as Lingeswara, which name stands more for His creative powers.

Historians believe that He was a pre-Vedic god who was admitted into the Vedic Pantheon because of His immense popularity during pre-vedic period. There is a theory that the seated yogi found on the seals of Indus Valley Civilization, was a prototype of Lord Shiva only. References to Him are found in the Rigveda.

In the Mahabharata we come across several references to Him. Both Arjuna and Krishna worshipped Him and obtained favours from Him. In the Ramayana too we come across several references to Him. Sage Valmiki depicted Ravana, the demon king and chief villain of the epic, as a great devotee and daily worshipper of Lord Shiva.

With the popularity of Shaivism a great deal of literature grew around Him, which came to be recognized as Agama literature. So great was His popularity and fame that Agama literature was placed on equal footing to even the Vedas by His followers.

Shaivism as a popular movement took shape mainly in South India because of the patronage of the Pallavas and the dedicated work of many great Tamil Saints, who built enormous bhakti or devotional literature in His honour and made His name a household name. Shiva is also referred as the Lord of the south as he faces the south always in his form as Dakshinamurthy.

Megasthenes mentioned the worship of Shiva in his book Indika. So did Patanjali, the composer of Yoga Sutras. Two great rulers of ancient India, Kanishka and Harshavardhana were His great followers. In the south the Pandiyas, Cholas and Pallavas built many temples in His honour.

Shiva and His Titles: He is known by many names and titles. As a god of anger, He is Rudra, the Red One, feared by one and all. As Kailasapathi, He is the Lord of Kailash, His Abode in the Himalayas. As Purusha, He is Iswara Himself. As the Lord of the beings, He is known as Pasupathinath. As the husband of Uma, the Mother Goddess, He is known as Umapathi or Parvathipathi.

As the bearer of the sacred river Ganges, He is known as Gangadhar. Because of His matted hair, He is dearly called as Jatadhari, by His ascetic followers. As a perfect being, He is Siddheshwar. With His Trident in His hands, He became popular as heroic and fearless Trishuladhari. As the world teacher, Adi Shankara eulogized him as Dakhshinamurthi in his famous book, "Hymns to Dakhshinamurthi".

To the connoisseurs of art, He is well known as Nataraja, master of all dance forms. As the perfect Yogi, He is credited with the source of all knowledge concerning the various yogas. Such was His powers and divinity, that Lord Vishnu in His incarnations as Rama and Krishna, worshipped Him with great reverence. He was dearer not only to gods but also to demons.

Many demons like Ravana, Bhasmasur and Surapathma were His ardent followers, to whom He gave several boons out of His unbound love and in the process invited great trouble for Himself and for others. Ever willing to help those who are in distress, He saved the cosmos and all the gods by partaking Halahal during the churning of the oceans.

It is interesting to note that while He is worshipped as he is the guru of Tantrics shashtras relating to kama, He is also known for destroying the physical form of Cupid, kama with His third eye when the latter tried to disturb Him during His meditation. Men and women love Him alike for his unsurpassed qualities of love and generosity. Even today many young and unmarried girls in India worship Him and pray to Him seeking a devoted husband like Him.

Because of His close association with Vishnu, He is also known as Hari Har. Combining in Himself both the male and female aspects of creation, He earned the popular name of Ardhanarishwara. As rider of the Bull Nandi, He is known to the world as Nandiswara.

Loved by His children Ganesha and Skanda, and followed by His dutiful wife Parvathi, He became a symbol of ideal householder to His devotees despite of His well-known image as an introvert and an ideal ascetic.

Shiva and Tantra: Shiva has been the object of worship by many schools of tantras, some of whom follow sexual cults and other different paths in search of self-realization.

The fact that a great mass of heterogeneous cults and practices came to be associated with Him, suggests that in His unlimited wisdom and boundless love as a World Teacher and Father of all, Lord Shiva gives immense freedom to His followers to chose whatever path they want to follow for their self-realization.

To the followers of Vira Shaiva cult, He is Vira Bhadra, valour personified. In His terrific forms, He is worshipped as Bhairavamurthy, Pataleswar and so on. He has many temples built all over India and in many other places in the world. He has shrines in almost every village or city, on the banks of every river and even in remote hilly areas of India.

Followers of Shaivism are familiar with three words pati, pasu and paasa. Pati is Shiva himself, the lord and husband. Pasu is the deluded self that is caught in the cycle of birth and death. Pasa is the bond that binds the pasu to this world and it gains liberation through devotion and surrender to pati.

His names are endless. So does His popularity. Even as early as the 2nd Century A.D., His fame spread beyond the boundaries of the Indian Subcontinent and spread to Central Asia. As the Hindu culture spread to far east, temples were built in His Honour in many places like Java, Champa (Indo-China), Kambhoja (present day Cambodia) and in the adjoining areas of the now south east Asian countries. Some of these temples were built there as early as 5th Century A.D.

Aspects of Lord Shiva: Shiva is known by several names and worshipped in various forms. We are mentioning below some of his most famous aspects:

Shivalingam: The Shivalingam is the symbolic of the Supreme Self. It is verily Maheswara Himself, the Highest Self and the Lord of the universe. In this aspect it has three parts. The lower part represents Brahma. The middle part, which is octagonal in shape, represents Vishnu. The upper part, which is cylindrical in shape, represents Rudra and is also called Pujabhaga.

Shivalingam literally means the body of Shiva. Next to the symbol of AUM, it is perhaps the most potent, powerful and popular symbol in entire Hinduism. In almost all the Shiva temples, worship is generally made to Shivalingas only. In the North part of India, we come across his images in the sanctum sanctorum of any Shiva temple. A Shivalingam is usually a round or cylindrical and protruding object. The cylindrical part is held firmly by a circular base.

On the physical plane, the object resembles the male sexual organ, suggestive of the creative power of Shiva. The octagonal base resembles that of the female, suggestive of his consort Parvathi. Physically a Shivalingam is a phallic symbol, representing the male and female sexual organs in a state of conjugal bliss.

Mentally it symbolizes the union of mind and body. Spiritually it represents the union between Purusha and Prakriti, the highest principles of the manifest universe.

The Shivalingas are normally found installed in the temples. But many devotees of Shiva keep them in their houses and offer regular worship. People are however cautioned not to keep Shivalingas in their houses without offering worship, since they are believed to be powerful sources of divine energy.

Shivalingas are either naturally found or made artificially. Different materials are used in their making, such as clay, gold, crystal, glass, diamonds, precious stones and wood.

The round and smooth stones found in the river beds of the Narmada or the Godavari are considered to be the most ideal for worship. Sometimes Shivlingas are made temporarily with clay or sandal paste and disposed of after worship. Some devotees wear Shivalingas on their bodies or around their necks. When Shivalingas are found fortuitously in the river beds and desolate places, it is considered to be a great omen.

They are housed in temples or houses and offered regular worship.

Shiva Murthy: Panchanana Shiva: In some temples Shiva is shown with five faces. Each of the faces has a name and represents a specific aspect. These five faces are Isana, Tatpurusa, Aghora, Vamadeva and Sadyojata. Isana faces south east and represents Iswara aspect of Shiva known as Sada Shiva, or the Eternal Shiva. Tatpurusha faces the east. He is Shiva in his aspect as a deluded purusha or ego. Aghora faces the south and represents the destructive and regenerative aspect of Shiva that, like fire, first devours life and then prepares the ground for its renewal. Vamadeva faces north. He is healer and preserver. Sadyojata faces west and represents the creative power of Shiva.

Anugrahamurthy: This is the milder or peaceful aspect of Lord Shiva when he is in the company of his beloved devotees or his family members.

Ugramurthy: Also known as Rudra, Bhairava, Kankala or Samharamurthy, this is the ferocious or angry form of Shiva, generally associated with the events during which Shiva assumed his terrible form to slay the demons or the wicked.

The following are his well known terrible forms:

Kankala-bhairava: The form which he assumed after cutting off the fifth head of Brahma.

Gajasura-vadha-murthy: The form he assumed while killing a demon named Nila.

Tripurantakmurthi: The form he assumed while destroying the three cities of gold, silver and iron built by the three sons of Andhakasura.

Sarabhesa-murthy: The form in which he allegedly fought and sanctified, Narasimha, the incarnation of Vishnu.

Kalari-murthy: The form in which he fought and defeated Yama to save his devotee Markandeya.

Kamantaka-murthy: The form in which he destroyed Manmadha, the god of lust, for disturbing him while doing penance.

Andhakasura-vadha-murthy: The form in which he defeated Andhakasura, who subsequently joined his forces as his commander and became popular as Bhringi.

Bhairava-murthy: The form generally found in connection with the cults of teaching the secrets of tantras, yantras, alchemy, magic and occult knowledge.

Slokam: With the hands in abhaya (protecting) and varada (boon giving) postures, with a pleasing and decorated expression, a blossomed face and eye, with the shadow created by moon on the crown, with an upright body, and feet in the same level, Coral like formed, holding the deer and axe, (He) stay in the lotus pedestal (of my heart)

Purana of the Deity

Chandrashekhar : moon ornamented Lord (bhoga murti)

Daksha had twenty seven stars as daughters. All of them were married to moon. But the moon had special attraction towards Rohini. So all the other wives complained it to the father daksha that their husband moon is not treating them fairly. Daksha got angry and cursed the moon to lose its luminance (kala) day by day. Everyday the moon started losing one luminance part (kala) out of his 16 parts. Afraid and ashamed moon disappeared into the ocean. There are many herbs that require the light of the moon to grow. Without moon, they were harmed. Consequently there was suffering in the world. To end the problem the celestials advised moon to take refuge in the Great Divine, Lord Shiva. Left with only one kala, he took refuge in Lord Shiva. Being the graceful Almighty, He wore the moon crescent on His head, making him grow for 15 days and decay for 15 days periodically. Thus Chandra-shekhar is considered a giver of refuge.

Kalayana Sundarar

Slokam: Red in colour (sindhuram), Three eyed, shoulders like yugas (four shouldered), wearing necklace and bracelet, colourful in divine wonderful dress, shining in the wedding robe, ornated, with enchanting body, salutations to that murti who is in marriage posture, with a hand of Devi in one lotus hand, with axe and deer in hands and ganga and moon on the wound-up hair.

Purana of the Murti

Kalyana Sundar : The beautiful (murti) in marriage (bhoga murti) Shakthi was born as Parvati, the daughter of the king of Himalayas. As a young child, She was not interested in playing like the other children. She was more inclined towards meditating on Lord Shiva in the mountains. She desired to marry Lord Shiva. For that she wanted to perform austerity in the snow covered Himalayas. Her parents hesitated, but finally had to subdue to the determination of Parvati. Parvati performed austerity from an ashram. Lord Shiva who was happy with Her worship, came as an old devotee to her place. Parvati offered Her respect to the Old bhakta of Her Beloved Lord.

Now, He tried to convince Her that She shouldn't waste Her youth doing tapas, but should enjoy life getting married! He further suggested that She could get married to Him, instead of desiring for Lord Shiva Who dances in the cemeteries and wears skulls and bones! Parvati, without knowing that He is God Himself, got very angry on hearing the Old man's words and told Him that She showed Him respect only because He seemed like a devotee and She would not want to hear any little blasphemy of God further. She asked the Old Man to leave the place immediately.

The Lord, pleased with Her determination and devotion, revealed who He is. Parvati was surprised and begged the pardon of God. However God had accepted Her scolding as the most pleasant hailing. Didn't it come from a very deep love for God?! He gave Her the boon She yearned for-getting married to Her.

The Himalayan king's family was delighted to see their beloved daughter's wedding. The region was decorated and shining with prosperity. The young beautiful Parvati was decorated with chosen best ornaments for the wedding. Now came the Groom-Lord Shiva-to the wedding place-on an old bull, with skull and bone ornaments, with the skin of the tiger as the clothing, accompanied by the roar of the buta ganas ! The mother of Parvati menai fainted to see the groom in such a form for her sweet daughter, softer than the flowers.

Now the Lord changed to the form, glittering in a beautiful wedding robe-with golden ornaments and splendid clothing! When menai woke up and saw the Groom she was thrilled to see such a beautiful form and was very pleased that He is "the suitable" groom for her daughter. The play of the Lord has no bounds! menai saw only the external appearance of the Groom. Other than the great Parvati who knows the glory of that Groom?! The enchanting Lord in the wedding robe got married to the Daughter of the mountains and this form of God is called kalyana sundharar

Kalyana Vratam (Panguni uththiram)

Kalyana vratam is one of the eight auspicious vratas. When the Sun is shining in the Pisces sign (mina raashi) that is in the month of panguni (mid of March to mid of April) on the uththara naxaththiram on the Moons growing face (shukla paxam), this vratam is observed. This is the day Shakthi married Lord Shiva after a great austerity in the Himalayas, as the daughter of Himavaan. It is also observed as the auspicious day when Lord Muruga married devasena. This vratam is explained in the skandha puranam.

In the morning after getting up, the observer of the vratam should meditate on the charming Lord Shiva in the wedding posture with Uma. After taking bath and through with other required deeds, should worship the Lord. The golden idol of the God and Goddess (who can afford to) should be anointed devotionally with holy substances.

Then decorating them should make the wedding ceremony of the Goddess with the God. Making the nice and sweet offerings to the divine Parents, should salute them. Inviting the spiritual people who think of good to all the creatures, who have learnt the Vedas and who are devotees of Lord Shiva, along with their wives, should host them a feast. Later should go to the Shiva temple, worship, circumambulate three times and prostrate in front of the Lord. In the night should dine along with the kind hearted devotees of Lord Shiva and eat the sweet dishes like fruits and Payasam. Should sleep on the dharbai grass. The next morning after regular deeds, should donate the golden idol of God and Goddess to disciplined love hearted people who are the devotees of Lord Shiva. Should eat only once that day.

Observing this vratam will get one the great boon of shri Lord Shankara's delight. It would bring much joy and comfort in life, lead to the abode of Lord Shiva and give the liberation. Maha Vishnu got wedded to Lakshmi sincerely observing this vratam Brahma wedded Saraswati, Indra wedded Indrani, moon wedded the 27 stars, sage Agastya wedded lobhamudra observing this vratam.

The two daughters of Vishnu namely amritavalli, saundaryavalli were married to the six faced Lord as devasena and valli. The daughter of vedanga Rishi called sukesi got married to nandi devar. The two daughters of sage satyapurnar purna, pushhkalai were wedded to maha sastha, kama got rati, Sita got Rama, Jambhavati got Krishna, sage Saupari got many princess' and so many more benefited all in the glory of this vratam. The man who observes this vratam will get the girl he likes and the woman gets beautiful man as her husband. The couple who observe this will get good offspring. Anybody who observes with devotion will get His grace.

Ardhanarishvarar

Slokam: In the form of male and female, matted hair with moon, axe, smeared in red (aruna), wearing snakes and the skin of tiger, embracing the bull and with a bent leg, this the right half, and the left black in colour, hand holding a (lily) flower close to the chest, with a silk like lotus foot, wearing gold ornaments, salutations to the Half female God.

Purana of the Deity

Ardhanarishvarar: Half female God (bhoga murti) Sage Bhringi is one of the ardent devotees of Lord Shiva. He used to worship only Lord Shiva and not Shakti. Goddess shakti, being the power as the name indicate, pulled out the energy from Bhringi maharishi's body. Now he was even unable to stand. He pleaded to God. God Shiva provided him with a stick. On its support he stood and still worshipped Lord Shiva alone. Goddess shakti wanted to become an inseparable part of Lord Shiva's form. She observed the Kedara mahamaha vrata austerity, which is now known as Deepawali. Pleased with her austerity, Lord Shiva granted her the boon of being part of His form. So the Lord now appeared male on the right side and female on the left side and hence became archanarishvara.

Significance of this Form

This is one of the very important form of God, Hindus worship. This is a much-hailed form in scriptures of various languages. Hindus do not say that the God is only male. God is male - female and neuter too ! Since God is conceptually beyond sex, though gets referred as He/She many times, it is more appropriate to refer as It, especially at Its intrinsic condition, as do many Hindu scriptures.

Philosophically, this form is quite associated with the Grace of God. Shiva and shakti are one and the same Supreme. The formless God is called parashiva. On Its own free-will for the benefit of pashus (souls), which are drowned in pasha (bondage), It thinks to create the worlds. Its dynamism of creation thus springs out of It, which is called shakti. Now Shiva and Its power shakti create everything. This is the form of their togetherness that springs out of Lord Shiva. Because of this the form is associated with the grace of God. Shiva and shakti though the same may also act independently. They are associated like the person and the action of the person. They are one and the same like the ice and the water - one becomes the other. For this reason scriptures describe that shakti to Shiva is a wife (they are together), mother (shakti becomes Shiva - so Shiva comes out of shakti) and daughter (Shiva become shakti). Poet Kalidasa hails them as inseparable like the word and its meaning, the letter and pronunciation.

Kedara (gauri) vratam - Deepawali

Kedara Gowri vradham familiarly known as Deepawali (Diwali) is celebrated throughout India in a grand manner. Without Caste creed, rich - poor differences people observe this festival. In fact very few people know that it is one of the important Saivite vratas. Bhringi rishi is a great Shiva bhaktha. When he prays to Lord, he prays only to Lord Shiva and ignores Shakti. Angered by his act Shakti devi removed the energy from his body. He was not able to stand. He prayed to Lord Shiva. God gave him a stick to support his body. Shakti wanted to become part of Lord's body. She observed the Kedara vrata, one of Gods favourite vratas. Pleased by Her austerities God gave the left part of His body to shakti and became ardha narishwara. The vrata is then called Kedara gauri vrata since Gowri observed it.

When Observed?

This Kedara vratam is observed for twenty one days starting

from shukla paxa dasami (Tenth moonday in its growing face) in the month of purattachi (mid Sep to mid Oct.). The final day (Deepawali) also should be observed in great devotion.

How to Observe this Vratam?

mantras to perform this Puja (Puja vidhanam)

Install Lord Kedarishwara Swami in a filled pot (kalasham). Make a roof (mantapa) above the kalasham. Make vrata threads - 21 fibers having 21 knots. The 16 courtasy worship has to be done for 21 days starting from the purattachi shukla paxa dasami to aipachi amarapaxa chaturdashi (Deepawali) or amavasya. On the culmination day (21st) in a clean decorated area devotionally install the kalasham over the grains spread in a banana leaf and offer various food and fruits to the Lord as offering and donate to others.

Glory

The glory of this vratam is very splendid as Shri Gauri Devi observed this vratam in full devotion and got to be in half the body of Lord Shiva !! Vishnu became Lord of vaikuntha observing this vratam. Brahma got hamsa vehicle, the guards of the eight directions got rid of the bane they got from brahma, bhagyavati and punyavati got lots of wealth all due to the glory of this vratam. One who observes this vratam with devotion pleases Lord Shiva.

Natarajar

Slokam: A face with four shoulders, three eyes, to the left destructive fire (in the hand), moon and leaves on the head, hand stretching downwards, the raised foot pointing down, to the right swastika earring, Damarukam (drum), ganga (in the head), and protection posture, salutations to that God of ceaseless dance whose matted hair is flowing, standing on the unconscious body (hyapasmara deham)

Purana of the Deity

Natarajar : King of dance (yoga murti) Lord Shiva dances during the creation, protection and destruction of the worlds, though the kind of His dance varies with respect to the action. (sandhya tandava, urdhva tandava, rudra tandava, samhara tandava etc.). The dance of the Lord takes place in every minute particle, for all of us to exist and act. That is the source of all the energy. His movement is shakti. Yogis hear and see the dance of the Lord by invoking the Kundalini shakti.

There were two ardent sages Vyagrapada and patanjali who were worshipping God to see Its blissful dance that energizes the worlds. Vyagrapada out of his devotion asked for the eyes and legs of the tiger, so that he could go very early in the dawn, even before the bees wake up, to pluck the flowers very fresh - not even touched by the bees to offer to God ! That is why he was called Vyagrapada. The other sage was the serpent Adisesha on which maha Vishnu reside, desired to see the glorious Dance of God. They were performing austerity at the holy place called thillai.

At the same time bhadrakali, the fierce form of goddess asked for a competition with God in dance. God and mahakali came to the thillai, where the sages were performing austerity to see His dance and there began the competition between Kali and Lord Shiva. The Lord, Who keeps dancing creating, protecting, destroying, hiding and blessing, won the play by acting the urdva tandava, raising His Feet to His Head. The gracious dance of the God filled the hearts of the sages and those who ardently seek Him. Lord Shiva danced in the five ambalams during various occasions. Out of them chithambaram is very much renowned. Lord danced here to fulfil the worship of patanjali and vyaghra pada maharishis.

Kalari

Slokam: Red in colour (sindhuram), Three eyed, shoulders like yugas (four shouldered), with hands holding up the shulam, noose, axe in hands, with frightening teeth, nice face, with the left foot standing up over the chest of kala (time - death), with cast down red matted hair, to that pashupati (Lord of creatures), kalantaka I prostrate.

Purana of the Deity

Kala Ari : The enemy of kala (vira murti) kala is the deva who is responsible for death. Taking the kala as time it can be said kalari represents the fact that God is beyond the limits of time (mrityujnjayan).

The sage Mrikandu did not have an offspring for quite a

long time. He performed tapas to get the blessings of Lord Shiva. God appeared in front of him. Now the sage had two choices - either a son indiscipline, cruel and dumb living for long or a son loving, intelligent and a gem of character living very short span of life. The sage chose the second one. His wife gave birth to a child Markandeya, out of a boon from Lord Shiva, by which Markandeya would be very intelligent but would live just for 16 years.

Young child Markandeya grew up learning the great scriptures, caring and loving, devotional towards God. His parents were very pleased with him. When he became 16, he found his parents weeping. He came to know that he would die at 16 and that was the cause of the gloom. Intelligent Markandeya realized that none other than the God, Who is beyond all the scopes of time and hailed as Mrityunjaya - who conquered the death, can save him from the strong clutches of death. Determined and devotional, he started doing Shiva Puja and surrendered himself completely to the Lord.

The yamadutas who came to take his life away were scared away by the flame of this young boy's devotion. As the attendants couldn't take away his life, kala the god of death, himself came. Young Markandeya did not loose his devotion even in the crisis moment. He embraced the Shiva Lingam. As kala still tried to take away Markandeya's life, the Lord appeared furious from the Shiva Lingam and kicked kala to death!! He blessed the sincere devotion of the young boy and made Markandeya to be in 16 always-deathless! All the gods pleaded to Lord to show mercy on kala. On their request, God gave kala life back and ordered him not to disturb His devotees.

thiruk kadavur is the temple associated with this valorous deed of Lord Shiva.

Daxinamurti

Slokam: The leg pressing over a demon, on the top of which the Embodiment of merits is sitting with one leg folded, the one who teaches difficult words (vedas) with ease, the sages enjoying (the teachings, sitting) on ground, with the (hand) posture of explaining, a fire pot, book and akshamala in the four hands, Who trembles away my ignorance, to That Dakshinamurti (salutations).

Purana of the Deity

Dakshina Murti: South faced Lord (yoga murti) The four sons, of Brahma, Shanaka, Sanandana, Sanatana, Sanat kumara did austere tapas and analysis, but they were unclear of the Supreme Truth. They finally decided to come to Lord Shiva to get the knowledge of the Truth. The Lord sat under the banyan tree, and the four sages also sat down around Him. Lord stayed in the yoga posture without saying a single word. The four sages got all their doubts cleared just by that posture. The form in which God appeared as a Supreme Guide is the form of wisdom Dakshinamurti.

This explains that the Truth cannot be explained in words and must be experienced. Including the great chinmudra posture, the posture of Shri Dakshinamurti, who is the teacher of all the teachers, indicates a lot of information that needs days to explain. As thirumular says, the posture of the guru is a thing to be thought about always. That is the clarity! (thelivu guruvuru chindhiththal thane).

Shiva as Nataraja

Tandavamurthy: Nataraja is Shiva who is hidden in all the rhythmic movements of the manifest creation, the so called cosmic dance that ensures the orderliness (Rta) of the universe, the movement of the earth and the heavens, the arrangement of the galaxies and the inter stellar spaces, on which depends precariously the whole balance.

His dance is a divine activity that suffers no conflicts. It entertains our suffering minds and dispels our ignorance. It destroys our illusions and burns the worlds of demons and darkness. Finally, at the end of creation it dissolves the entire universe into a mysterious period of ekanda, a suspended activity.

Lord Shiva is a master of dance forms. He is the author of all dance forms. The science of dance (Natya shastra) dealing with the 108 types of classical Indian dance forms said to have originated from him just as all the yogic postures.

In case of Lord Shiva all dance is a form of expression, which he uses either to destroy the evil or alleviate the sufferings of his devotees.

About nine forms of Shiva in dancing mode are described, of which the most popular form is Nataraja (the king of dance). Though we have a number of icons of Shiva as Nataraja, he is rarely worshipped in this form either in the temples or in the households.

His other dance forms include, Ananda-tandava-murhty, dancing in a pleasant and cheerful mood, Uma-tandava-murhty, dancing in the company of Parvathi, Tripura-tandava-murthy, dancing while slaying Tripurasura and Urdhva-tandava-murhty, dancing in the air. The Apsmarapurusha (the forgotten and deluded self), on whose body he rests his feet in the image of Nataraja symbolizes this fact. And for Shiva this whole wide world of apasmarapurushas is a stage on which he enacts his dance drama.

Dakshinamurthy: This is Shiva in his aspect as the universal teacher, teaching the secrets of yoga, tantras, yantras, alchemy, magic, occult knowledge, arts and sciences, ancient history or knowledge of the future to the sages and saints, gods and goddesses and his highly qualified devotees.

He is called Dakshinamurthy, because he does his teachings sitting on the snowy mountains of Himalayas and facing towards the Indian subcontinent, which is in the southerly direction to him. The images of Dakshinamurthy, depict Shiva in his pleasant mood, seated on a high seat, with one leg folded while the other rests on the Apasmarapurusha, the deluded self.

Two of his arms hold a snake or rosary or both in one hand and fire in the other. The snake is a symbol of tantric knowledge and the fire is a symbol of enlightenment. Of the remaining two one is in abhayamudra (posture of assurance) and the other holds a scripture in gnanamudra (posture of presenting knowledge).

Lingodhbhava-murthy: This image signifies the importance of Shiva in the form of Linga as the Supreme Self, without a beginning and without an end. According to Hindu mythology, Shiva once revealed his infinity to Brahma and Vishnu in the form of a pillar of fire that could not be scaled by either of them from one end to the other. As Lingodhbava-murthy, Shiva appears seated in the heart of a Linga, with four arms, while Brahma and Vishnu adore him from the two sides.

Bhikshatana-murthi: This is Shiva in his ascetic aspect, wandering from place to place, with a begging bowl made of human skull, doing penance or lost in his own thoughts. Even today we can see some followers of Shiva going around the villages in India in this form. Some of them even do a little magic to attract our attention or scare away the trailing children.

Hridaya-murthy: This is Shiva in a mood of reconciliation and friendship with Vishnu. Also known as Harihara or Shankaranarayana. The images show the right half of Shiva on the right side of the image and the left half of Vishnu on the left side.

Ardhanarishwara: This Shiva and Parvathi together in one form signifying the unity of Purusha and Prorate. The feminine left half of Parvathi is fused with the masculine right half of Shiva in one continuous form, sometimes standing with the Bull Nandi in the background, or sitting on a pedestal and blessing the worlds, with eyes open or closed.

Shiva Pariwar: These are part of Shiva's Retinue. The most important of them are Nandi, Bhringi, Virabhadra and Chandesvara.

Nandi: Nandi, the Bull, is Shiva's vehicle. Nandi is invariably found sitting right infront of the sanctum sanctorum in every Shiva temple facing the image and looking at him all the time. In fact no one is supposed to see the chief deity in a Shiva temple without paying homage first to the seated Nandi and looking at Shiva from a far through the space between the ears and the top of his head.

There are some temples in India which are exclusively built for Nandi like the famous Nandiswara temple in Karnataka. Nandiswara in his anthromorphic form appears just like Shiva, with three eyes and four hands of which two are permanently dedicated to the veneration of Shiva while the other two carry his weapons.

Symbolically Nandi represents the passion and love of Shiva for beings. Nandi is well versed in all scriptural knowledge. Nandi is the first disciple of Lord Shiva and he imparted the teachings of Shiva to this world. He is the Guru of the great saint Thirumular and he imported the knowledge of devotion to Hanuman. It is a tradition in many parts of rural India to let a Bull roam free in each village as a mark of respect to Nandi and to inseminate the cows in the village.

Bhringi: He was originally a demon named Andhaka, who was transformed by Shiva into a humble devotee and admitted into his force as a commander of his armies. Bhringisa was so loyal to Shiva that in his state of devotion he would not offer his worship to any one including Parvathi. It is said that when he saw once Shiva in his Ardhanarishwara form, he tried to bore through the middle of the body in the form of a bee to complete his obeisance to only the Shiva side of the form, much to the annoyance of Parvathi. Bhringi who got his name thus was made to realize his mistake and change his behaviour by Lord Shiva.

Virabhadra: He is Shiva in his ferocious mood. Shiva manifested himself as Virabhadra, when Daksha, his father in law, ill treated and insulted his wife Sati, Daksha's own daughter, infront of a large gathering. Unable to cope with the insult, Sati immolated herself. This angered Shiva so much, that he descended upon the place of Daksha with his large army and beheaded Daksha's.

The images of Virabhadra depict the anger and ferocity of Shiva in that destructive mood, wearing a garland of skulls, and with four arms holding four different kinds of weapons.

Virabhadra is a warrior god who was worshipped during wars in ancient and medieval periods. He is also the principal deity of Virasaiva movement and still worshipped by many in the Karnataka region of India.

Chandesvara: He is an aspect of Chandi in human form later elevated to the status of divinity, to signify the connection between Shiva and Chandi, or Durga. Chandesvara is a ferocious god, holding weapons of war and ready to do battle for a divine cause. His images are generally found in a corner in all the Shiva temples. As in case of Nandi, devotees usually visit him and pay their respectsat the worship of the Shivalingam in the sanctum sanctorum.

Famous Saints of Shaivism: Shaivism is a very ancient sect of Hinduism with a known history of at least 3000 years. It is a historical fact that though Shaivism found its adherents in the early Vedic works such as the Svetavatara Upanishad, it took shape mainly in southern India in the remote past. Many great devotees of Lord Shiva who hailed from the land of Tamils, enriched Shaivism with their devotional fervour and meritorious religious compositions.

They brought Hinduism out of the closed door policy of castism by taking religion to the masses and teaching them the path of selfless devotion as a way of salvation.

They countered the attacks from monastic religions like Buddhism and Jainism, and defied the social order of their times by often initiating people from the lowest castes into Shaivism.

They created a body of entirely new religious literature, of great devotional merit and deep philosophical truths.

Just like many aspects of ancient Indian history, we have little information about the early Shaiva saints who shaped Shaivism into a great religious movement.

We come across few names like the famous sage Thirumula, Agastya, Manickavasaga, Sundarar, Appar and Thirugnanasambandar. They probably lived during post vedic and later Vedic periods. They were ardent devotees of Lord Shiva, and remembered in the scriptures for their devotion and contribution to Shaivism.

Tirumular: An ardent devotee of Lord Shiva and a disciple of Nandi, he lived sometime during the sixth century A.D, was endowed with supernatural powers and composed about 3000 poems in the name of Thirumantiram.

Manikkavachaka: First among the four greatest ancient teachers of Shaivism, he is considered as the founder of the path of truth or 'sat marga'. Known for his intelligence from an early age, he worked as a chief minister in the court of a Pandya king for sometime before he became a true enunciate. Gifted with poetical abilities, which earned him the title of Mannikkavachaka, which literally means he whose utterances are gems, he composed many songs in honor of Lord Shiva. His work Tiruvachakam is considered to be a pioneering work in Shaivism.

Appar: A contemporary of the Pallava King Mahendra1, and reckoned as the second greatest ancient teacher of Shaivism, he lived about 7th Century A.D. He is credited with the discovery of dasamarga or the path of the servant in Shaivism. Originally a follower of Jainism he became subsequently a great devotee of Lord Shiva and spent considerable time rendering bodily service (dasa seva) to him.

He also composed many poems out of which only a few are available today. He is often compared to the legendary Prahlada for his devotion to Lord Shiva.

Gnana Sambandha: He was a disciple of Appar. He is considered as the third greatest ancient teacher of Shaivism, who found the path of satputra marga or the path of the son and therefore he is regarded as the father of the Shaiva sect.

A precocious child, he was dedicated to Lord Shiva and Parvathi from a very early age. He was blessed with the divine feeding of the mother of universe, Parvathi.

He and Appar toured many places in South India and said to have performed many miracles. He composed many beautiful poems extolling Shiva and Parvathi. But only a few poems are available today.

If Sambandha had a great teacher in the form of Appar, he also had a great disciple in the form of Tirunilakanda Yalpanar who accompanied him always in his tours and sing along with him.

Kannappa: Kannappa lived in the region near Kalahasti in the present day Andhra Pradesh. A hunter by profession, he was totally dedicated to Lord Shiva. He worshipped Shiva regularly every day, with intense love, sometimes offering him such things as flowers and even meat.

Overwhelmed with intense devotion, once he said to have plucked out one of his eyes and offered it to Lord Shiva as a symbol of sacrifice. He tried to pluck out the other eye also immersed totally in his devotion, when Lord Shiva said to have appeared infront of him and prevented him from proceeding further.

Sundaramurthi: He is the last among the four greatest ancient teachers of Shaivism. He founded sahamarga or the path of the friend. He led a very unusual life. He became a renunciate just before his marriage and thereafter travelled to many places singing songs in praise of Lord Shiva. But strangely after sometime, he married a beautiful non Brahmin, maiden named Paravai. He stayed with her for sometime as she was also a great devotee of Lord Shiva. But their association did not last for long. A few miles north of Chennai, he married again, this time to a Brahmin virgin. Subsequently he lost vision in both of his eyes and said to have suffered greatly.

But he regained his lost vision through intense spiritual discipline and devotion. He composed many thousands of devotional poems of which very few are available today.

Karikkal Ammaiyar: Her devotion to Lord Shiva can be compared in someway with that of Mira Bai, the famous devotee of Lord Krishna. Born into a princely family, she was married to a wealthy merchant at an early age.

Seeing her devotional fervour and spiritual yearning, her husband decided to leave her to herself and married another woman. But Ammaiyar, though devoted to Lord Shiva from an early age, could not overcome her traditional respect and love for her husband initially.

But seeing her husband in his new role, she overcame that afterwards and dedicated her life completely to Lord Shiva. She also composed many devotional poems which reflect the depth of her devotion to Lord Shiva.

Auvai: Another famous woman saint of Shaivism, she was endowed with great literary talents and devotional fervour. She composed many verses which immortalized her name in Tamil religious literature.

Meypporul Nayanar: A king by birth he sacrificed his life out of love for Lord Shiva.

Sakya Nayanar: Originally a Buddhist, he later embraced Shaivism and was said to have been blessed with a vision of Lord Shiva and Parvathi.

Nandanar: An untouchable by birth, he was a great devotee of Lord Shiva who won the recognition of many learned people and was even admitted into the precincts of the Chidambaram temple which at that time was not open to people from his caste.

Meykandar: Initiated into Shaivism at the early age of three by a sage, he is credited with the composition of the famous work Shiva-Jnana-bodham, which contains twelve famous Shiva Sutras or aphorisms.

Meykandar is known in the history of Shaivism as the seer of Truth and his life is a shining example of knowledge and devotion coming together in total dedication to God.

Arundai Shivachariar: He became a disciple of Meykandar, after the latter opened his eyes in a famous encounter to the world of devotion and self-surrender. He composed Shiva-Jnana-sittiyar, according to the wishes of his guru, explaining the truths hidden in the aphorisms of the latter.

Marai-Gnanasambandar : Arundai Shivachariar also remembered in Shaiva tradition for his initiation of Marai-gnanasambandar into Shaivism. The latter though hailed from an untouchable caste was blessed with great literary talent and devotional fervour.

Umapathi Shivam: Marai-gnanasambandar in turn initiated another famous Shaiva saint, named Umapathi Shivam and helped him attain self-realization. Umapathi Shivam contributed greatly to Shaiva literature in Tamil. He wrote eight philosophical treatises on Shaivism, apart from a short biographical work on the famous 63 Shaiva saints.

Pattinathar: A rich merchant by birth, he turned to spiritualism in strange circumstances when he realized that all his wealth would not accompany him beyond his death. He along with his princely friend Bhadragiri composed many devotional poems, exhorting people to renounce their worldly ways and enter the world of devotion and self-surrender. He lived about tenth century in Tamil Nadu.

Arunagiri: He lived about fifteenth century. Early in his life, he led a very sinful life, giving himself up entirely to the pleasures of the world. But later a great transformation took place in him and he became a great devotee of Lord Murugan, the first divine child of Lord Shiva. Tiruppugal is one of his famous compositions which is known for its lyrical beauty and devotional depths.

Tayumanavar: He lived in the seventeenth century, and belonged to the priestly family which was attached to the Shiva temple at Vedaranyam, in Tamil Nadu. He lived and worked for some time at the court of a Naik ruler from Tiruchinapalli, before he renounced his worldly life and became a great devotee of Lord Shiva. He expounded the philosophy of Shaivism from a Vedantic point of view and tried to reconcile the existing contradictions.

Lingayat Saints: Mention may also be made of the five famous Lingayat Saints of Virasaivism path, namely Shivaprakasa 1, Santalinga, Kumaradeva and Shivaprakasa 2. They were men of great religious and spiritual merit, who lived during the seventeenth century and composed many religious songs and treatises.

The meaning of Samkara and Shankara: The word "samkara" or "Shankara" is a combination of two words: "sam"+"kara". "Sam" means good and "kara" means doer and therefore "samkara" means doer of good deeds.

According to another interpretation, "sam" means the "sam" of "samadhi" or the state of complete self absorption or self realization. According to this interpretation, the word "samkara" means the cause of union or self realization.

The word "sam" also means harmony, as in the word "sam/veda" or "sama/veda". Of all the Vedas, Samaveda contains the most musical hymns and are actually sung according to a set melody. Probably for this reason, Lord Krishna declared in the Bhagwad Gita that of all the Vedas He would be found in the Samaveda, signifying the harmony and melody hidden in the hymns. If we go by this meaning, the word "samkara" means creator of harmony or music. Indeed Lord Shiva is very much the master of sounds and music as symbolized by the dhamru he carries. There is no true equivalent to the Sanskrit letter "sa" of the word "samkara" in English. The nearest rendering of it is "Sha". In practice Lord Shiva is pronounced as "Shankara" or "Shankar" not "Samkara" or "Samkar".

If we take the word as "Shankara" instead of "samkara", we come across two more interpretations. The word "Shankara" is a combination of two words, namely "shanka" and "hara". "Shanka" means doubt and "hara" means destroyer. Thus the word "Shankara" means, He who destroys or defeats doubt.

Shankara destroys the animal nature in man, which is represented by the tamasic and rajasic qualities. These two qualities are primarily responsible for his lower nature, his egoistic disbeliefs and profound ignorance. By destroying these qualities and thereby our lower nature, Shiva establishes the conditions conducive to the emergence of divine nature in man.

It is interesting to note that in the Hindu mythology, most of the demons, such as Ravana of the Ramayana, Surapathma or Bhasmasur and many others, were great devotees of Shiva, who despite of their excessive wickedness, showed immense faith in Shiva.

These stories tend to suggest that only Shiva can transform such individuals, who are characterized by excessive rajas and tamas, through His immense powers. The moral of these stories is that if you have excessive rajas and tamas in you, should invariably worship Lord Shiva in order to overcome these impediments.

13

Vishnu: God of Preservation

Vishnu represents that aspect of the divine reality that maintains and sustains the creation. The endless creative force of Brahma gives life to all beings, and Vishnu's infinite sustaining force protects this life. Just as the feminine Supreme Energy, Vishnu has a "thousands names" which symbolize in fact just as many of his aspects. The daily repetition of Vishnu's thousand names is a living proof of his devotee's faith and ardour. Vishnu's blue body is often depicted in blue. The colour blue symbolizes the infinite. Vishnu is represented as an infinite force. He has no form, no name, and he is incommensurable.

The garland of flowers around Vishnu's neck is a symbol of God's worship. The precious stone decorating his neck indicates that Vishnu fulfils his worshipper's desires and the crown is a symbol of the Divine's power and supreme authority. His two earrings stand for the dual nature of creation. Vishnu wears yellow clothing. The yellow colour is associated with the terrestrial life. The dress of Vishnu, therefore, symbolizes his incarnations as a man, fighting for justice and destruction of the evil. "Vishnu, the Preserver, sustains the whole creation and has the power of manifesting himself under numerous forms. In the great Cosmic Ocean, He sustains both the sun of the infinite and the eternal spirit of existence, which is the master of the universe."

Vishnu Purana

Vishnu the Preserver, is often depicted as lying on Ananta, a many-headed serpent. He lives on Meru with his wife Lakshmi. Vishnu usually rides through the heavens on Garuda, a man-bird, endowed with highly unusual powers, which spreads courage and Vedic knowledge. Very often, Vishnu appears under the form of a young, very handsome man, with four arms (several arms is an indication of the divine, showing that they can perform several functions in the same time).

In his hands, Vishnu is shown holding a shell, a disk, a lotus, and a sceptre. The symbolism of the shell is two-folded: on one hand it represents Vishnu's relationship with the primordial waters and its use as a musical instrument, reminiscent of the primordial waters, and on the other hand the shell represents the five elements, and consequently the origin of manifestation.

The lotus is a symbol of the spiritual development and cosmic harmony. It also signifies the appearance of life on the neutral immensity of the primordial waters.

The opening of the lotus bud represents the realization of the possibilities contained in the "seed" of the human being. The sceptre is a symbol of power and authority.

The disk is a solar symbol, and the classical image of Vishnu, the ascendant, unifying, intellectual tendency of a human being. It represents the power that destroys the ignorance and the darkness, just as it is a symbol of a killing weapon, and of the sun. It destroys the evil through the process of illumination.

Vishnu is more a god of love. For a Vaishnavite, salvation is usually won by bhakti, a loving devotion to God as preserver. Vishnu is considered the guardian of mankind and the keeper of the Dharma. He preserves the order in the universe. Every time the humanity decays, Vishnu takes on the form of an avatar, a divine model coming on earth, to show people new paths for spiritual development. He has taken nine incarnations.

His first incarnation was a fish, Matsya; the second a turtle, Kurma; the third a wild boar, Varaha; the fourth a lion; the fifth a dwarf, Vamana; the sixth a warrior, Parasurama; the seventh a hero, Rama; the eighth Krishna; the ninth Buddha.

Vishnu's tenth incarnation, Kalki, is supposed to come about at the end of this age, Kali Yuga. He is said to be the cosmic rider of Apocalypse, who will take on the role of destroyer of what is evil on earth. The most important incarnations of Vishnu are Rama and Krishna.

To Hindus, Rama, who is nearly always noble and righteous, is the ideal man. Sita, incarnation of Lakshmi and his loyal wife, is the ideal woman. All sects reverence Rama. No name is more commonly given to Hindu children, and all Hindus would like to die with his name on their lips. When Mahatma Gandhi fell, mortally wounded by a fanatic assassin, he murmured "Ai Ram, Ai Ram" (O Rama, O Rama).

Krishna, even more popular and lovable, is the subject of countless stories and legends. As a youth Krishna flirts with the Gopi milk maidens and has an affair with one, Radha. These erotic experiences are interpreted symbolically. Individual souls are drawn to God as the milkmaidens were attracted to Krishna, and one should give one's self to God in complete surrender as Radha did to Krishna.

VAISHNAVISM IN THE SOUTH

The ancient Vaishnava mystics and saints in the South were known as Alvars, and the Vaishnavism teachers as Acharayas. They had a powerful exponent of these views in Ramanuja, who attacked the Advaita interpretation of the Upanishads and gave recognition to three ultimate realities, God, Soul and Matter, the last two being dependent on the first.

As early as the 2nd century B.C. the renowned Besnagar Column had been erected by a Greek named Heliodorous, who had been converted to the Bhagavata or Vaishnava faith of which the Pancharatra doctrines then formed an integral part; its scriptures were Satvata Samhita, the Mahabharata, and the Bhagavata and Vishnu Puranas. The origin of the Pancharatra doctrines which form the basis of Sri Vaishnava culture has be Pancharatra entraced further back to the well known Purusasukta of the Rig-Veda.

The Satapatha Brahmana refers to the Pancharatra sacrifices performed by the primoval Narayana, the idea of Nara and Narayana (Primordial man and the deity Vishnu) being an integral part of ancient Indian thought. There are more than a dozen Vaishnava Upanishads. It was in the period from the 10th century up to the 17th that many Vaishnava works were produced. The Vaishnavas regard the Pancharatra literature as almost equal to the Vedas.

The Vaishnava Samhitas and other works insist on knowledge of and devotion to, the supreme Godhead rather than on Vedic studies or sacrifices. It is worthy of note that in the Bhagavata Purana (11th Skanda) the Alwars were prefigured or adverted to; several great devotees of Vishnu, the Purana states, would appear on the banks of the Tamraparni, Kritamala (Vaigai), Payasvin (Palar), Kaveri (Cauvery), and Mahanadi (Periyar).

The Alvars lived between the 5th and the 12th centuries. The first group included Saroyogin or Poygaiyal var, Bhatayogin or Bhutattalvar, Mahadyogin or Peyalvr and Bhaktisara or Tirumalisai-Puran. Nammalvar or Satakopa, who came in the next group, was perhaps the greatest of the Alvars. Others in this group included Madhurakaviyalvar, Kulasekhara Perumal, Vishnuchitta (or Periyalvar) and Andal, his adopted daughter. In the last of the groups were Bhaktanghrirenu (Tondaradippodiyalvar), Yogivahana (Tiruppanalvar) and Parakala (Tirumangaiyalvar). The Divya Prabhandha constitutes the collection of the Alvars' compositions in the Tamil language.

VAISHNAVISM IN THE NORTH

One of the most influential Vaishnava cults was founded by Vallabhacarya, a Telugu Brahmin who lived in the 15th century. He migrated to the North and in his numerous works in the North he gave an interpretation of the Vedanta differing from that of Ramanuja, as also of Shankara. He called his doctrine Suddha Advaita, pure non-dualism. The world is real, and not an illusion. God is Nimitta-Karana, the causative being.

Discarding the Maya theory Vallabhacharya asserts that God cannot be described by negatives but only by his holy and gracious attributes, and is personified in Krishna He is not only karta, creator, but also Bhokta, enjoyer. Though he has no need to assume a bodily form, he often does so to please his devotees.

Regarding Bhakti as the chief means of salvation and superior to Jnana, (knowledge) Vallabha opposed all kinds of asceticism. The body is the temple of God, he said. The famous Upanisadic precept Tatvamasi was by an ingenious interpretation, modified by Vallabha as Atatvamasi, "That thou art not". Vallabhacharya's doctrines were fully interpreted and expounded by his son Vitthala.

Later, in Northern India, there arose the Chaitanya movement. Nimbarka had already elevated Radha, the consort of Krishna, to the highest position. Jayadeva, the author of Gita-Govinda, and other poets like Vidyapati, Umapati and Chandidas, adopted the Radha-Krishna cult.

Chaitanya, the great Vaishnava teacher of the 15th century transformed the Vaishnava faith and extended his influence in most parts of Northern India. He accepted converts from Islam, the foremost among them being Haridas, Rupa and Sanatana. Salvation, according to his doctrine, consists in the eternal experience of God's love. Chaitanya exercised great influence over later Indian thought.

Chaitanya Mahaprabhu was born in Mayapur in the town of Nadia just after sunset on the evening of the 23rd Phalguna 1407 Sakabda, answering to the 18th of February, 1486, of the Christian Era. The moon was eclipsed at the time of his birth, and the people of Nadia were then engaged, as was usual on such occasions, in bathing in the Bhagirathi with loud cheers of Haribol. His father, Jagannath Mishra, a poor brahmana of the Vedic order, and his mother, Sachi-devi, a model good woman, both descended from brahmana stock originally residing in Sylhet. Mahaprabhu was a beautiful child, and the ladies of the town came to see him with presents. His mother's father, Pandita Nilambara Chakravarti, a renowned astrologer, foretold that the child would be a great personage in time; and he, therefore, gave him the name Vishvambhara.

The ladies of the neighbourhood styled him Gaurahari on account of his golden complexion, and his mother called him Nimai on account of the nimba tree near which he was born. Beautiful as the lad was, everyone heartily loved to see him every day. As he grew up he became a whimsical and frolicsome lad. After his fifth year, he was admitted into a pathasala where he picked up Bengali in a very short time.

Most of his contemporary biographers have mentioned certain anecdotes regarding Chaitanya which are simple records of his early miracles. It is said that when he was an infant in his mother's arms he wept continually, and when the neighbouring ladies cried Haribol he used to stop. Thus there was a continuation of the utterance of Haribol in the house, foreshewing the future mission of the hero.

It has also been stated that when his mother once gave him sweetmeats to eat, he ate clay instead of the food. His mother asking for the reason, he stated that as every sweetmeat was nothing but clay transformed, he could eat clay as well. His mother, who was also the consort of a Pandita, explained that every article in a special state was adapted to a special use.

Earth, while in the state of a jug, could be used as a water pot, but in the state of a brick such a use was not possible. Clay, therefore, in the form of sweetmeats was usable as food, but clay in its other states was not. The lad was convinced and admitted his stupidity in eating clay and agreed to avoid the mistake in the future. Another miraculous act has been related. It is said that a brahmana on pilgrimage became a guest in his house, cooked food and read grace with meditation upon Krishna. In the meantime the lad came and ate up the cooked rice.

The brahmana, astonished at the lad's act, cooked again at the request of Jagannath Mishra. The lad again ate up the cooked rice while the brahmana was offering the rice to Krishna with meditation. The brahmana was persuaded to cook for the third time. This time all the inmates of the house had fallen asleep, and the lad shewed himself as Krishna to the traveller and blessed him. The brahmana was then lost in ecstasy at the appearance of the object of his worship. It has also been stated that two thieves stole away the lad from his father's door with a view to purloin his jewels and gave him sweetmeats on the way.

The lad exercised his illusory energy and deceived the thieves back towards his own house. The thieves, for fear of detection, left the boy there and fled. Another miraculous act that has been described is the lad's demanding and getting from Hiranya and Jagadisha all the offerings they had collected for worshipping Krishna on the day of Ekadasi. When only four years of age he sat on rejected cooking pots which were considered unholy by his mother. He explained to his mother that there was no question of holiness and unholiness as regards earthen pots thrown away after the cooking was over. These anecdotes relate to his tender age up to the fifth year.

In his eighth year, he was admitted into the tola of Gangadasa Pandita in Ganganagara close by the village of Mayapur. In two years he became well read in Sanskrit grammar and rhetoric. His readings after that were of the nature of self-study in his own house, where he had found all-important books belonging to his father, who was a Pandita himself. It appears that he read the smriti in his own study, and the nyaya also, in competition with his friends, who were then studying under the celebrated Pandita Raghunatha Shiromani.

Now, after the tenth year of his age, Chaitanya became a passable scholar in grammar, rhetoric, the smriti and the nyaya. It was after this that his elder brother Visvarupa left his house and accepted the ashrama (status) of a sanyasi (ascetic). Chaitanya, though a very young boy, consoled his parents, saying that he would serve them with a view to please God. Just after that, his father left this world. His mother was exceedingly sorry, and Mahaprabhu, with his usual contented appearance, consoled his widowed mother.

It was at the age of 14 or 15 that Mahaprabhu was married to Lakshmidevi, the daughter of Vallabhacharya, also of Nadia. He was at this age considered one of the best scholars of Nadia, the renowned seat of nyaya philosophy and Sanskrit learning. Not to speak of the smarta panditas, the Naiyayikas were all afraid of confronting him in literary discussions. Being a married man, he went to Eastern Bengal on the banks of the Padma for acquirement of wealth. There he displayed his learning and obtained a good sum of money.

It was at this time that he preached Vaishnavism at intervals. After teaching him the principles of Vaishnavism, he ordered Tapana Mishra to go to and live in Benares. During his residence in East Bengal, his wife Lakshmidevi left this world from the effects of snakebite. On returning home, he found his mother in a mourning state. He consoled her with a lecture on the uncertainty of human affairs. It was at his mother's request that he married Vishnupriya, the daughter of Raja Pandita Sanatana Mishra. His comrades joined him on his return from pravasa or sojourn. He was now so renowned that he was considered to be the best Pandita in Nadia. Keshava Mishra of Kashmir, who had called himself the Great Digvijayi, came to Nadia with a view to discuss with the panditas of that place. Afraid of the so-called conquering Pandita, the tola professors of Nadia left their town on pretence of Invitation. Keshava met Mahaprabhu at the Barokona-ghata in Mayapur, and after a very short discussion with him he was defeated by the boy, and mortification obliged him to decamp. Nimai Pandita was now the most important Pandita of his times.

It was at the age of 16 or 17 that he travelled to Gaya with a host to sing the holy name of Hari in the streets and bazaars. This created a sensation and roused different feelings in different quarters. The bhaktas were highly pleased. The smarta brahmanas became jealous of Nimai Pandita's success and complained to Chand Kazi against the character of Chaitanya as un-Hindu. The Kazi came to Srivasa Pandita's house and broke a mridanga (khola drum) there and declared that unless Nimai Pandita ceased to make noise about his queer religion he would be obliged to enforce Mohammedanism on him and his followers. This was brought to Mahaprabhu's notice. He ordered the townspeople to appear in the evening, each with a torch in his hand. This groups, and on his arrival in the Kazi's house, he held a long conversation with the Kazi and in the end communicated into his heart his Vaishnava influence by touching his body. The Kazi then wept and admitted that he had felt a keen spiritual influence which had cleared up his doubts and produced in him a religious sentiment which gave him the highest ecstasy. The Kazi then joined the sankirtana party. The world was astonished at the spiritual power of the Great Lord, and hundreds and hundreds of heretics converted and joined the banner of Vishvambhara after this affair.

It was after this that some of the jealous and low-minded brahmanas of Kulia picked a quarrel with Mahaprabhu and collected a party to oppose him. Nimai Pandita was naturally a soft-hearted person, though strong in his principles. He declared that party feelings and sectarianism were the two great enemies of progress and that as long as he should continue to be an inhabitant of Nadia belonging to a certain family, his mission would not meet with complete success. He then resolved to be a citizen of the world by cutting his connection with his particular family, caste and creed, and with this resolution he embraced the position of a sanyasi at Katwa, under the guidance of Keshava Bharati of that town, on the 24th year of his age.

His mother and wife wept bitterly for his separation, but our hero, though soft in heart, was a strong person in principle. He left his little world in his house for the unlimited spiritual world of Krishna with man in general.

After his sannyasa, he was induced to visit the house of Advaita Prabhu in Santipura. Advaita managed to invite all his friends and admirers from Nadia and brought Sachidevi to see her son. Both pleasure and pain invaded her heart when she saw her son in the attire of a sanyasi. As a sanyasi, Krishna Chaitanya put on nothing but a kaupina and a bahirvasa (outer covering). His head was without hair, and his hands bore a danda (stick) and a kamandalu (hermit's water pot). The holy son fell at the feet of his beloved mother and said, "Mother! This body is yours, and I must obey your orders. Permit me to go to Vrindavana for my spiritual attainments." The mother, in consultation with Advaita and others, asked her son to reside in Puri (the town of Jagannath) so that she might obtain his information now and then.

Mahaprabhu agreed to that proposition and in a few days left Santipura for Orissa. His biographers have described the journey of Krishna Chaitanya (that was the name he got after his sannyasa) from Santipura to Puri in great detail. He travelled along the side of the Bhagirathi as far as Chatrabhoga, situated now in Thana Mathurapura, Diamond Harbour, 24 Parganas. There he took a boat and went as far as Prayaga-ghata in the Midnapura District. Thence he walked through Balasore and Cuttack to Puri, seeing the temple of Bhubaneshvara on his way. Upon his arrival at Puri he saw Jagannath in the temple and resided with Sarvabhauma at the request of the latter.

Sarvabhauma was a gigantic Pandita of the day. His readings knew no bounds. He was the best naiyayika of the times and was known as the most erudite scholar in the Vedanta philosophy of the school of Shankaracharya. He was born in Nadia (Vidyanagara) and taught innumerable pupils in the nyaya philosophy in his tola there. He had left for Puri some time before the birth of Nimai Pandita. His brother in law Gopinatha Mishra introduced our new sanyasi to Sarvabhauma, who was astonished at his personal beauty and feared that it would be difficult for the young man to maintain sannyasa dharma during the long run of his life. Gopinatha, who had known Mahaprabhu from Nadia, had a great reverence for him and declared that the sanyasi was not a common human being.

On this point Gopinatha and Sarvabhauma had a hot discussion. Sarvabhauma then requested Mahaprabhu to hear his recitation of the Vedanta-sutras, and the latter tacitly submitted. Chaitanya heard with silence what the great Sarvabhauma uttered with gravity for seven days, at the end of which the latter said, "Krishna Chaitanya! I think you do not understand the Vedanta, for you do not say anything after hearing my recitation and explanations." The reply of Chaitanya was that he understood the sutras very well, but he could not make out what Shankaracharya meant by his commentaries. Astonished at this, Sarvabhauma said, "How is it that you understand the meanings of the sutras and do not understand the commentaries which explain the sutras? All well! If you understand the sutras, please let me have your interpretations." Mahaprabhu thereon explained all the sutras in his own way without touching the pantheistic commentary of Shankara.

The keen understanding of Sarvabhauma saw the truth, beauty and harmony of arguments in the explanations given by Chaitanya and obliged him to utter that it was the first time that he had found one who could explain the Brahma-sutras in such a simple manner. He admitted also that the commentaries of Shankara never gave such natural explanations of the Vedanta-sutras as he had obtained from Mahaprabhu. He then submitted himself as an advocate and follower. In a few days Sarvabhauma turned out to be one of the best Vaishnavas of the time. When reports of this came out, the whole of Orissa sang the praise of Krishna Chaitanya, and hundreds and hundreds came to him and became his followers. In the meantime Mahaprabhu thought of visiting Southern India, and he started with one Krishnadasa Brahmana for the journey.

His biographers have given us a detail of the journey. He went first to Kurmaksetra, where he performed a miracle by curing a leper named Vasudeva. He met Ramananda Raya, the Governor of Vidyanagara, on the banks of the Godavari and had a philosophical conversation with him on the subject of prema-bhakti. He worked another miracle by touching (making them immediately disappear) the seven tala trees through which Ramachandra, the son of Dasaratha, had shot his arrow and killed the great Bali Raja. He preached Vaishnavism and nama-sankirtana throughout the journey.

At Rangaksetra he stayed for four months in the house of one Venkata Bhatta in order to spend the rainy season. There he converted the whole family of Venkata from Ramanuja Vaishnavism to Krishna-bhakṭi, along with the son of Venkata, a boy of ten years named Gopala, who afterwards came to Vrndavana and became one of the six Gosvamis or prophets serving under their leader Sri Krishna Chaitanya. Trained up in Sanskrit by his uncle Prabodhananda Saraswati, Gopala wrote several books on Vaishnavism.

Chaitanya visited numerous places in Southern India as far as Cape Comorin and returned to Puri in two years by Pandepura on the Bhima. In this latter place he spiritualized one Tukarama, who became from that time a religious preacher himself. This fact has been admitted in his abhangas, which have been collected in a volume by Mr. Satyendra Nath Tagore of the Bombay Civil Service. During his journey he had discussions with the Buddhists, the Jains and the Mayavadis in several places and converted his opponents to Vaishnavism.

Upon his return to Puri, Raja Prataparudra-deva and several Pandita brahmanas joined the banner of Chaitanya Mahaprabhu. He was now twenty-seven years of age. In his twenty-eighth year he went to Bengal as far as Gauda in Malda. There he picked up two great personages named Rupa and Sanatana. Though descended from the lines of the Karnatic brahmanas, these two brothers turned demi-Moslems by their continual contact with Hussain Shah, the then Emperor of Gauda. Their names had been changed by the Emperor into Dabira Khasa and Sakara Mallika, and their master loved them heartily since they were both learned in Persian, Arabic and Sanskrit and were loyal servants of the state. The two gentlemen had found no way to come back as regular Hindus and had written to Mahaprabhu for spiritual help while he was at Puri. Mahaprabhu had written in reply that he would come to them and extricate them from their spiritual difficulties. Now that he had come to Gauda, both the brothers appeared before him with their long-standing prayer. Mahaprabhu ordered them to go to Vrndavana and meet him there.

Chaitanya returned to Puri through Santipura, where he again met his dear mother. After a short stay at Puri he left for Vrndavana. This time he was accompanied by one Balabhadra Bhattacarya. He visited Vrndavana and came down to Prayaga (Allahabad), converting a large number of Mohammedans to Vaishnavism by argument from the Koran. The descendants of those converts are still known as Pathana Vaishnavas. Rupa Gosvami met him at Allahabad. Chaitanya trained him up in spirituality in ten days and directed him to go to Vrndavana on missions. His first mission was to write theological works explaining scientifically pure bhakti and prema. The second mission was to revive the places where Krishnacandra had in the end of Dvapara-yuga exhibited His spiritual lila (pastimes) for the benefit of the religious world. Rupa Gosvami left Allahabad for Vrndavana, and Mahaprabhu came down to Benares.

There he resided in the house of Chandrashekhar and accepted his daily bhiksa (meal) in the house of Tapana Mishra. Here it was that Sanatana Gosvami joined him and took instruction for two months in spiritual matters. The biographers, especially Krishnadasa Kaviraja, have given us details of Chaitanya's teachings to Rupa and Sanatana. Krishnadasa was not a contemporary writer, but he gathered his information from the Gosvamis themselves, the direct disciples of Mahaprabhu. Jiva Gosvami, who was nephew of Sanatana and Rupa and who has left us his invaluable work the Sat-sandarbha, has philosophized on the precepts of his great leader. We have gathered and summarized the precepts of Chaitanya from the books of those great writers.

While at Benares, Chaitanya had an interview with the learned sannyasis of that town in the house of a Maratha brahmana who had invited all the sannyasis for entertainment. At this interview, Chaitanya shewed a miracle which attracted all the sannyasis to him. Then ensued reciprocal conversation. The sannyasis were headed by their most learned leader Prakasananda Saraswati. After a short controversy, they submitted to Mahaprabhu and admitted that they had been misled by the commentaries of Shankaracharya.

It was impossible even for learned scholars to oppose Chaitanya for a long time, for there was some spell in him which touched their hearts and made them weep for their spiritual improvement. The sannyasis of Benares soon fell at the feet of Chaitanya and asked for his grace (krpa). Chaitanya then preached pure bhakti and instilled into their hearts spiritual love for Krishna which obliged them to give up sectarian feelings. The whole population of Benares, on this wonderful conversion of the sannyasis, turned Vaishnavas, and they made a master sankirtana with their new Lord. After sending Sanatana to Vrndavana, Mahaprabhu went to Puri again through the jungles with his comrade Balabhadra. Balabhadra reported that Mahaprabhu had shown a good many miracles on his way to Puri, such as making tigers and elephants dance on hearing the name of Krishna.

From this time, that is, from his 31st year, Mahaprabhu continually lived in Puri in the house of Kasi Mishra until his disappearance in his forty-eighth year at the time of sankirtana in the temple of Tota-gopinatha. During these 18 years, his life was one of settled love and piety. He was surrounded by numerous followers, all of whom were of the highest order of Vaishnavas and who were distinguished from the common people by their purest character and learning, firm religious principles and spiritual love of Radha-Krishna. Svarupa Damodara, who had been known by the name of Purushottamacarya while Mahaprabhu was in Nadia, joined him from Benares and accepted service as his secretary. No production of any poet or philosopher could be laid before Mahaprabhu unless Svarupa had passed it as pure and useful. Raya Ramananda was his second mate.

Both he and Svarupa would sing while Mahaprabhu expressed his sentiments on a certain point of worship. Paramananda Puri was his minister in matters of religion. There are hundreds of anecdotes described by his biographers which we do not think it meet here to reproduce. Mahaprabhu slept short. His sentiments carried him far and wide in the firmament of spirituality every day and night, and all his admirers and followers watched him throughout. He worshipped, communicated with his missionaries at Vrndavana, and conversed with those religious men who newly came to visit him. He sang and danced, took no care of himself and oft times lost himself in religious beatitude.

All who came to him believed in him as the all-beautiful God appearing in the nether world for the benefit of mankind. He loved his mother all along and sent her mahaprasada now and then with those who went to Nadia. He was most amiable in nature. Humility was personified in him. His sweet appearance gave cheer to all who came in contact with him. He appointed Prabhu Nityananda as the missionary in charge of Bengal. He dispatched six disciples (Gosvamis) to Vrndavana to preach love in the upcountry. He punished all of his disciples who deviated from a holy life. This he markedly did in the case of Junior Haridasa. He never lacked in giving proper instructions in life to those who solicited them. This will be seen in his teachings to Raghunatha dasa Gosvami. His treatment to Haridasa (senior) will show how he loved spiritual men and how he defied caste distinction in spiritual brotherhood.

Bibliography

Agrawala, V. S. : *Siva Mahadeva: The Great God*, Veda Academy, Varanasi, 1966.

Aiyar, R. Krishnaswami: *Outlines of Vedaanta*, Chetana, Bombay, 1978.

Aurobindo, Sri: *Vyasa and Valmiki*, Acharya Press, Pondicherry, 1956.

Banerjea, J. N. : *Pauranic and Tantric Religion*, University of Calcutta, Calcutta, 1966.

Berreman, Gerald D.: *Hindus of the Himalayas*, University of California Press, Berkeley, 1963.

Bose, D. N.: *Dharmashastra: Their Philosophy and Occult Secrets*, Kali Press, Calcutta, 1965.

Chaturvedi, M.D. : *Hinduism, The Eternal Religion*, Bharatiya Vidya Bhavan, Bombay, 1992 .

Devaraja, N.K.: *An Introduction to Shankara's Theory of Knowledge*, Motilal Banarsi Dass, Delhi, 1962.

Flood, Gavin. : *An Introduction to Hinduism*, Cambridge University Press, England, 1996.

Harding, Elizabeth: *Kali: The Black Goddess of Dakshineshwar*, Nicolas-Hays, York Beach, 1993.

Harman, William: *The Sacred Marriage of a Hindu Goddess*, Indiana University Press, Bloomington, 1989.

Jain, G.: *The Hindu Phenomenon*, UBSPD, Delhi 1994.

Kaviraj, Gopinath : *Aspects of Indian Thought*, University of Burdwan, Calcutta, 1966.

Keith, Arthur Berriedale: *The Religion and Philosophy of the Veda and Upanishads*, MacMillan, Delhi, 1925.

Kinsley, David R. : *Hinduism A Cultural Perspective*, Prentice-Hall, Inc., New Jersey, 1993.

Klostermaier, Klaus K. : *A Survey of Hinduism*, State University of New York Press, Albany, 1989.

Levy, John: *The Nature of Man According to Vedanta*, Routledge & Kegan Paul, London, 1956.

Morgan, Kenneth W. : *The Religion of the Hindus*, The Ronald Press Company, New York, 1953.

Organ, Troy W. : *Hinduism: Its Historical Development*, Barron's Educational Series, Inc., New York, 1974.

Payne, E. : *The Shaktas: An Introduction and Comparative Study*, Calcutta, 1933.

Renou, Louis : *The Nature of Hinduism*, Walker and Co., New York, 1963.

Rocher, L.: *The Puranas*, , Motilal Banarsidass, Delhi, 1984.

Satyapal Verma: *Role of Reason in Sankara Vedanta*, Parimal Publication, Delhi, 1992.

Schweitzer, A.: *Indian Thought and its Development* Charles E. B. Russell, Boston, 1936.

Singh, Ram Pratab: *The Vedanta of Shankara: A Metaphysics of Value*, Bharat Publishing House, Jaipur, 1949.

Srinivas, M. N. : *Religion and Society among the Coorgs of South India*, Clarendon Press Oxford, 1952.

Thomas, P.: *Kama Kalpa or the Hindu Ritual of Love,* D. B. Taraporevala Sons, Bombay, 1965.

Trilok, C.: *Sadhus and Saints of India and Nepal*, Tecpress, Bangkok, 1996.

Vihari, D.: *The Essentials of Advaitism, Suresvara's Naishkarmyasiddhi Explained in English*, Punjab Oriental Series, Lahore, 1933.

Wendy Doniger: *Siva: The Erotic Ascetic,* Oxford University Press, Delhi, 1998.

Zaehner, Richard C. : *Hinduism*, Oxford University Press, New York, 1966.

Zimmer, Heinrich : *Myths and Symbols in Indian Art and Civilization*, Bollingen Series/ Pantheon/Random House, New York, 1946.